Performance Measurement of New Product Development Teams

Also by Magdy Abdel-Kader

ENTERPRISE RESOURCE PLANNING
Implementation and Management Accounting Change in a Transitional
Country *(with A. Kholeif and M. Sherer)*

BEHAVIOURAL ASPECTS OF AUDITORS' EVIDENCE EVALUATION
(with M. Abou-Seada)

INVESTMENT DECISIONS IN ADVANCED MANUFACTURING TECHNOLOGY
A Fuzzy Set Theory Approach *(with D. Dugdale and P. Taylor)*

NON-FINANCIAL PERFORMANCE MEASUREMENT AND MANAGEMENT
PRACTICES IN MANUFACTURING FIRMS
A Comparative International Analysis *(with A. Abdel-Maksoud)*

Performance Measurement of New Product Development Teams

A Case of the High-Tech Sector

Magdy G. Abdel-Kader
Senior Lecturer, Brunel Business School, Brunel University, UK.

and

Erin Yu-Ching Lin
PricewaterhouseCoopers, Taipei, Taiwan

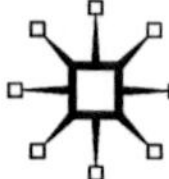

First published 2009 by
PALGRAVE MACMILLAN

Palgrave Macmillan in the UK is an imprint of Macmillan Publishers Limited, registered in England, company number 785998, of Houndmills, Basingstoke, Hampshire RG21 6XS.

Palgrave Macmillan in the US is a division of St Martin's Press LLC, 175 Fifth Avenue, New York, NY 10010.

Palgrave Macmillan is the global academic imprint of the above companies and has companies and representatives throughout the world.

Palgrave® and Macmillan® are registered trademarks in the United States, the United Kingdom, Europe and other countries.

ISBN-13: 978-0-230-57384-0   hardback
ISBN-10: 0-230-57384-3   hardback

This book is printed on paper suitable for recycling and made from fully managed and sustained forest sources. Logging, pulping and manufacturing processes are expected to conform to the environmental regulations of the country of origin.

A catalogue record for this book is available from the British Library.

A catalogue record for this book is available from the Library of Congress.

10   9   8   7   6   5   4   3   2   1
18 17 16 15 14 13 12 11 10 09

Printed and bound in Great Britain by
CPI Antony Rowe, Chippenham and Eastbourne

This book is dedicated to our families ...
Magda Abou-Seada and Mohamed Abdel-Kader ... (MAK)
My father, My mother and My two younger brothers
and their wives ... (EYL)

Contents

List of Tables

List of Figures

List of Abbreviations

AVP	Associate Vice President
BC	Budget-constrained
BP	Budget-profit
BSC	Balanced Scorecard
BU	Business Units
CEO	Corporate Executive Officer
CNN	Cable News Network
DFA	Design For Assembly
DFM	Design For Manufacturing
DFR	Design For Reliability
DFT	Design For Testing
DMAICR	Define, Measure, Analyse, Improve, Control, Record
FMEA	Failure Management Evaluating Analysis
HDD	Hard Disk Drives
HR	Human Resource Manager
ICT	Information and Communication Technologies
IRR	Internal Rate of Return
ISIC	International Standard Industrial Classification
KPI	Key Performance Indicators
M Form	Geographic Organisation
MR	Market Researcher/Marketing Business Person
NA	Non-accounting
NPD	New Product Development
OECD	Organisation for Economic Co-operation and Development
PC	Profit-conscious
PDTC	Planning and Preparation, Design, Testing and Modification and Commercialisation
PM	Project Manager
QA	Quality Assurance
QRE	Quality and Reliability Engineering
QT	Quality Technology
R&D	Research & Development
ROC	Republic of China
ROI	Return On Investment
SBUs	Strategic Business Units

SQE	Software Quality Engineering
STI	Science, Technology and Industry
TSEC	Taiwan Stock Exchange Corporation
U Form	Functional Organisation
VP	Vice President

Preface

The survival of a business in today's extremely competitive markets depends on its ability to produce a constant flow of high quality new products that meet its customers' needs. Further, the dramatic changes in consumption and consumer patterns together with the growth of international mega-brand products have put heavy pressure on companies to improve the process of New Product Development (NPD) (Chaturvedi and Rajan, 2000). Consequently, the role of management accounting and accountants has changed, especially concerning the NPD process, the cross-functional project team and cross-functional project team performance measurement. Development of new products – especially in high-technology sectors – is a high-risk task. About 46% of the resources invested in NPD resulted in unsuccessful projects (Booz-Allen and Hamilton, 1982), and 35% of launched new products failed commercially (Cooper and Kleinschmidt, 1987a). Thus, understanding the factors that contribute to new product success/failure is vital to gain insights that should help in the planning of new product projects.

It is argued that the essence of the NPD process is the project team. Introducing teamwork and team-based activities into an organisation is a complex process, which involves multifunctional interactive processes that are frequently complicated to control and, hence, difficult to appropriately align with incentives. Positivistic agency theory, from an economic perspective, and stewardship theory, from a sociological perspective, are utilised in this study to explain the control systems that diminish the agency problem. Additionally, social identity theory and self-categorisation theory are employed, from psychological and sociological perspectives, to clarify the cognitive, evaluative and emotional processes which motivate individuals to unite cohesive teams and augment their abilities.

In this book we investigate the extent to which the project team performance measurement system affects new product success/failure. We conducted in-depth interviews with project managers, project team-members, human resource managers and senior managers – such as CEOs or vice presidents – in four Taiwanese multinational computer companies. In each company we focused only on one project team, which designed and produced a breakthrough product.

The intention of this study is not to dispute whether incentives work or not; conversely, the purpose is to realise how to make incentives work. We adopt a conceptual framework that takes into account the interaction of incentive and team effort, team effort and team effectiveness, team effectiveness and team performance and team performance and new product success/failure. We also adopt a naturalistic methodology using a qualitative case study approach due to its capability of exploring the holistic quality of project teams and the practices of human actors. Key findings show that an open and non-discriminatory performance measurement system is the dominant incentive that motivates and influences performance of members of teams and in turn affects new product success or failure in the four cases.

This book is organised in nine chapters. Chapters 1 and 2 are introductory chapters, which give an overview of the area and review the relevant literature on NPD teams. Chapter 3 explains the organisational architecture that encompasses three systems: the assignment of decision rights to NPD participants within the company, rewarding and punishing new product project members and the performance measurement system. The conceptual framework of this research is developed in Chapter 4. This framework draws on the four theories of agency, stewardship, social identity and self-categorisation to understand the relationships of incentive-effort, effort-effectiveness, effort-performance and performance-success. The research methodology and methods used to collect empirical data are described and justified in Chapter 5. The empirical data are analysed and discussed in Chapters 6, 7 and 8. Chapter 9 concludes the study with a set of general implications and recommendations for theory and practice.

Magdy Abdel-Kader and Erin Lin
Authors

1
Introduction

1.0   Introduction

The essence of the new product development (NPD) process and the focus of much NPD literature are the project teams (as referred to cross-functional project teams, multifunctional teams, or NPD project teams). Although project teams have become increasingly popular in practice in high-technology sectors, introducing teamwork and team-based activities into an organisation is a complex process which involves multifunctional, interactive processes that are frequently complicated to control and difficult to appropriately align with incentives. Positivist agency theory, at an economic level, and stewardship theory, from a sociological viewpoint, are utilised in this study to explain the control systems that diminish the agency problem. Also, social identity theory and self-categorisation theory are employed, from psychological and sociological perspectives, to clarify the cognitive, evaluative and emotional processes that motivate individuals to unite cohesive teams and augment their ability to contribute to their teams, which would be required for many team tasks.

This chapter gives an overview of the book and it is organised as follows:

- Background to the study
- High-technology industry in Taiwan
- The role of management accounting and management accountants
- The gap between theory and practice in management accounting
- Objective and research questions
- Significance of the study
- Conclusion and book structure

1.1 Background to the study

March and Simon (1993) suggest three broad functions of the role of management accounting within business organisations. These functions are scorekeeping, direction attention, and assisting in problem solving. Traditionally, management accounting acts as a scorekeeping function in the production stage rather than directing attention and assisting in problem solving in the NPD stages of organisations. Nowadays, faced with a fast-paced, extremely competitive environment, almost all companies, alongside their executives, are being influenced by the concepts of reducing cost, improving quality and shortening NPD time in this competitive environment (Cooper, 1995; Nixon, 1998). In order to survive in today's extremely competitive markets, the future of companies relies on their ability to produce a constant flow of quality new products that meet their customers' needs.

'The dramatic changes in consumption and consumer patterns together with the growth of international megabrand products have put heavy pressure on industry to change its way of doing business, especially its NPD.' (Chaturvedi and Rajan, 2000: 788). Currently, as a consequence of the rapid transmission of technological skill, the role of management accounting and accountants has changed, especially concerning the NPD process (Nixon, 1998), the cross-functional project team (Parker, 1994) and cross-functional project team performance measurement (Rowe, 2004). 'The rules of the game in NPD are changing' (Takeuchi and Nonaka, 1986: 137) and it is time to pay attention to accelerating the quality of NPD in today's business environment (Eisenhardt and Tabrizi, 1995), not least because running NPD is, to a large extent, a process of separating the winners from the losers (Cooper and Kleinschmidt, 1995).

Successful new product innovation is essential to business success in a dynamic and highly competitive environment, such as the high-technology sectors. But, new products are high-risk deeds as well; around 46% of the resources invested in NPD and commer-cialisation was applied to unsuccessful projects (Booz-Allen and Hamilton, 1982), and 35% of launched new products fail commercially (Cooper and Kleinschmidt, 1987a). The intelligence of new product success or failure factors is vital for two reasons, it gives guiding principles for the planning of new product projects and it pilots how insights into the new product project should be administered.

A study by Takeuchi and Nonaka (1986) examined the NPD process of six *successful*, specific products. However, the result could be misleading because failed products may share some similarity as successful products. Without comparing the results of successful and unsuccessful products we cannot identify the unique success factors. For example if we assume a researcher attempts to observe the success factors of gold medal winners in the Athens 2004 Olympic Games in Greece. After interviewing 51 gold medal athletes from the USA and Japan the researcher concluded that each gold medal winner has a coach. But, the other 11,048 athletes have coaches too – some may even have two coaches!

A concept of 'heavyweight team leaders' was introduced by Clark and Fujimoto (1991). Heavyweight team leaders manage the activities of a cross-functional project team and work with senior management to construct an overarching product concept. Thus, executives can put into effect 'subtle control' techniques through the employment of such team leaders, who direct their cross-functional project teams in the perspective of a product vision. Clark and Fujimoto's (1991) findings show that heavyweight team leaders can and do know how to gain resources, respect from authority, and impact upon traditional functional loyalties whilst simultaneously constructing a strong product vision. However, there are three shortcomings. To begin with, the heavyweight team leaders appear as if they are stronger than *Spiderman* in talents, tasks, and *time*. Secondly, as Brown and Eisenhardt (1995) critique, there is a shortfall in political and psychological practicality. From a political viewpoint, the dependence of project teams on external processes for resources needs to be explored. Alternatively, from a psychological perspective, the methods used to actually motivate the employees of the team and to make the project team work and communicate with internal team mates and external actors are not addressed. Thirdly, understanding how senior managers affect NPD activities and how the responsibilities of senior management are distinct from the responsibilities of project managers is still vague and incomplete in the literature.

Imai, Ikujiro, and Takeuchi (1985) study seven successful NPD efforts in five different Japanese companies across several industries, and examine a problem-solving strategy involving cross-functional project teams that assisted successful NPD. They note that the senior management level should become involved in subtle control rather than just playing a supportive role for teams. The main inspiration behind subtle control is that successful project team-members uphold the balance between allowing ambiguity to facilitate problem solving at the project team level and exercising sufficient control to fit in with the overall corporate competencies and strategy. Briefly, for the best performance results, senior management should be involved in subtle control by communicating a clear vision and objectives to project teams concurrently by providing team-members with the freedom to work autonomously within the remit of that vision.

Imai *et al.*'s (1985) argument can be criticised because the concept of 'subtle control' has not been adequately expounded and remains as a vague concept (Brown and Eisenhardt, 1995). This lack of clarity impairs the usefulness of the perspective. In addition, is it appropriate to assume that executives or project managers are responsible for securing whether new products are synergistic with the core competencies of the company? (Leonard-Barton, 1992).

To investigate whether there is a relationship between the project team performance measurement system and the success/failure of new products, we conducted an in-depth study based on open-ended, face-to-face interviews with project managers, project team-members, human resource managers, and senior managers such as CEO's or vice presidents in four Taiwanese brand-name multinational computer companies in the Hsinchu Science-Based Industrial Park. We selected one project team from each sample company; each project team designed and produced a breakthrough product. We consider each breakthrough product on the basis of its bang, its visibility within each sample company as part of a breakthrough development process, the innovation of the product features at the time, and accessibility of its breakthrough product's data and its output – the breakthrough product.

1.2   High-technology industry in Taiwan

Taiwan is a place of contradictions; a small island called Formosa 240 miles long, home to 22.7 million people (January 2005 est.). From a *population* standpoint, Taiwan is a 'small' country. In contrast to Taiwan, the USA has 293 million people, Japan has 127.3 million people, and Mainland China has 1,298.8 million people. Using China as an example, it has an immense population, so it has the capability to manufacture products for other countries such as the USA, Taiwan, using low-skilled Chinese workers. In contrast to China, Taiwan is extremely small cannot compete with China in manufacturing capacity. Thus, Taiwan must use high-technology capabilities in order to remain competitive in the international market.[1]

Taiwan's high-technology industry has some attributes that make it suitable to study new products. To begin with, the disciplines involved in Taiwan's high-technology industry mean that technological uncertainties may be greater than in other industries; repeatedly product innovation is required in high precision, miniature electronic products and even in assembled products.

Secondly, Taiwan's high-technology industry requires high research and development (R&D)-intensity and knowledge-intensity characteristics. NPD requires linking management disciplines and product innovation with the market; in addition, the success of new products depends on the NPD process and management. Taiwanese brand-name international computer companies assemble project teams to produce their own computer brands, and these project teams work together with management disciplines and functional departments professional employees. Therefore, there is brand-name high-technology industry and higher possibilities for employing cross-functional breakthrough product project teams than in other industries.

Thirdly, there is an extensive practice of successful NPD in Taiwan's high-technology industry. The high-technology industry in Taiwan is characterised by several large and well-known technology-based Taiwanese companies. Many of these well-known companies have been dedicated to R&D, technology and product innovation for breakthroughs. New products seem to be the key to overall corporate success in Taiwan's high-technology industry, possibly more than in most other industries; and management disciplines, specified expertise, technology and teamwork permeate all the way through the corporate culture and vision.

---

[1] In order to control for the variations in industries' characteristics we conduct our study on one-industry only. As will be shown in the literature review, the SAPPHO studies, the Stanford Innovation Project, and the Project Newprod are major success-versus-failure research studies, but these studies cut across a broad array of industries rather than referring explicitly to any one industry (Cooper and Kleinschmidt, 1993). The results of these studies could be misleading. For example, a success factor such as 'high-rate of product innovation' might be central to success in an emerging, high-technology industry that produces semiconductors or high precision, miniature electronic products, but might not be important at all in a commodity chemical industry (Hayes, Pisano, Upton, and Wheelwright, 2005). Cross-industry-studies tend not to reveal these differences (Cooper and Kleinschmidt, 1993).

1.2.1 Key definitions of high-technology industry

Technology endeavour is a decisive cause of productivity growth and international competitiveness (OECD, 2003). Every country creates policies concerning high-technology to deal with increasing social, economic and environmental problems. The aim of a policy, such as encouraging entrepreneurship and innovation, the development of new products and so on, is to make the national innovation system adaptive enough to conquer these problems. However, the conception of high-technology is still not a well-defined term (Grupp, Münt, and Schmoch, 1996).

A high-technology industry classification is defined by the International Standard Industrial Classification, ISIC Revision 2 industry classifications (OECD, 2003). ISIC uses three indicators of technology intensity reflecting 'technology-producer' and 'technology-user' aspects. The three technology intensity indicators are: (1) R&D expenditures divided by value added, (2) R&D expenditures divided by production, and (3) R&D expenditures plus technology embodied in intermediate and investment goods divided by production. These indicators are evaluated for 1990 and for the aggregate of the ten Organisation for Economic Co-operation and Development (OECD) countries for which a measure of embodied technology is available, using 1990 USD purchasing power parities (Hatzichronoglou, 1997; OECD, 2003).

A simplified classification of manufacturing industries based on direct R&D intensities is presented in the last edition of OECD[2] using the STI (Science, Technology and Industry) Scoreboard. OECD STI uses the ISIC Revision 3 R&D expenditure and output data to develop an updated technology classification based on an evaluation of R&D intensities for 13 OECD countries for the period 1991–1997, to define what high-technology industry is. According to OECD, high-technology industry includes: aircraft and spacecraft (ISIC 353); pharmaceuticals (ISIC 2423); office, accounting and computing machinery (ISIC 30); radio, television and communication equipment (ISIC 32); and medical, precision and optical instruments (ISIC 33).

The Department of Statistics in the Ministry of Finance, Republic of China (ROC) promulgates *the Custom Import Tariff and Import and Export Commodity Classification of the Republic of China* to define the high-technology industry of Taiwan. The characteristics of the high-

---

[2] A multilateral institution made up of 30 market democracies from North America, Europe, and the Pacific Rim.

technology industry include that it employs high product value-added, complicated technologies, high-skill workers and a high ratio of R&D investment – such as chemistry, electrical machinery and equipment, electronics-telecommunications and transportation. Also, a company's core competence and bases of innovation rely on the company's phase of evolution from a small technology-based endeavour to a chief high-volume producer (OECD, 2003).

1.2.2   Distinctiveness of new products

New products are essential because they contribute to a company's growth and profitability and to its ability to compete in international markets (Crawford and Di Benedetto, 2003). New product innovations could be radical (discontinuous) or incremental (continuous) innovations, depending on the nature of the new knowledge created (Tushman and Anderson, 1986). In fact, radical new products play an imperative role in building competitive advantage and can contribute considerably to a company's development and profitability (Ali, 1994; Kleinschmidt and Cooper, 1991). That is, radical products are the goldmine and the key success factor (Cooper, 1979b) for companies.

Although most of the NPD literature has focused on incremental innovations and the NPD process as it concerns product improvements, upgrades, and line extensions, there has been extremely little research focused on radical new products (Veryzer, 1998). Even now, it is not ascertainable whether the best practices involved with incremental new products apply to radical new products as well or whether some of the practices are in reality counterproductive in this situation (Lynn, Morone, and Paulson, 1996; Morone, 1993; Veryzer, 1998). The development of radical products and discontinuous innovations are always the golden rules for high-technology companies (Cooper, 1979b). Therefore, an understanding of the distinctions between the radical and incremental new products, and their NPD processes are indispensable if the progress of radical new products is to be managed efficiently (Veryzer, 1998).

Kleinschmidt and Cooper (1991) define three categories of innovativeness: high, medium, and low, which reflects the degree to which technology is applied in a new way and to some extent the degree to which it is based on an existing product. Also, Wheelwright and Clark (1992) suggest that the degree of change, including manufacturing process change, represented by a product is the most useful way to classify NPD projects. Ali's (1994) argument is consistent with Tushman and Nadler's (1986) categorisation of radical innovation as the application of noteworthy technologies or ideas for making pioneering or new-to-the-world products. Otherwise, Meyers and Tucker (1989) hold that radical innovations encompass both the development of new technology and the introduction of a product into the market in a way that is unusual within the product class, and the highlighting of breakthrough products which entail remarkable leaps in terms of the customers' perceptions.

Veryzer (1998: 307) uses a 'Technological Capability' dimension and a 'Product Capability' dimension to delineate four levels of innovation. The *Technological Capability* dimension alludes to the degree to which the product implicates expanding (technological) capabilities (the way customers perceive the product functions) beyond existing (technology and product functionality) boundaries. The *Product Capability* dimension highlights the benefits (e.g. functionality) of the product as perceived by customers. Figure 1.1 describes the four levels of innovation.

Briefly, the term *new* products can be distinguished from either discontinuous/revolutionary, radical (Veryzer, 1998), original (Bart, 1999) or continuous/evolutionary, incremental (Veryzer, 1998), imitative (Bart, 1999). That is, terms such as radical, breakthrough, revolutionary, really new, game-changing, and boundary expanding have all been used to describe products that involve impressive departures from existing products or their logical extensions (Veryzer, 1998). The authors use the term 'breakthrough' to represent the *new* products in this book.

Briefly, breakthrough products generally signify the first entry of a new product class or category and are referred to as *new* to the world, *new* to the market, and *new* to the producing company (Bart, 1991 & 1999). The most breakthrough products involve advanced capabilities that

---

I. **Same** Technological Capability + **Same** Product Capability
= Continuous Products

II. **Advanced** Technological Capability + **Same** Product Capability
= Technological Discontinuous Products

III. **Same** Technological Capability + **Enhanced** Product Capability
= Commercially Discontinuous Products

IV. **Advanced** Technological Capability + **Enhanced** Product Capability
= Technological and Commercially Discontinuous Products
and New Product is Emerged

Figure 1.1   Formulations of Types of Product Innovation

do not exist in current products and cannot be achieved through the extension of existing technology. That is, the most breakthrough products bring significant new technologies and offer significantly enhanced benefits from a customer's perspective. For instance, personal computers, notebooks, cell phones, and pagers were breakthrough products when they were first introduced to the market.

The term *new product*, in this book, is narrowed down to a specific definition. It refers to physical, discrete, radical, and engineering products, such as personal computers and notebook computers. The importance of service settings where customers interact directly with the operating environment cannot be ignored. Particularly, online trading is obviously a breakthrough service in the financial services industry and, assessing its increasing volume, it has been a very successful service (financial product) innovation (Hayes *et al.*, 2005). However, although much of the study applies to products of all kinds, the development of physical products has been selected as the focus of this study. Therefore, four project teams that all produced breakthrough products, namely, Taiwanese brand-name notebook computers, are the focus of this study.

1.3   The role of management accounting and management accountants

Horngren, Bhimani, Foster, and Datar (1999: 5) argue that 'Management accounting measures and reports financial as well as other types of information that are primarily intended to assist managers in fulfilling the goals of the organisation.' In addition, Drury (2004: 7) defines that 'Management [a]ccounting is concerned with the provision of information to people within the organization to help them make better decisions and improve the efficiency and effectiveness[3] of existing operations ....' Simply, in theory, academic textbooks portray that accounting information should be suitable and helpful to the needs of users internal to the business and can be used to assist their managerial decision-making. However, Ryan, Scapens, and Theobald (2002: 68) argue that 'management accounting researchers were developing sophisticated mathematical models which practitioners considered too abstract and

---

[3]Emmanuel, Otley, and Merchant (1990: 29) define that '*Effectiveness* is concerned with the attainment of objectives; an action is effective to the extent that it achieves what it was intended to achieve. *Efficiency* is concerned with achieving a given result with a minimum use of resources.' In this book, the terms effectiveness and efficiency will be used as defined by Emmanuel *et al.*

unrelated to their needs.' In fact, in 1979, Chiu and Chang argued that due to the lack of adequate knowledge about some management accounting techniques and too complicated for staff to apply, some managers in Taiwan may not appreciate and decide to abandon these techniques used in the companies previously. In addition, practitioners study American academic management accounting textbooks and apply the management accounting techniques to their companies. However, few ask whether American management accounting techniques can be transferred and used successfully in the companies of a developing country, such as Taiwan (Chiu and Chang, 1979).

Historically, practitioners treat management accounting as a series of techniques and simply view the role of management accounting and accountants in very general terms, such as meeting management's needs for accounting information (Drury, 2004; Horngren *et al.*, 1999; Ryan *et al.*, 2002). Nevertheless, today's high-technology companies face an environment of intense competition, rapid change and uncertainty, so the role of management accounting and accountants has changed (Nixon, 1998). In today's complex economy, one of managers' missions is to search for new management accounting techniques and efficient management control systems to help their companies act in response and attain competitive advantage in the market. According to Scapens (1991: 9), 'The professional view appears to be that management accountants should be concerned with all aspects of accounting, except the external audit.'

In a classical textbook, Horngren (1975) distinguishes the role of cost accountant and management accountant. The cost accountants pursue *absolute truth*, i.e. to get as accurate or precise costs as possible. Conversely, management accounting stresses that different costs are for different purposes and management accountants attempt to find *conditional truth*. The traditional role of the management accountant is to collect and present the financial data, and the traditional role of management accounting systems is focused on transaction-heavy inspection and reconciliation engines (Maskell and Baggaley, 2001). However, Johnson and Kaplan (1987: 1) argue that 'Today's management accounting information, driven by the procedures and cycle of the organization's financial reporting system, is too late, too aggregated, and too distorted to be relevant for managers' planning and control decisions.'

After observing important changes in the nature of management accounting practice, Bromwich and Bhimani (1989) argue that due to increasing use of multi-disciplinary (cross-functional) teams, management accountants are now more integrated into the functional areas of the organisation. The role of management accountants has been changed to comprise managers and others drawn from different functions altogether to tackle particularly complex decision problems. Bromwich and Bhimani (1989) also argue that management accountants are now more directly involved in day-to-day decisions through the provision of informal or non-routine information. Also, there is increasing recognition of the need for management accountants to be outward-looking (for example, to identify competitors' cost structures and the company's own) and to report non-quantitative information (for example, information about quality, innovations, and so on). In conclusion, in today's teamwork environment, the role of management accountants should move to team-member and change-agent, and the role of management accounting systems should move to lean and vital providers of business insight (Maskell and Baggaley, 2001).

1.4   The gap between theory and practice in management accounting

According to Ryan *et al.* (2002) and Scapens (1991), the so-called *theory* of management accounting could be treated as a set of the management accounting concepts and techniques that portrayed in current academic textbooks. However, the *practice* of management accounting is frequently changed to facilitate the organisational response. Conventional wisdom holds that high-technology companies that are technology-intensive tend to be more innovative and creative and pay higher salaries to their employees. Conventional wisdom also holds that there is intense competition to motivate and to attract such high-technology professional employees under the assumption that they can be an engine for company's growth, serving by instance and diffusion to raise performance levels across all functions of company. Thus, it is essential that companies should apropos evaluate employees' performance and timely adjust their rewards based on their performance.

Based on the above argument, management certainly needs a management system (not only a performance measurement system) that enables the organisation to attract, encourage, and keep its professional employees. That is to say, it is possible that executives need to change previous or traditional management concepts and techniques such as performance measures that portrayed in current academic management accounting textbooks so that they can properly evaluate their employees. Therefore, expectably, there could be a gap between management accounting theory and practices concerning the performance measurement systems of the four breakthrough product project teams.

Such a gap is apparent and came to be recognised by management accounting researchers, although some researchers claim that the reason could be simply because of the time lag between theory and practice (Scapens, 1991). At this time, the role of management accounting researchers is to study both the extent and the context of theory (i.e. academic textbooks) and practice (i.e. what is going on in organisation). On the contrary, the role of management accountants is to look for accounting innovations and/or techniques relevant for the needs of modern business enterprises.

In their book of *The Rise and Fall of Management Accounting*, Johnson and Kaplan (1987) observe that the management accounting techniques were developed through the practical innovations of entrepreneurs and businessmen. For example, the Du Pont Power Company develops return on investment (ROI) as a measure of the commercial success of operating units. In the 1920s, the company's chief financial officer, F. Donaldson Brown, decomposes ROI into two parts – an operating return (return on sales) and asset turnover (sales to assets). Such techniques are still widely used in practice. However, not all techniques of management accounting textbooks are so popular in practice. Coates, Smith, and Stacey (1983) observe little formal analysis of cost behaviour in the day-to-day operation of management accounting systems and little use of marginal cost analysis in most of their sample companies.

In addition, even though many management accounting textbooks describe mathematical techniques or models for determining economic order quantities and stock levels, Gregory and Piper (1983) find that only simple techniques being used in practice. Even though numerous management articles describe the balanced scorecard for assisting companies in applying best practices in balanced scorecard and performance measurement for strategic management and transformation, still most of Taiwanese companies do not comprehend how to translate an organisation's vision and strategy into action and literally most of Taiwanese companies do not apply the balanced scorecard.

1.5   Objective and research questions

The velocity of international market and technological revolutions has sped up in the preceding decade. Essential to competitive success in the current tumultuous environment is the company's capability to R&D and launch new products. However, NPD activities in high-technology sectors are characterised by an amplified speed of innovation, shortened product life cycles, fast progresses in information and communication technologies (ICT), and the globalisation of NPD projects or teams (Godener and Söderquist, 2004; Söderquist and Nellore, 2000; Tomkovich and Miller, 2000). That is, there are still several dilemmas that are in need of solutions. Recently, there has been a call for further research into the factors or determinants of new product success/failure (González and Palacios, 2002).

Understandably, a comprehensible understanding of the new product success/failure factors is desirable so as to facilitate companies to optimise the company's resources devoted to the NPD process and amplify the market demand for a company's new products. However, there is little research on the impact of project team performance measurement systems on the success/failure of NPD (Brown and Eisenhardt, 1995; Godener and Söderquist, 2004; Millson and Wilemon, 2002). Accordingly, our objective is to explore whether there is a relationship between project team performance measurement systems and new product success/failure in four Taiwanese brand-name computer companies.

The importance of this objective stems from three major reasons. First, this study helps to explore the dominant incentive which aligns the interests of employees of project teams and shareholders of companies. NPD is important because new products are critical to companies' growth and organisational survival and new products are the outcomes of project teams. The use of teams in modern organisations has considerably increased over the last years (Cohen and Bailey, 1997). Organisations reported numerous benefits in using teams, including greater participation and contribution, augmented concentration to process improvements, and improved employee satisfaction (Wellins, Byham, and Dixon, 1994). Yet, from a decision rights theory, incentive contracting and performance measurement viewpoint, the teamwork setting remains a challenge (Towry, 2003).

Project teams perform non-routine tasks that span the broader processes such as the NPD process or value chain (Anderson, Hesford, and Young, 2002; Ittner and Larcker, 1995; Wruck and Jensen, 1994) and manage in dynamic environments, such as high-technology sectors, in which it is complicated to suitably align incentives (Rowe, 2004). When appropriate performance measures of individual contributions are not accessible, incentive contracting may not be helpful for encouraging employees to direct their efforts toward the organisation's goals. As a substitute, the utilisation of team incentives can bring about free-rider problems and then professional employees feel uncomfortable and upset.

After a while, these professional employees may leave their companies. Consequently, the problem of losing professional employees can occur.

Second, several researchers have pointed out that NPD processes are important to maintain a company's profitability and organisational survival in today's competitive business environment.[4] Many studies suggest that either important relationship exists between proficiently performed NPD activities and the success of new products (Cooper and Kleinschmidt, 1986, 1987a, 1990, 1991) or between organisational integration and new product success or failure (Kahn, 1996; Song, Neeley, and Zhao, 1996). Millson and Wilemon (2002) combined earlier research involving NPD proficiency and organisational integration and brought it up to date using empirical data from three major capital goods industries to investigate how NPD teams can be more successful in developing new products. But the key incentive of motivating people has still not been addressed.

In addition, Bourgeois and Eisenhardt (1988) and Hackman (1990) emphasise in their work some of the management processes that may lead team-members to be motivated to work as a team. However, these findings appear to lack intelligibility concerning *how teams work*; these researchers focus on how teams can be managed effectively without describing *what teamwork really is*. Thus, managers perhaps go along the recommended processes, but may also carry on with other activities that are counterproductive to the underlying psychological processes indispensable to teamwork (Lembke and Wilson, 1998). Exploring how companies form project teams, how to make project teams work and how to measure project teams' performance properly, from economic, sociological and psychological approaches is essential.

Third, most NPD studies have analysed successful North American firms, Japanese companies, or European companies (Brown and Eisenhardt, 1995; Cohen and Bailey, 1997), but it is possible that their results may not extend to other developing countries such as Taiwan or other kinds of companies such as computer companies. Furthermore, many widespread studies have relied on a Japanese standpoint. The Japanese have created several successful Japanese brand-name high-technology products and, Japanese comparisons have also been significant in improving thinking and helping research. However, Japanese industrial domination occasionally makes it unclear as to which features are essential to NPD and which are just relevant to Japanese industry.

---

[4]See, for example, Cooper, 1996; Cooper and Kleinschmidt, 1991, 1993; and Nixon, 1998.

The need for examining the factors involved in new product success or failure is clear but there have been limitations in previous research, which will be discussed in Chapters 2 and 3. Thus, to achieve the objective of this study, the following research questions are addressed:

RQ1: In computer companies' settings, how are project teams formed and how do they work, including preparation before forming the teams, and to what extent is authority delegated to the teams?

RQ2: In what areas is performance measured for project teams, and how are internal project team performance measurement systems operated and compared to the theoretical recommendations of the literature?

RQ3: Are the uses or purposes of project team performance measurement results and their impact realised in practice?

RQ4: What are the key impacts of the NPD performance measurement results on the behaviour of the members of the project teams and functional departments?

These four research questions incorporate the interaction of agency, stewardship, social identity, and self-categorisation theories as well as the organisational architecture of the sample companies under study in order to achieve the research objective – to investigate the relationship between project team performance measurement systems and the success/failure of a team's output – the new product. The first research question looks at social identity and self-categorisation theories as well as the decision allocation systems of companies by introducing how to form project teams and the practices of teamwork. The second, third, and fourth research questions examine whether performance measurement systems are effective and observe interactions with decision allocation and reward systems. The authors show how the project team performance measurement system affects the success/failure of a new product and why project team performance measurement systems are the main cause of the success/failure of the new product. In the next section, the significance of this study is discussed in more details.

1.6   Significance of the study

Huberman and Miles (1994) criticise the purported myth that only controlled quantitative experiments can establish causal relationships. In contrast, Huberman and Miles (1994: 434) argue that 'causality is an unworkable concept in human behaviour' and 'qualitative studies ... are especially well suited to finding causal relationships.' However, recent researchers such as Rowe (2004) still prefer quantitative experiments. In addition, Tomkins and Groves (1983a: 364) argue that 'most academics do not often seem to use their practical experience in guiding their research in terms of topic coverage or method of investigation; at least not with respect to that published in leading academic journals.' This could be one of basic reasons why practitioners may perceive academic accounting research as divorced from practices (Ashton, Hopper, and Scapens, 1995).

One of the authors used a two-year practical working experience in a Taiwanese multinational computer company to this NPD project team research. Utilising an exploratory and explanatory multiple-case design in order to study how practitioners (e.g. cross-functional project team-members) perceive their work environment (e.g. corporate culture and the reality of teamwork). Specific areas addressed include; what issues they feel are of concern (e.g. authority, pay structure, performance measurement), and how they recognise their influence upon accounting practices and whether they have been influenced by accounting practices to witness the influence of performance measurement on human behaviour and to consequently address the gap in the performance measurement-new product success/failure relationship in NPD literature.

Although the existing literature on NPD is intensive, ranging from broad-brush explorations to in-depth case studies and across several types of product, firm, and industry, there are still many gaps remaining (Brown and Eisenhardt, 1995). For example, there is a widespread dependence on products, firms, and industries from the USA, Japan, and Europe, but not Taiwan. Thus, Taiwanese brand-name computer companies were used as sample companies in this study to gain a different viewpoint from the USA, Japan, and Europe. Also, the actual use of performance measurement results and the resulting impact on team-member behaviour and functional departments have been neglected.

Brown and Eisenhardt (1995) emphasise that project teams were found to enhance project success. But, the aspect of *how* project teams enhance project success is missing. In addition, it is reasonable that senior management only support potential promising projects, because of limited corporate resources such as budget and time. The authors selected two project teams from two successful sample companies which have increased sales on their new products, and two project teams from two unsuccessful sample companies which have decreased sales on their new products to examine whether project team performance measurement systems are a key factor in new product success/failure.

Particular organisations, surrounded by wide-ranging organisational categories, differ along many dimensions such as authority, compensation, performance measurement, capital structure, distribution, and sales practices (Jensen, 1983; Milgrom and Roberts, 1992). There is a lack of understanding why specific organisations differ along these dimensions, and if NPD business is considerably influenced by organisational architecture, then without a basic and comprehensive understanding of the connection among organisational structures scholars cannot gain a whole picture of why NPD differ across organisations (Jensen, 1983).

A core problem with cross-functional project teams is that, in a teamwork environment, individuals work within a rigorously controlled environment in which it is difficult to appropriately align incentives (Rowe, 2004). The literature has voiced that trade-offs between formal economic incentives and informal control mechanisms demonstrates that social control mechanisms such as trust, team identification and collectivism can mitigate the free-rider problems (Evans, Hannan, Krishnan, and Moser, 2001; Rowe, 2004; Towry, 2003). Rowe (2004) demonstrates that if the cross-functional team structure and the process-level accounting report structure support group framing, the cross-functional team structure can help to mitigate the free-rider problem indirectly by inducing informal control mechanisms. But the authors pay attention to how to structure a team that accomplishes the team purpose of achieving adequate integration through business environment consideration, new product strategy, and appropriate organisational architecture.

1.7 Conclusion and book structure

There are many academic debates regarding whether the incentive works in improving performance, or the effectiveness of monetary incentives to individuals, or the role of incentive in organisations and the like. These debates aim to find out the usefulness of incentives, but the authors place emphasis on how to make the incentive useful to organisations and aim to uncover the key incentive cause of motivating employees to improve performance. In this book, we attempt to bridge the gap regarding the relationship between new product project team performance measurement systems and new product success/failure. By bridging this gap, we suggest a way for employers to effectively motivate and retain their professional employees of teams, to improve performance and effectiveness of new product project teams, and in turn enhancing new product success.

The remainder of this book consists of eight chapters. The next chapter provides an extensive review of previous research in the area of new product success/failure. It explores the role of performance measurements of cross-functional project teams in Taiwan's high-technology sector in new product success/failure factors and their interaction of organisational architecture within companies.

Chapter 3 overviews the company's organisational architecture. It encompasses three systems: the system of assignment of decision rights to NPD participants within the company, the system of rewarding/ punishing new product project members and the performance measurement system to evaluate the corporate executive officer (CEO), business units, and project teams. The importance of these systems of organisations has been recognised by many writers and researchers in economics and management.

Chapter 4 develops a theoretical framework that will be used to analyse empirical data. The chapter examines different theories and evidence concerning the effects of incentives on team effort, team performance, and team outcome – on new products. This framework draws on theories of agency, stewardship, social identity, and self-categorisation to understand the relationships of incentive-effort, effort-effectiveness, effort-performance, and performance-success.

Chapter 5 details the research methodology and methods used to collect empirical data. It discusses alternative methodologies and methods and selects the most suitable methodology and methods to address the research questions. The chapter also introduces the case study design, including the preparation tasks and case study sites.

Chapter 6 provides within case studies analysis and interpretation. After managing and organising the raw data from interviews and documents, the authors set a list of themes as the code and direction for each case. Following these themes, we describe and explain the process of each breakthrough product project team to provide an understanding of the causality of the project team performance measurement system and new product success/failure.

Chapter 7 compares and summarises assumptions and findings across the four cases and illustrate an empirical framework so that the external validity can be extended and increased and the findings could be used for further research and practice.

Chapter 8 discusses the important issues related to the four cases reported in earlier chapters. In this chapter we argue, based on empirical findings, that the performance measurement system will eventually affect the behaviour of the agent and the steward.

Chapter 9 explains the links between theoretical assumptions and speculations, the significance, contributions, implications, limitations, and empirical findings of this study. It also explains some opportunities for future research.

2
New Product Development Success Factors

2.0 Introduction

In this chapter we review recent literature related to the success factors of outputs of NPD project teams and performance measurements of project teams in Taiwan's high-technology sector. The literature shows that considerable previous research exists in the area of new product success/failure. However, there is no agreement among scholars on the degree of importance and the influence of these factors on the success/ failure of new products.

This chapter is organised as follows:

- Overview of new product development research
- New product innovation: past evidence and present application
- Conclusion

2.1 Overview of new product development research

There have been several review articles in the area of NPD (Balachandra and Friar, 1997; Brown and Eisenhardt, 1995; Cusumano and Nobeoka, 1992; Griffin and Hauser, 1996; Krishnan and Ulrich, 2001). There are at least five common perspectives: marketing, organisations, engineering design, operations management, and decision perspectives. Often, there are great differences between these perspectives in the level of construct at which these researchers studied NPD, not only in the methodology used and assumptions made, but in the abstraction of how NPD is carried out (Krishnan and Ulrich, 2001). For example, much of the marketing and engineering design literature is at a more in depth abstraction, with the focal point being the individual product engineer or the market researcher and the matters challenging them (Shocker and Srinivasan, 1979).

The project team performance measurement system is the focal point in this study in order to see whether it could be a critical factor of new product success. Thus, we concentrate only on the organisational perspective, paying attention at a comparatively aggregate level to the determinants of project success. From an organisations-oriented perspective, focusing at a micro level on how specific new products are developed, Brown and Eisenhardt (1995) organise NPD literature into three research streams: NPD as a rational plan, communication web, and for disciplined problem solving.

The rational plan stream focuses on exploring which factors, out of an extremely broad variety of factors, were linked with the financial success of a new product, whereas the communication web stream concentrates on the narrow but deep effects of communication on the project team. In addition, disciplined problem solving work centres on the effects of a new product – a project team, its suppliers, and project team leaders on the real NPD process. These three streams are developed from different foundations and are centred on rather particular parts of NPD. It can be noticed that the research within each stream is theoretically and methodologically similar, and they offer complementary and occasionally overlapping insights into NPD (Brown and Eisenhardt, 1995). These three streams contribute to our understanding of the NPD process and its success but each stream encountered different shortcomings.

For example, the shortcomings of the rational plan stream include: (1) too many important findings (Griffin and Page, 1993) and too much factor analysis (over 75 measures); (2) the methodological approach relies heavily on single informants; (3) results do not relying on well-defined constructs and without reporting non-significant findings. Undeniably, the rational plan stream largely defines the relevant factors for NPD literature by a comprehensive overview of the NPD process. Thus, in order to avoid such shortcomings in this study we, first, focus on investigating the relationship between the project team performance measurement system and new product success, second, collect data from multiple sources – interviews with project team-members, leaders, and related senior managers, and finally, preparing a case study protocol and database.

Conversely, the shortcomings of communication web work include: (1) it excessively focuses on communication by project team-members and ignores other factors such as the organisation of the work and product attributes; (2) it focuses on subjective performance measures; (3) it does not distinguish the types of products. But, the in-depth focus of the communication web (size depth emphasised) balances the across-the-board (breadth emphasised) outlook of the rational plan by looking inside of the project team. Thus, in order to avoid such shortcomings in this study we consider (1) other factors such as team identification, incentives, and organisational architecture; (2) objective performance measures such as product profitability; and (3) breakthrough products.

The shortcomings of disciplined problem solving research include: (1) a lack of political and psychological realism; (2) some concepts which are challenging to comprehend; (3) extensive reliance on the Japanese view. Compared to the rational plan stream, this stream is more specific about the effective organisation of work and is more focused on the NPD process and product concept than on the financial success of the new product. In comparison to the communication web stream, this stream has a broader reach and considers the role of suppliers, senior management, project leaders, and project teams. Thus, in order to avoid such shortcomings in this study we focus on (1) economic, sociological, and psychological perspectives; (2) clear concepts such as core competence, organisational culture, long-term strategy; and (3) The Taiwanese viewpoint.

From the above discussion we can see that these three streams focus on somehow overlapping and complementary sets of constructs but in this study we attempt to retain the benefits of each stream and improve on its shortcomings.

The most relevant studies in NPD literature are highlighted in Table 2.1. Reviewing the NPD literature, most NPD studies analyse successful North American, Japanese, and European firms. However, as far as is known none of previous studies analyses Taiwanese companies, though the significance and influence of Taiwanese high-technology companies in international markets is recognised. Therefore, the context of this study is focused on Taiwanese companies.

2.2 New product innovation: past evidence and present application

The last decade has seen considerable changes in the business environment including fast and breakthrough technological developments in computers, telecommunication, and information sciences, globalisation of business, continuing mergers, acquisitions and strategic alliances, increased government and public analysis of business decisions,

Table 2.1 Summary of Selected Studies in NPD Literature

Author(s)	Sample	Context
Rothwell (1972) Rothwell, Freeman, Horsley, Jervis, Robertson, and Townsend (1974)	43 success or failure productpairs – SAPPHO	United Kingdom (UK) chemical and instrument firms
Allen (1971, 1977)	345 R&D professional employees in 60 projects	Large USA R&D laboratories
Cooper (1979b)	102 successful and 93 failed new products	The Project Newprod in 103 Canadian industrial firms
Katz (1982)	50 R&D project teams	One large USA R&D laboratory
Katz and Allen (1985)	86 R&D project teams	Nine technology-based, major USA firms
Maidique and Zirger (1984, 1985) Zirger and Maidique (1990)	The Stanford Innovation Project – 70 product pairs 86 product pairs	21 case studies in California firms 86 USA Fortune 1000 electronics firms
Imai *et al.* (1985) Takeuchi and Nonaka (1986)	Seven successful NPD projects	Five Japanese companies
Clark, Chew, and Fujimoto (1987) Clark and Fujimoto (1991) Hayes, Wheelwright, and Clark (1988)	Harvard Auto Study 29 NPD projects	20 firms in the auto industry – the USA, Japan, and Europe
Iansiti (1992, 1993)	27 NPD projects	Firms in mainframe computer industry – the USA, Europe, Japan
Subramaniam, Rosenthal, and Hatten (1998)	Project teams, global NPD processes	13 multi-national firms – Seven Japanese, three American, two European firms, one joint venture Japan and the USA
Davila (2000)	12 business units	Seven companies – Europe, the USA

Table 2.1 Summary of Selected Studies in NPD Literature – *continued*

Author(s)	Sample	Context
González and Palacios (2002)	365 firms were contacted 195 firms – sample companies	195 firms in electric and electronic equipment, and transport equipment manufacturing industry – Spain
Godener and Söderquist (2004)	Three electronic companies	The high-technology sector in French

increased deregulation, privatisation, and cooperation between businesses and government, and changes in business practices such as downsizing, outsourcing and re-engineering (Wind and Mahajan, 1997). However, regardless of these striking changes, NPD practices have only seen few changes (Krishnan and Ulrich, 2001).

Production innovation is a major way to increase a company's profitability. However, it is not an easy task to create successful new products. For example, the Wall Street Journal (1992) reports that, of the practically 16,000 new products introduced in 1991, approximately 90% did not accomplish their business objectives. Even though many studies have attempted to find out the important factors that can designate the success or failure of new product projects, it is still difficult to predict why some new products succeed while most fail, because NPD is notoriously risky (Hopkins, 1980) and also a complex and difficult task to most of companies (Balachandra and Friar, 1997).

The importance of effective NPD is recognised in both the marketing (Shocker and Srinivasan, 1979; Wind and Mahajan, 1997), and the innovation literature (Rothwell, 1972; Veryzer, 1998). Krishnan and Ulrich (2001:1) define 'NPD as the transformation of a market opportunity and a set of assumptions about product technology into a product available for sale.' Successful NPD needs an organisation-wide information accumulation and communicate process designed to diminish possibilities of uncertainty in meeting customers needs (Moenaert and Souder, 1990). Explicitly, executives who aim to improve NPD performance should involve and promote effective participation of all departments and professional employees with potential influence on the outcome of the NPD project team.

Many studies have been carried out to examine the NPD process (Cooper and Kleinschmidt, 1987a; Griffin and Hauser, 1996; Hughes and Chafin, 1996; Wind and Mahajan, 1997), to identify what steps a company ought to conduct (Cooper, 1988a, 1990; Crawford and Di Benedetto, 2003), to document what impact each step has on the outputs – new products (Cooper, 1990; Cooper and Kleinschmidt, 1986), and \to assess the role of models in supporting and improving the NPD pro-cess (Mahajan and Wind, 1986). Cooper (1988b, 1996) explains that the NPD process is a goal directed, stepwise process, involving a series of information acquisition activities and evaluation points. Cooper (1988b: 250) further argues that adopting a 'systematic new product process … is one solution to correct the serious deficiencies that are common to many firm's new product efforts.'

However, a systematic new product process seems to be not enough for improving companies' new product efforts. Some studies (e.g., Cooper, 1988a; Millson and Wilemon, 2002; Wind and Mahajan, 1997) have noted that companies often fail in their new product efforts because of their negligence of integration processes needed for successful NPD; the omission of important activities from their NPD processes; and their repeatedly ineffective and incompetent performance of NPD tasks. NPD needs the full involvement of most of the departments such as R&D, marketing, manufacturing, procurement, quality assurance; and the management disciplines including operations, human resources, and finance (Wind and Mahajan, 1997). Therefore, it is necessary to fully integrate these various perspectives for successful NPD (Moenaert and Souder, 1990).

Previous research increasingly highlights the significance of 'teams' for managerial success in the contemporary economy. Four types of team have been identified by Cohen and Bailey (1997). These types are work teams (Wellins, Byham, and Wilson, 1991), parallel teams (Bushe and Shani, 1991), project teams (Parker, 1994), and management teams (Nadler and Ancona, 1992; Mohrman, Cohen, and Mohrman, 1995). Work teams are ongoing work units responsible for producing products (e.g. computer manufacturing teams) or providing services (e.g. government audit teams); the members of work teams are stable, full-time, and cross-trained in various skills relevant to the tasks they do. Parallel teams draw together personnel from diverse work units to carry out functions that a regular organisation is not prepared to do well (Bushe and Shani, 1991); the members of parallel teams are responsible for problem-solving and improvement-oriented activities (Cohen and Bailey, 1997). Project teams produce one-time outputs such as a new product within a limited time (e.g. NPD teams in high-technology firms or R&D teams in pharmaceutical industry). Management teams manage and give direction to the sub-units under their jurisdiction, creatively integrating interdependent sub-units across key business processes (Mohrman *et al.*, 1995); the members of management teams are responsible for the overall performance of a business unit.

Typically, high-technology companies draw the team-members from different disciplines and functional departments so that esoteric expertise can be relevant to the new product project. In addition, new product project team-members share responsibility for outputs – new products. However, a work team includes a set of people who work together to do a task, and the members share a common goal, are also coordinated by a leader, but their performance is evaluated using individual performance measurements (Wellins *et al.*, 1991). Therefore, work teams, and parallel teams are irrelevant to this study.

New product project team-members are the personnel who actually do the work of NPD and who have specialist expertise as well. For example, the R&D members of the project team should have abilities to transform vague ideas, concepts, and product specifications into the R&D of new products. The marketing members within the project team should be professional marketing employees who are familiar with the advances in marketing research and modelling, and are experienced in using these techniques (Wind and Mahajan, 1997). That is, the project team-members are not managers from senior management, so management teams are not relevant either. Naturally, the project team is the central of this study.

2.2.1   Key definitions of new product success/failure

A key to maintain a competitive advantage in the market is the ability to repeatedly commercialise successful new products, including both physical goods and services (Griffin and Page, 1996). Thus, before discussing the new product success or failure factors, it is important to set up a clear definition or criterion by which to judge success or failure of a new product. The success and failure of new product innovation is difficult to define, because it composites several measures; subjective and objective (Balachandra and Friar, 1997).

Hopkins (1980: 4) agues that 'a major new product was taken to be a success if it met management's original expectations for it in all important respects' and *vice versa*. Such a major new product frequently sustains sales, but the severe possibility is that its performance proves so unacceptable that it is in fact withdrawn from the market. In Cooper and Kleinschmidt's (1988: 251) study, 'success and failure are defined from a profitability standpoint, i.e. the degree to which the new product exceeded (or fell short of) the acceptable profitability level for this type of investment.' Furthermore, Millson and Wilemon (2002: 3) define new product success as 'how well a new product effort exceeds or falls short of expectations stipulated by the new product developing firm.' They examined 'four measures of new product market success – profits, sales, the ability to enter existing markets, and the ability to create and enter new markets.'

Griffin and Page (1993) demonstrate different views about the complication of the definition of success in NPD. They explain that project success comprises three independent categories: consumer acceptance, financial performance, and technical success. Every company launches a new product and hopes to achieve overall success – the product is accepted by customers, brings enormous financial return to the company, and also, is technically elegant which provides a competitive advantage to the company, namely, it is commercialised efficiently. However, they argue that such a perfect NPD project does not exist, and emphasise that companies normally have to sacrifice some level of success in one category to achieve success in another. Specifically, one new product could simultaneously be a success and failure, and that is why it is difficult to assess product success. For example:

> The Xerox Mouse is ... a technical and customer success, but a financial failure. Xerox invented the mouse at their Palo Alto Research Corporation laboratories in the mid-1970s. The product, like Post-it Notes™, is now almost ubiquitous. Nearly everywhere there is a personal computer, there is a mouse. However, the mouse on your desk does not say Xerox. Apple, Microsoft ... firms have all profited from Xerox's development, although Xerox has not. Xerox did not commercialise the mouse – for them the product is a failure because ... no financial return on the investment. (Griffin and Page, 1996: 480)

The above discussion suggests that there is no clear scale for measuring new product success and failure, since there is no single common measure of success (Balachandra and Friar, 1997). Also, success is a composite of a number of objective, perceptions, behavioural and attitudinal measures (Cohen and Bailey, 1997). However, using Veryzer's (1998) definition of the breakthrough product, really breakthrough products are advanced technological capability and enhanced product capability, i.e. technological and commercially discontinuous products.

Additionally, according to the Taiwan Stock Exchange Corporation (TSEC) Criteria for Review of Securities Listings, an issuing domestic high-technology company applying for listing its stock must meet product or technology innovation and profitability criteria.[1]

In this study we use the TSEC Criteria in assessing the success of a new product. As will be seen later our four sample teams under study all produced breakthrough products as defined by Veryzer of the breakthrough product, i.e., the four sample company had innovated at least a product or a technology with market potential. However, the four companies must meet profitability criterion as well to be successful based on TSEC criteria. Thus, profitability,[2] i.e. financial success is the measure of new product success in this study.

2.2.2 New products: key success factors versus failure factors

After almost four decades of studies, there is still not a prescribed common criterion that can explain how successful new products are created (Poolton and Barclay, 1998). The pioneering Project SAPPHO (Rothwell *et al.*, 1974), which employs a success-versus-failure comparison methodology, was the first effort to analytically compare commercially successful and unsuccessful innovations from the same market. The SAPPHO research identifies that successful companies should have a much better understanding of customer needs, attend more to marketing and advertising, perform NPD work more effectively, encourage more use of outside specific expertise, and authorise and promote responsible and experienced professional employees to senior manage-

---

[1]TSEC Criteria for Review of Securities Listings, Chapter II The Listing of Domestic Securities, Section 1 The Listing of Stock, Article 5,

'Where the central authority in charge of the enterprise concerned has issued an unequivocal opinion certifying that the issuing company applying for the listing of its stock is a technology-based enterprise and the said issuing company meets the criteria listed below, this Corporation will agree to list its stock:

1. ...

2. It has successfully developed a product or a technology with market potential, and the company has obtained an appraisal opinion from the central authority in charge of the enterprise concerned.

3. ...

4. Its net worth in both its most recent financial report and in its financial report for the most recent fiscal year represents two-thirds or greater of the amount of its paid-in capital.

5. ...' (TSEC, accessed 14 February 2006)

[2]The four sample companies define profitability measures as a project team's ability to generate revenues in excess of the costs incurred in producing those revenues. In this study, we do not intend to measure business success.

ment levels. Their conclusion was that professional employees and good management techniques are the keys of success.

Rubenstein *et al.* (1976) concentrate on defining the barriers (e.g. too much management support) and facilitators in the NPD process. The finding was that there is no one factor governing success, because in some cases one company's barrier could be another company's facilitator. They identify that the formal aspects, such as organisational architecture, control mechanisms and formal decision-making processes, are shown to have little effect on new product success. Individuals are found to be important at the outset, during the progress and at the end of a new product project. However, Rubenstein *et al.* (1976) categorise both technical and commercial success into three groups: the market orientation, open communication, and the support of senior management.

The Project Newprod (Cooper, 1979b) is an exploratory study aimed to categorise those characteristics that separate 102 new product successes from 93 failures in 103 Canadian industrial firms. Cooper (1979b) develops a list of 77 factors that are considered to motivate new product outcomes. Respondents were required to distinguish each venture on the 77 factors. The use of factor analysis and multiple regression analysis revealed a set of success factors: 11 factors in terms of three keys to success, three barriers, three facilitators and two weakly related factors (see Figure 2.1). The results indicate that new product projects that scored high in all of the three success factors have a 90% chance of success. However, 93% of new product projects that are low on all three success factors had a chance of success.

Cooper's (1979b) findings are offered in much more detail than other studies, in that they are more adapted to the product and market aspects and little emphasis is placed on the management, communication, and

Three success factors	Three barriers	Three facilitators	Two weakly related factors
• Introducing a unique and superior product. • Market knowledge and marketing efficiency. • Technical or production synergy and proficiency.	• High priced product relative to competition. • Being in a dynamic market. • Entering a highly competitive market.	• A good 'product or company fit' with respect to managerial and marketing resources. • Strong marketing communication and launch effort. • Being in a large, growing, high need market.	• Avoiding products new to the firm. • Having a market derived idea with considerable investment involved.

Figure 2.1   Project Newprod: 11 Factors

people perspectives. A following study by Cooper and Kleinschmidt (1987a) expanded on Cooper's earlier work – the Project Newprod, using a structured interview questionnaire completed by managers of about 203 products in a total of 125 Canadian manufacturing firms, including 123 successes and 80 failures. Cooper and Kleinschmidt (1987a) find that new products which entered into large and growing markets and/or launched into markets with low overall intensity of competition had more possibility of being successful. Additionally, they identify 11 success- versus-failure factors, typically including financial measures such as profitability, sales, relative revenues, and market share.

Furthermore, Cooper and Kleinschmidt (1993) conduct another piece of Newprod NPD research to examine the success-versus-failure issue by an in depth study of 103 new product projects in the chemical industry in North America and Europe. They found that product differential advantage is most strongly related with commercially successful products. Contrary to their earlier work (1987b), Cooper and Kleinschmidt (1993) found that market competitiveness has no relationship with product success. These contradicting results support the need for further study (Brown and Eisenhardt, 1995) on the effect of market competitiveness on new product project outcomes.

Montoya-Weiss and Calantone (1994) review and summarise factors found to drive new product success at the project level (see Figure 2.2). Cooper and Kleinschmidt (1995) agree that these factors considerably impact new product management (Crawford and Di Benedetto, 2003) for many companies, because these companies re-engineered their NPD processes, building in project success factors. Also, links to new product success are useful in screening or project selection and prioritisation criteria, as companies have to forfeit minor projects and focus on being more proficient in their project portfolio management efforts (Griffin and Page, 1996). However, Cooper and Kleinschmidt (1995) argue that a broader macro view of the determinants of success is missing in Montoya-Weiss and Calantone's (1994) analysis.

A study by Terwiesch, Loch, and Niederkofler (1998) aimed to identify the relationship between NPD performance and business success. Their study was based on Brown and Eisenhardt's (1995) work which observed the omission of market context factors in NPD performance research. Terwiesch *et al.* (1998) conducted a study of 86 business units in 12 different electronics industries worldwide, by developing a market contingency framework for understanding the impact of NPD performance on a company's profitability. They also suggest that the overall relevance of NPD

Strategic Factors	• Product advantage • Technological synergy • Marketing synergy • Company resources • Strategy of product
Development Process Factors	• Proficiency of technical activities • Proficiency of marketing activities • Proficiency of up-front or homework activ • Protocol (product definition) • Top management support • Speed to market • Financial or business analysis
Market Environment Factors	• Marketing potential size • Market competitiveness • External environment
Organisational Factors	• Internal and/or external relations • Organisational factors

Figure 2.2   Typical Success Factors Found at the Project Level

performance to business success relies on the company's competitive industry environment.

The results revealed that industry membership accounts for 23% of the variance in profits, with 18% of the variance determined by industry profitability and 5% by the market share, market growth, and external context dimensions of market context. Terwiesch *et al.* (1998) found that NPD performance has the most considerable effect in slow-growth and with long product life cycle markets. Also, in stable industries, low R&D intensity, product line freshness, and technical product performance increase profitability. Finally, Terwiesch *et al.* (1998) found that there is no significant relationship between NPD performance and profitability in industries with fast growth or short product life cycles; and large companies can much influence their financial performance through NPD, whereas the profitability of small firms is motivated mainly by their market environment.

We argue that cross-functional project teams are critical and central to NPD process performance (Brown and Eisenhardt, 1995; Clark and Fujimoto, 1991; Zirger and Maidique, 1990). Also, in reality, project team usually consists of less than 20 members, and come from different functions. The multi-functional diversity of project teams increases the amount and variety of information available to help project team-members to understand the NPD process more quickly and improve

NPD performance for producing new products. Specifically, an empowered project team, a strong NPD process, an attractive new product, and a munificent market are supposed to lead to a financially successful new product.

Terwiesch *et al.* (1998) attempted to find out a relationship between NPD performance and business success. Business success or corporate success is a broad area as there are many factors such as senior management investment policy which can influence business success. Explicitly, financially successful NPD cannot guarantee business success, whereas business failure does not mean NPD failure. Although Terwiesch *et al.* (1998) aimed at identifying the impact of NPD performance on a company's profitability; their hypothesis and analysis were too vague.

The Stanford Innovation Project began in 1982 as a long-term study, surveying 70 product success-failure pairs and conducting 21 case studies mainly with California electronic firms and emphasising product advantages, market attractiveness, and internal organisation (Maidique and Zirger, 1984, 1985). The Stanford Innovation Project focused on the USA electronic industry because of its continual rapid technological change. The project emphasised the uniqueness and cost or quality competences of new products, the importance of market knowledge, high internal communication between teams, and senior management support. The most important result was the association between the profitability of the product with new product success.

There are some studies such as Imai *et al.* (1985), Takeuchi and Nonaka (1986), Harvard Auto Study (Clark *et al.*, 1987; Clark and Fujimoto, 1991; Hayes *et al.*, 1988) emphasise senior management 'involvement' not just 'support.' But, one of common constraints or bureaucratic barriers on innovation in larger companies is senior management isolation – many senior executives have little contact with conditions in the factory or with customers who are delivered the outcomes of new products (Ulwick, 2002) which might influence their approach towards breakthrough innovations. Since risk perceptions are inversely related to familiarity and experience, commercially successful oriented senior executives are prone to perceive breakthrough innovations as more problematic than acquisitions that are perhaps just as uncertain but that appear more familiar (Quinn, 1985). Thus, senior management 'involvement' is broader than 'support' and is helpful to technological innovations, especially in breakthrough projects.

Indeed, several empirical studies have identified new product success versus failure factors (Cooper and Kleinschmidt, 1995, 1996; González and Palacios, 2002; Millson and Wilemon, 2002), have proposed what factors separate successors from failures (Cooper, 1979a; Cooper and Kleinschmidt, 1987a, 1990, 1995), have extended review of the relevant literature to generalise comments about the success-failure factors (Balachandra and Friar, 1997; Brown and Eisenhardt, 1995; Griffin and Page, 1993), and have highlighted the need for developing tools and procedures that provide means to better run the NPD process (Crawford and Di Benedetto, 2003). Also, studies concerning NPD, product, and process innovation, such as enhancing productivity capacity, quality and the utilisation of different approaches for managing innovation opportunities, have been increased (Ali, 1994; Morone, 1993).

Although numerous studies have been pinpointed understanding the managerial processes related to NPD (Cooper and Kleinschmidt, 1986; Griffin and Hauser, 1996; Griffin and Page, 1993; Hughes and Chafin, 1996), these studies simply focus on the nature of incremental NPD innovations. Certainly, on the one hand, incremental NPD research has clarified and explained the NPD process; however, on the other hand, it has mostly neglected the NPD process as it concerns new products involving breakthrough innovations (Cooper and Kleinschmidt, 1991; Veryzer, 1998). This study focuses on breakthrough innovations.

2.2.3 New product development processes and project teams

The literature shows different processes of NPD. Figure 2.3 shows a series of logical steps which begin with idea screening and eventually lead to testing and commercialisation as introduced by different studies. However, breakthrough innovation involves a very high degree of technological uncertainty, a sequence of innovations, long development times (Lynn *et al.*, 1996; Morone, 1993), an uncertainty as to the appropriate instruments for the new technology and a greater distance from the market in terms of time and customer familiarity with the new product (Veryzer, 1998). Affected by these uncertain factors, the NPD process of breakthrough products may not follow the same way described and is not particularly amenable to being managed according to the NPD process for more incremental products.

Veryzer (1998) designs an overlapping breakthrough NPD process (see Figure 2.3, E) which is initiated by the convergence of developing new technologies, various environmental factors, and the vision of a strong product champion (Wind and Mahajan, 1997), and then formulates into a product instrument for the new technology in order that the direction and feasibility of the product may be determined. Based on this logic, the formative prototype phase is used to examine and formulate the technological part of the breakthrough product,

A. Cooper and Kleinschmidt (1986: 1–13)(1988a: I–III)	B. Jenkins et al. (1997)	C. Kotler (1997)	D. Ulrich and Eppinger (2004)	E. Veryzer (1998)
I. Pre-development Activities 1. Initial Screening 2. Preliminary Market Assessment 3. Preliminary Technical Assessments (Design and Manufacturing)	1. Define/ Know New Product Strategy 2. Generate Ideas 3. Screen/Evaluate Concept 4. Specification and Planning	1. Idea Generation 2. Idea Screening 3. Concept Testing 4. Marketing Strategy Development 5. Business Analysis	0. Planning 1. Concept Development	1. Convergence (Dynamic Drifting) (Contextual Factors and Visionary: Technology and Market) 2. Formulation 3. Preliminary Design (Formal Evaluation Screen)
II. Product Development and Testing 4. Detailed Market Study/Research 5. Business/Financial Analysis 6. Product Development (Formation of Prototypes and Pilot Run Products) 7. In-house Product Testing 8. Customer Product Tests	5. Prototype Development 6. Test and Evaluate Design	6. Product Development 7. Market Testing	2. System-Level Design 3. Detail Design 4. Testing and Refinement	4. Formative Prototype 5. Lead User Testing 6. Design Modification 7. Prototype 8. Commercialisation Activities
III. Commercialization 9. Test Market/Local Sell 10. Trial Production 11. Precommercialisation Business Analysis 12. Production Start-up 13. Market Lunch	7. Volume Manufacture	8. Commercialization	5. Production Ramp-Up	

Figure 2.3   Comparisons of the Process of NPD

develop an application for the new technology and to allow subsequent activities such as opportunity analysis and target market selection to be undertaken (Veryzer, 1998). Namely, the breakthrough NPD process still involves market assessment and financial or business analysis, just unlike the incremental NPD process does – prior to beginning development.

As will be explained later we examine project teams and their outputs – breakthrough products; therefore, Veryzer's (1998) NPD process is used as the model for this study. Detailed phases of the breakthrough development process cannot be used as a stand-alone process but instead are used as a set of tools that must be integrated with other management disciplines and utilised throughout the NPD process (Wind and Mahajan, 1997). Indeed, successful companies do have universal elements, including a commitment to innovation throughout all levels of the organisation, the ability to forestall future market lacks, and a managed NPD process, which is constantly used and continuously improved (Jenkins, Forbes, and Durrani, 1997). In addition, the aim of an effective NPD process is to improve the quality and efficiency of NPD, to maximise the success rate for new products, and so ensuring continuous growth.

The multi-functional nature of NPD has significant implications for involving, integrating, and communicating between project team-members, process engineers, financial personnel, senior managements, customers and suppliers. As Millson and Wilemon (2002) argue, the internal organisational integration between NPD project teams and the functional departments throughout the overlapping NPD process are found to be important to new product success. Suppliers and customers need to be integrated and coordinated with NPD project teams throughout the NPD process as well. The relationship between the breakthrough NPD process and the cross-functional project team is depicted in Figure 2.4.

NPD is a strategic activity. An effective strategy takes a long time to formulating and implement and also requires concentrating a company's efforts and resources, so once in position, a company expects that a strategy is commonly shared and endured. A strategy directs how the company is supposed to behave toward its employees, customers, suppliers, and teams. As defined by Hayes *et al.* (2005: 34–36), there are three types of management-related strategies. *Corporate strategy*, the first level, includes decisions concerning the industries and markets in which it enters, how it structures itself to enter those markets, and how it acquires and allocates key corporate resources to various activities

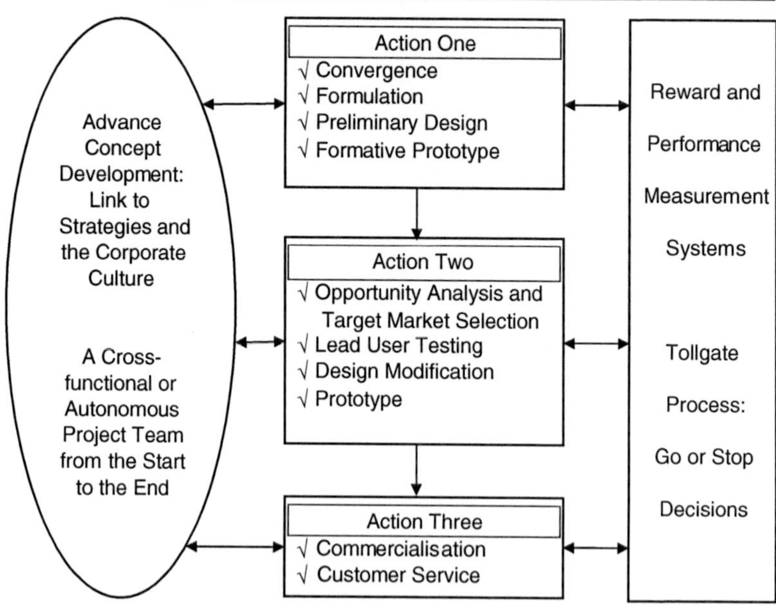

Figure 2.4   NPD Process versus Cross-Functional Project Team

and teams. A company is a corporation that has many strategic business units (SBUs) such as a subsidiary, division or product line. *Business strategy*, the second level, associates with each of the corporation's SBUs. Each SBU might have its own business strategy, which specifies the scope of its business and relationship to the corporation as a whole; and how it positions itself within its particular industry to achieve and maintain a competitive advantage. The third level, *Functional strategy*, such as a marketing or sales strategy, an operations strategy, a financial or control strategy, and a research or development strategy comprises of the pattern of decisions actually made to support the type of competitive advantage being pursued. For example, decisions regarding the degree of product innovation and technologies to be pursued, whether to be an industrial leader or follower, and whether to stress breakthrough engineering or basic research all comprise subparts of the R&D strategy.

A corporate culture, which ties personnel together, guides efforts of personnel throughout an organisation, encourages employee involvement and participation, and gives meaning and purposes to employees' work (Hayes *et al.*, 2005; Levi and Slem, 1995), is necessary for teamwork. Explicitly, not only a strategy but also a corporate culture is developed to support team work and is difficult to change. Therefore, in Figure 2.4, strategies and a corporate culture are considered to guide the project team. In addition, NPD participants – usually customers, suppliers, internal functional departments, senior managements, and project teams, are required to integrate and communicate during each NPD process to increase new product success (Balachandra and Friar, 1997; Millson and Wilemon, 2002; Wind and Mahajan, 1997).

The results of measurement provide team-members with feedback on job achievement, decide whether the new product project can continue or should stop, as well as determine rewards and sanctions – cash, wages, bonuses, reassignments, and dismissals. In addition, team-members are evaluated every three months to get feedback on job accomplishment that provide important information on whether team-members might need additional training in particular areas to improve performance, as well as on the level of bonuses team-members should obtain (Milgrom and Roberts, 1992). Thus, the double-headed arrows in Figure 2.4 are thought to hold for each individual NPD process to provide important information on go or stop decisions and feedback on whether project team-members and process engineers follow strategies and the corporate culture. In addition, the direction of single-headed arrows is thought to show the steps of overlapping NPD process.

Many of the NPD books and articles concentrate on developing an appropriate organisational architecture such as corporate culture, team structure, corporate roles, professional employees, technology, as well as performance measures and incentives that advances the probabilities of successful new products (Griffin and Hauser, 1996; Jensen and Meckling, 1995; March and Simon, 1993; Milgrom and Roberts, 1992; Millson and Wilemon, 2002; Wind and Mahajan, 1997). However, the real challenge is how to design the organisational architecture as a flexible and adaptable system that encourages the organisation's NPD objectives (Wind and Mahajan, 1997).

2.2.4 External business environment and organisation

Milgrom and Roberts (1992) argue that optimal organisational architectures differ across companies; otherwise, companies operating in the same industry tend to develop similar architectures. Explicitly, if an industry's external business environment – technology, markets, and regulation – changes, most companies in that industry will respond by readjusting their decision rights, reward, and performance measurement systems. Technologies influence the production of or expectation for new products, the approaches of production, and the information systems. In high-technology industry, not only do both product and process technologies evolve rapidly, breakthrough products cannot be commercialised without breakthroughs in process technology (Hayes *et al.*, 2005).

As discussed earlier, there is no single common measure of new product success, due to the complexity of definitions and divergence of views about success in NPD. In addition, after understanding the relationships between the external business environment, strategy, organisational architecture, and company value, it is reasonable to categorise the large number of success factors using an alternative method. This categorisation is used in marketing strategy studies to systematise information – market, technology, environment, and/or organisation (Aaker, 2005; Balachandra and Friar, 1997). The following review of the relevant NPD literature is structured into these four major perspectives.

I.   Market: customers, competitors, and suppliers

There is a general agreement that there should be a strong market for the new product under consideration or for the outcome of the new product project (Balachandra and Friar, 1997). Many researchers give high importance to the strength of market based on the market analysis – usually on the potential market size, the expected market share, and the profitability of the new product and suggest a good market analysis should be done early (Cooper, 1979b; Jenkins *et al.*, 1997; Millson and Wilemon, 2002; Rothwell *et al.*, 1974; Rubenstein *et al.*, 1976; Song *et al.*, 1996). Conversely, Wheelwright and Clark (1992) note that market analysis is likely to direct new product projects toward existing markets with small, incremental innovations rather than to undeveloped markets with breakthrough innovations.

The need for market analysis and the existence of a strong market is supported for both incremental and breakthrough innovations (Balachandra and Friar, 1997). Undeniably, it is difficult to get good information on potential customer needs for breakthrough products in potential markets because customer preferences may not be known by the customers themselves (Leonard-Barton and Wilson, 1994). Besides, many companies do ask and listen to customers regarding what they would like to see and want in new products and do deliver these tangibles, and customers, very often and much to everyone's chagrin, just do not buy (Ulwick, 2002). The reality is that market analysis can only show customer preferences and concerns in products and concepts that customers have a good knowledge of (Veryzer, 1998).

Balachandra and Friar (1997) consider competitors to be a part of market analysis. Most of the researchers categorised competition as a part of market factors (Brown and Eisenhardt, 1995; González and Palacios, 2002; Milgrom and Roberts, 1992). However, when the product is a breakthrough product with unknown competitors, few researchers (Cooper and Kleinschmidt, 1995) include competitors in the environmental characteristics. The product life cycle and the degree of importance that innovation has over the competitiveness in the industry may influence new product success (González and Palacios, 2002). Zirger and Maidique (1990) find that companies that enter low competitive markets have a better chance of providing a significant value to the customer; alternatively, large and growing markets are positively related to successful outcomes.

Finally, the third key player in market perspective is the suppliers. Prior studies have indicated that early and extensive (Clark and Fujimoto, 1991; Imai *et al.*, 1985) supplier involvement leads to a more competent NPD process (Brown and Eisenhardt, 1995). As González and Palacios (2002) argue, with the use of suppliers' networks, suppliers can gain a very high level of technological skill in a specialised area, which allows suppliers to accomplish unusual or rapid requests quickly and effectively.

From the above discussion, obviously, the market is a composite perspective, including customers, competitors, and suppliers, and these factors may contribute positively to new product success in some situations but negatively in others. It relies on whether the new product is entering an established market or is a breakthrough product for which there is unknown market (Balachandra and Friar, 1997).

II.   *Technology*

Many researchers (e.g. Cooper, 1979b; Mahajan and Wind, 1986; Maidique and Zirger, 1984) find that an innovative product has a greater chance of success in the market. Alternatively, Rothwell *et al.* (1974) finds that innovative products are much more likely than less innovative products to fail. Thus, the nature of the product to be designed and the degree of innovation expected, i.e. the innovativeness of the technology, are important considerations from the technology perspective. In addition, in Cooper and Kleinschmidt's (1996) research, the climate and culture for innovation within a company was a success factor, but not as strong as others.

Technology is an intangible asset, the intellectual property and reputation of a company. For example, Company AA is able to develop suitable technologies for a specific customer – BB, then AA gains specialised expertise for BB's exclusive needs, and BB will not switch to alternative suppliers. This advantage can reduce NPD cycle time and accrue much profit for the company. Thus, it is not strange that some research studies included patentability of the product or use of strong technology in the product as an important factor for success (Rubenstein *et al.*, 1976).

III. *Environment*

A new product cannot succeed if the environment is not supportive. The environment consists of many different features, such as availability of resources e.g. raw materials, government regulations, industry restructure opportunity, political/social factors, risk distribution, public interest in the product, and social acceptability of the product (Balachandra and Friar, 1997). In addition, designing a physical environment to encourage interaction among all members of the extended project team is important for reducing NPD cycle time (Wind and Mahajan, 1997). Also, different environments require different organisational architectures, so it is essential to recognise any differences in the environments of the benchmarked companies and to consider these differences when analysing the data on companies' policy choices (Milgrom and Roberts, 1992).

IV. *Organisation*

Even with the consideration of market, technological, and environmental perspectives, the new product could still fail if organisation factors – such as technology ties to business strategy, senior management support, NPD process planning, commitment and communication of NPD members, an experienced project manager, and a practiced project team – are not considered. Then, companies still cannot launch new products into the markets successfully (Balachandra and Friar, 1997). Similarly, Wind and Mahajan (1997) argue that the organisation has responsibilities in designing NPD around multiple project teams; locating project teams in different time zones and linking them electronically via satellite to take advantage of 24-hour developments; designing an organisation that encourages the integration of market requirements with technology and operations; empowering the project teams and instituting reward structures that promote risk taking and innovation; if the company longs to reduce NPD cycle time.

2.3 Conclusion

A review of previous literature on NPD reveals a lengthy list of studies of new product success/failure factors that are supposed to increase NPD competence, and to help companies in NPD related decision-making. However, new products still continue to fail at an upsetting rate (González and Palacios, 2002). The current studies show new product success rates at launch to be less than 60%; 54.3% for the UK (Edgett, Shipley, and Forbes, 1992), 59% for the USA (Griffin, 1997), 59.8% for Japan (Edgett *et al.*, 1992) and 49% for Spain (González and Palacios, 2002). This highlights the needs for improving NPD process.

Breakthrough products are contributors to the company's survival, but there have been few studies on the breakthrough innovation disproportionate to the significance of breakthrough products (Wind and Mahajan, 1997; Veryzer, 1998). Thus, it cannot be ensured whether existing studies about new product success/failure factors improve breakthrough innovation. After reviewing the literature, the authors attempt to find out new management concepts and devices that can increase the possibility of successful breakthrough innovation.

The next chapter introduces three systems of organisational architecture – the assignment of decision rights, the reward and punishment system, and the structure of systems to evaluate the performance of both individuals of the team and the project teams.

3
The Organisational Architecture

3.0 Introduction

One of the basic elements for developing a breakthrough innovation is 'the organisational architecture: the process, culture, structure, people, resources, technology, and incentives.' (Wind and Mahajan, 1997: 3) The company's organisational architecture encompasses the assignment of decision rights to NPD participants within the company, the system of rewarding and punishing new product project members, and the performance measurement system to evaluate the corporate executive officer (CEO); business units; and project teams. The importance of these systems for organisations has been recognised by many writers in economics and management (e.g., Brickley, Smith, and Zimmerman, 2004; Jensen, 1983; Jensen and Meckling, 1995; Milgrom and Roberts, 1992; Robey, 1991).

This chapter reviews the literature related to the organisation architecture. The remaining of this chapter is organised as follows:

- Assignment of decision rights
- Reward and punishment system
- Performance measurement system
- Conclusion

3.1 Assignment of decision rights

In stable environments, companies can use centralised decision-making and concentrate on gaining economies of scale through large-scale standardised production; whilst, not surprisingly, in today's business – a fast-paced, global economy – only companies that can foresee and understand customer needs and deliver new products to market faster than their competitors (Wheelwright and Clark, 1992) can survive effectively. Consequently, due to globalisation, technological capability to the level where it reaches their market potential, improvement of product quality, customer service, and efficiency, the decentralisation demand is indispensable and necessary. However, within companies, there are no automatic systems for assigning decision rights to individuals to achieve a company's objectives. Decision rights are assigned to employees through formal and informal job descriptions (Milgrom and Roberts, 1992). An important role of senior management is to determine how to assign decision rights among employees of the company, since the appropriate reward and performance measurement systems depend on the allocation of decision rights – centralised or decentralised (Brickley *et al.*, 2004). Since modern companies increasingly use a team-based approach (Cohen and Bailey, 1997; Towry, 2003), it is popular to accompany decentralisation with a broadened stress on performance and incentive compensation to motivate the team-members (Milgrom and Roberts, 1992).

3.1.1   Authority[1] versus responsibility

'Freedom is only part of the story and half the truth ... That is why I recommend that the Statue of Liberty on the East Coast be supplanted by a Statue of Responsibility on the West Coast.' (Frankl, 1984: 134)

Brown and Eisenhardt (1995) argue that the NPD literature conceptualises only two levels of management: a project manager and senior management. Yet in reality, normally there are several levels of management with apparently different authorities and responsibilities. To understand the assignment of decision rights, there are three different organisational structures: the functional organisation (U form), the product and geographic organisation (M form), and the matrix organisation (Milgrom and Roberts, 1992).

The U form organisational structure groups jobs by functional specialty (e.g. R&D department, quality assurance department, procurement department, sales department, product marketing department, customer value department, finance department, etc.). Namely, an

---

[1]Authority, in this study, does not mean the right to discipline the work of others, but rather, to self-discipline, to diminish unwanted administrative intervention, to maintain a position in the formal and informal hierarchical level (Hansen, 1995).

individual job is characterised by the specialised task assignment. For example, all the R&D jobs in the company are grouped together to form an R&D department, etc. The functional background of managers represents the expertise available to the senior managers who participate in making specific strategic decisions with the CEO, the board of directors and the general manager, as well as sharing common goals (Cohen and Bailey, 1997). The responsibilities of senior management are defining the architecture, coordinating activities across departments, making key operating decisions, and setting strategy (Milgrom and Roberts, 1992).

In the M form structure, a company is organised into product or geographic organisation, and then divided into divisions (business units) such as monitor tech division, motherboard design division, supply chain management division, and so on. Each of these divisions has its own functional departments such as sales department and product marketing department, which focus on the particular products of the division. Operating decisions are decentralised to the managers of business units. Senior executives are responsible for major strategic decisions, including organisational architecture and the allocation of resources among the business units (Brickley *et al.*, 2004; Milgrom and Roberts, 1992).

The matrix organisational structures are employed to improve the effectiveness of the cross-functional project teams (subunits) (Jenkins *et al.*, 1997). The matrix organisation has functional departments such as finance, R&D, manufacturing, procurement, quality assurance, etc. Personnel from these functional departments are also assigned to subunits organised around product, geography, or some special projects such as NPD projects. A potential drawback of the matrix structures of organisation is that every cross-functional project team-member is reporting to two managers – the project manager and the functional manager (Milgrom and Roberts, 1992). This conflict of loyalty results from the intersecting lines of authority, which is usually designed in favour of the functional departments. NPD projects will be completed but the functional departments hold responsibilities for evaluating the performance (Jenkins *et al.*, 1997; Milgrom and Roberts, 1992). Thus, NPD projects are seen as being of secondary importance for cross-functional project team-members, since it is the functional managers who have the power for their immediate career development. Fortunately, this drawback can be mitigated by appropriate design of the reward and performance measurement systems (Milgrom and Roberts, 1992).

Although the empowered project team and project manager are essential in the NPD process, senior management support is significant to the successful NPD process as well (Balachandra and Friar, 1997; Brown and Eisenhardt, 1995; Wind and Mahajan, 1997; Zirger and Maidique, 1990). *Support* means the provision of both financial and political resources to the project teams, because this support is essential for obtaining the resources necessary to attract team-members to the project, to gain project approval to go ahead, and to provide the funding necessary to foster the NPD effort (Brown and Eisenhardt, 1995). In addition, since NPD projects focus on new products and NPD processes that are anticipated to give the company a competitive advantage, NPD projects have strategic implications and the senior management support of specific prospective NPD projects is a form of strategic leadership as well (Green, 1995; Hayes *et al.*, 2005).

NPD is an activity which involves every level, including the CEO, of a whole organisation, so it is essential for the company to develop a culture of discipline that ejects those who do not share the values and standards of an organisation and gives personnel more freedom to experiment and find their own best path to NPD results (Collins, 2001). For example, one of senior executives' most important tasks in dealing with any NPD project is to create a corporate environment that encourages honest disclosure about budget expenditures and completion timetables (Davis, 1985). The major responsibilities and roles of senior management are making strategic decisions about the astute management of new technological developments such as which technological paths should be followed and which promising projects have the potential for significant strategic impact (Green, 1995).

Hayes *et al.* (2005: 237–239) introduced four different types of project team in practice. The first type falls to one extreme and is the purely functional team – each functional department takes responsibility for a different part of the new product project. Few managerial mechanisms are available to integrate and coordinate problem-solving decisions across functional departments. The second is the lightweight team – relatively few resources and little decision-making authority over the team (Brown and Eisenhardt, 1995; Cohen and Bailey, 1997) which acts mainly as a medium for information exchange across functional departments. The lightweight project manager, who is a junior person with little control over the team and is usually assigned to multiple projects and is responsible for coordinating schedules, organising meetings, tracking progress, and identifying problems that need resolution (Hayes *et al.*, 2005). However, if there is a conflict between project team-members, or substantive issues involving design, operations or marketing, only senior functional managers have the authority to solve these problems.

The third type is the heavyweight team – with a greater degree of authority to integrate, coordinate and improve the NPD process across the functions (Clark and Fujimoto, 1991). The full-time members of a heavyweight project team are not just representatives from their departments, but instead are active in shaping project-level decisions. The heavyweight project manager, who is akin to a general manager and usually is dedicated to just one project, not just a coordinator, but an active and authoritative manager of both the project team and the NPD process (Clark *et al.*, 1987; Clark and Fujimoto, 1991; Hayes *et al.*, 1988). Hence, the project manager is fully responsible for the new product project success.

Finally, the autonomous team – formed for certain types of projects, and separated from the existing organisation, often is the ancestor to a new business unit (Hayes *et al.*, 2005). Even in the heavyweight project team, team-members are still located in and work for their departments and then report to both functional managers and the project manager. Consequently, there might be a conflict between the NPD project and functional performance and usually the NPD project will be sacrificed. To overcome the drawback of the heavyweight project team, many high-technology companies utilise the autonomous team to benefit the projects requiring completely new technological and commercial capabilities for the companies.

The empowered project manager is the linking bridge between the cross-functional project team and senior executive (Brown and Eisenhardt, 1995; Clark and Fujimoto, 1991; Cohen and Bailey, 1997; Cooper and Kleinschmidt, 1996; Iansiti, 1992, 1993). The empowered project manager refers to those project managers with significant decision-making responsibility, organisation-wide authority, and a high hierarchical level; it is supposed that such project managers are highly effective in obtaining resources such as more personnel and larger budgets for the cross-functional project team and are able to improve NPD process performance (Brown and Eisenhardt, 1995; Clark and Fujimoto, 1991).

An important characteristic of the project manager is vision which 'involves the cognitive ability to mesh a variety of factors together to create an effective, holistic view and to communicate it to others.' (Brown and Eisenhardt, 1995: 370). In the case of NPD, vision means fitting together the company's core competencies (e.g. strengths of technologies and markets) and strategies with the needs of the market (e.g. customer preferences for new product appearance and style) to create an effective product concept. Senior executives and the project manager often work together in developing and communicating a distinctive, coherent product concept, because the project manager is central to the creation of the product concept (Clark and Fujimoto, 1991).

The above review of literature suggests that different new product projects have different definitions and scopes of product and project, formations of project teams, structures and flows of NPD processes, and senior management involvement. Figure 3.1 summarises the above discussion by aligning each of the essential NPD performance factors with three different types of project or product to develop strategies for new product project executions (Hayes *et al.*, 2005).

3.1.2   Formation and integration of project team

Teams are formed because they are more successful at assembling specialised knowledge for decision making than are alternative

Type of Product or Project	Derivative	Platform	Breakthrough
Project Definition	1. Narrow specified requirements 2. Focus on existing processes or customer or market segments 3. Lever age existing platform	Definition involves goals and requirements of an anticipated future stream of derivative projects	1. Exploratory, high risk nature of project inhibits tightly defined specification 2. Project definition articulates broader concept, evolves through early stages
Project Team	Functional or Lightweight	Heavyweight	Heavyweight or Autonomous
NPD Process	1. Low technical and commercial uncertainty enables tight specification of process 2. Focus on ensuring conformance to narrow goals	1. Structured around key milestones 2. Early stages of process focus on systems architecture	1. High levels of technological and market uncertainty require highly flexible process 2. Focus on experimentation and adapting project to new information
Senior Management Involvement	1. Front-end senior management to ensure scope and focus 2. Monitor execution and performance of team leader	1. Frequent reviews throughout 2. Emphasis on ensuring appropriate integration across functions and approval of major changes	1. Act as a project's board of directors, provide broad oversight and approve major investments 2. Focus on risk management

Figure 3.1   Strategies for Three Types of Product Project Execution
Source: Adapted from Hayes *et al.* (2005)

methods that might be used to pass the knowledge through the traditional hierarchy. (Milgrom and Roberts, 1992: 434)

Selections of NPD project authority and the staffing of the project team considerably influence the performance of NPD projects (Hayes *et al.*, 2005). Usually, certain types of NPD project authority selections are very explicit. For example, a multi-functional team (Eisenhardt and Tabrizi, 1995); a fully dedicated project team (Hayes *et al.*, 2005); or a cross-functional project team (Parker, 1994). However, responsibilities of each team-member of the project team are usually very implicit. For example, design engineers are eventually responsible for getting the design right; and manufacturing representatives are responsible for getting the production job done.

In today's dynamic business environment, the traditional hands-off approach – having done the jobs – is not appropriate for producing a breakthrough product. In contrast, the team method brings together professional employees from R&D, manufacturing, quality assurance, marketing, and other functional departments so that they can work together on an NPD project from start to finish (Pelled and Adler, 1994). Since specialised new knowledge from a broader choice of functional departments is brought into the NPD process in its early phases, the functional heterogeneity in such project teams is prospectively an asset for a company (Hayes *et al.*, 1988). The challenge here is how a company utilises and manages this prospective asset.

As described earlier, faced with ever-tighter schedules, NPD professional employees utilise a range of methods for keeping 'one step ahead' of the challenge (Lundqvist, Sundgren, and Trygg, 1996), because habitually potential customers cannot appreciate or accept too modern technology that exceeds their imagination. Specifically, an autonomous, cross-functional project team proposes an efficient structure for aligning the occasionally conflicting objectives of the timely delivery of a high-quality, easily manufactured product (Lundqvist *et al.*, 1996). The literature on project teams is supportive to explore the implications of team settings, as well as to examine the areas of job design, team composition, conflict and communication in project teams.

I.   Job Design

(1)   Product distinctiveness

In a company, many different product project teams (Hayes *et al.*, 2005) are involved in NPD, so product distinctiveness and characteristics could be expected to have an impact on job design and eventually project team performance (Cohen and Bailey, 1997). Emmanuelides (1993) takes product characteristics in the model of NPD performance and proposes that the newness of the product and the complexity of the product are both associated with longer lead-time due to the increased information processing needed. Keller (1994) examines, among 98 R&D groups, the first fit between a project team's level of task technology 'nonroutineness' and the amount of information being processed and finds that this fit is the best predictor of project quality but does not predict budget-schedule performance. Also, Keller (1994) examines the second fit between a technology's unanalysability and the amount of processing carried out by the project team and finds that this second measures of fit predicted neither project quality nor budget-schedule performance.

(2)   Autonomy

Autonomy is not found to be associated with higher performance among project teams (Cohen and Bailey, 1997). Eisenhardt and Tabrizi (1995) examine 72 NPD projects drawn from European, Asian, and the USA computer companies in the high-velocity computer industry and found that using an experiential strategy of multiple design iterations, extensive testing, frequent project milestones, a powerful project leader, and a multi-national team, accelerated NPD. In addition, the project leader power, which concerns whether the project manager reported to SBU manager, is associated with accelerating NPD time. In contrast, the compression strategy of supplier involvement, use of computer-aided design (CAD), and overlapping NPD process were only useful for accelerating NPD in mature industry segments.

Overall, the above studies argue that product distinctiveness or characteristics should be taken into consideration when determining how to coordinate and integrate project team activities. If job design of a project team is properly considered with reference to product characteristics, team performance can be high, and *vice versa*. Regarding the autonomy issue, in the long term, it is a meaningful target for high-technology companies to support self-management and consensus decision-making for some issues such as 'one step ahead' breakthrough innovations, but forcing every project team to adopt this autonomous approach irrespective of different project types is badly chosen. Additionally, autonomy is helpful if the breakthrough project team has a respectful project manager.

II.   Team Composition

(1)   Diversity

Brown and Eisenhardt (1995) organise the empirical literature on NPD in western organisations, which was published in major North American and Europe journals, and synthesised their findings into a model of factors that affect the success of NPD. In this model, the project team is the focal point. Brown and Eisenhardt (1995) argue that team composition of the project team affected problem-solving and eventually influenced NPD performance. In addition, Eisenhardt and Tabrizi (1995) find that functional diversity, which enabled NPD processes to be integrated, linking technical, marketing, and manufacturing activities, is associated with faster time-to-market for NPD efforts in the computer industry.

(2)   Gatekeeper

The gatekeeper is the second project team composition factor – probably less important in cross-functional teams because the team-members have ordinary external contacts in their functional departments, but the gatekeeper obviously increases the external information reaching the team (Brown and Eisenhardt, 1995). The gatekeeper is an individual who regularly obtains diverse external information and then shares it within the project team. Similar to diversity, the gatekeeper affects NPD process performance by increasing the amount and variety of information – such as new technological developments occurring outside the team – available in the NPD process (Allen, 1971, 1977; Brown and Eisenhardt, 1995).

(3)   Team tenure

Finally, team tenure is a third team composition factor that influences NPD process performance (Brown and Eisenhardt, 1995). Katz (1982) found out that when team tenure is at moderate levels, team-members are most likely to undertake both extensive internal and external communications and to receive maximum benefit; all together NPD process performance is highest and eventually leads to higher project performance.

III.   Communication

(1)   Internal Processes

Katz and Allen (1985) found out that team-members of an established project team communicate less habitually with personnel outside the team and patterns of communication depend on organisational structure and project type. Imai *et al.* (1985) and Zirger and Maidique (1990) indicate that effective communication increases information and consequently is essential for improving NPD process performance. In addition, Clark and Fujimoto (1991) reveal that successful NPD depends on intensive communication between upstream and downstream team-members. Keller (1994) found out that internal processes such as cooperation, internal communication, and task process are positively associated with managers' assessments of performance.

Wheelwright and Clark (1992) argue that communication does not need to be enhanced everywhere within a project, but communication should be improved when and where it is supposed to affect the success of NPD projects. Ancona and Caldwell (1992) define team processes as the team's ability to develop plans, define goals, and prioritise work and state that team processes are positively related to team ratings of overall efficiency.

(2)   External processes

Frequent communication outside of the team with people such as customers, suppliers, and other organisational personnel brings new information from diverse viewpoints to the project team (Brown and Eisenhardt, 1995; Clark and Fujimoto, 1991; Imai *et al.*, 1985; Katz, 1982). Ancona and Caldwell (1992) reveal that the functions of external communication in the form of political activities such as lobbying for resources, engaging in impression management, and seeking senior management support for the project; as well as external communication are positively associated with managers' ratings. Keller (1994) reached similar results from 98 R&D teams.

As discussed earlier, NPD projects face challenges in coordinating and integrating cross-functional teams due to several barriers to communication within such teams, which come from organisational structures (Milgrom and Roberts, 1992), incentive systems (Towry, 2003), geographical location (Hayes, *et al.*, 2005), cultural differences (Pelled and Adler, 1994), leadership styles (Collins, 2001), and project management practices (Hayes *et al.*, 2005). Companies can improve their profits, quality, and customer satisfaction through employee empowerment and other changes in their decision-making systems, but, authorising the decision rights to the individuals who actually make the decisions risks some information being uncoordinated (Brickley *et al.*, 2004). Thus, an important role of senior management in a decentralised decision system is to promote information flows and coordination among decision-makers in the company (Milgrom and Roberts, 1992).

In addition, corporate culture and organisational structure usually cover the ways task and authority – decision rights – are arranged, the ways personnel are rewarded and performance measured, as well as the ways corporate slogans are decided. Arguably, appropriate assignment of decision rights can affect the success or failure of new product. Also, factors such as product distinctiveness, autonomy, diversity, gatekeeper, team tenure, internal processes, and external processes can also affect the success or failure of projects and should be considered before forming a team and delegating authority.

The assignment of decision rights and results of performance measurement should be the basis to reward or punish employees. Therefore, the reward and punishment system is discussed in next.

3.2   Reward and punishment system

Indeed, almost every company faces a distressing management problem: how to attract, recruit and keep professional employees and how to motivate them to be more creative within companies (Quinn, 1985). Companies should construct well-designed compensation contracts or plans that not only facilitate companies to attract, recruit and keep professional employees but also are designed to provide incentives to enhance the values of companies (Milgrom and Roberts, 1992). Undoubtedly, in today's high-velocity business environment, interdependence between different SBUs and organisational functions, as well as the need for customer service and quality, make incentive compensation more appropriate than it used to be (Beer, 1993; Quinn, 1985).

However, some companies may ask the wrong question: 'How should we design the incentive system in order to obtain the desired behaviour?' (Beer, 1993: 39). Indeed, the incentive system is important, but firstly, the incentive system cannot create the desired behaviour from the wrong people (Collins, 2001). Secondly, a more appropriate question here should be: What role should incentive play?

3.2.1   The role of incentive and motivation

'One day Deng Xiaoping decided to take his grandson to visit Mao. "Call me granduncle," Mao offered warmly. "Oh, I certainly couldn't do that, Chairman Mao," the awe-struck child replied. "Why don't you give him an apple?" suggested Deng. No sooner had Mao done so then the boy happily chirped, "Oh thank you, Granduncle."

"You see," said Deng, "what incentives can achieve."' (Time, 1984: 62)

Manipulation through incentive plans is attractive to many managers as a cheap way to improve performance by providing individuals with incentives to work harder, especially, companies that are under intense stress to improve efficient productivity, quality of new products to meet customers' expectations, and when their corporate resources are severely limited (Hayes *et al.*, 2005). Appelbaum (1993) admits that aiming to improve performance by fiddling incentive plans has proven counterproductive. But, Appelbaum (1993) also argues that it relies on the role incentives really play in team production in the USA companies. Recognising the work process to exploit employee skills and involvement has improved performance, mostly in combination with employment security, gain-sharing, and incentives to participate in training. Thus, from the human resource practice viewpoint, incentive plans are necessary for companies to support high-performance work processes.

Beer (1993) considers a certain practical problem – the pay-for-performance dilemma to see the role of incentive pay in motivation. For example, in some industries, such as insurance industry or organisational functions such as sales department, incentive compensation is the current practice. Without paying for performance, a company will lose its professional employees. Alternatively, by paying for performance, employees act for self-interests as opposed to organisational commitments. But if there is no better solution, then the current one is the best: for example, when the leader of a breakthrough product project is an independent SBU placed a long way from headquarters and does not have a motivating manager-subordinate relationship.

Furthermore, Milgrom and Roberts (1992) argue that the prospect of a long-term relationship the company motivates people to work in support of the company, because a long-term relationship decreases the possibility of dysfunctional activities and increases the flexibility that a company retains in designing compensation plans to motivate employee effort. Having a fair internal labour market in the company may motivate employees to stay and work hard. For creative and ambitious professional R&D employees – who create major innovations, if the company can offer clear opportunities such as established career paths to fulfil all their economic, psychological, and career goals at once, then they will not move to other companies with only monetary goals (Quinn, 1985).

Research studies show that the results of incentives, motivations, or rewards are to some extent varied. For example, R&D professional employees habitually long to reach a technological contribution for either intangible or tangible personal rewards such as recognition, power, or simply money (Quinn, 1985). Kohn (1993) indicates that rewards may destroy cooperation and commitment to teamwork where professional R&D employees' individual efforts are integrated into the success or failure of the team. In addition, Kohn (1993) maintains that incentive plans must fail, since rewards are based on an obviously inadequate theory of motivation. He also indicates that companies should pay employees well and fairly on compensation, and then do everything possible to help them to forget money. This statement is based on the premise that companies have the right people who are capable of their jobs.

If as Kohn (1993: 62) implies that employees are the right people ('they work because they love what they do'), then supposedly 'the right people will do the right things and deliver the best results they are capable of, *regardless of the incentive system*' (Collins 2001: 50, *emphasis added*). Kohn (1993) explains that pay is not a motivator; rewards and punishments, rupture relationships, discourage risk-taking, and undermine interest. Further, Kohn (1993: 55) states that incentives 'do not create an endur-ing *commitment* to any value or action' but just temporarily change employees' behaviours. Eventually, incentive plans cannot work.

We argue against Kohn's (1993) criticism to incentive plans. Even professional employees, the right people, still expect rewards because an effective compensation plan consists of a fixed but low salary plus one or more performance-contingent incentives. That is, professional employees under normal circumstances wish to get the reward and expect the reward constantly and reliably rooted into given actions (e.g. objective performance evaluation) and results (e.g. the reward equal to the effort that produced it) (Wolters, 1993).

In October 1990, Du Pont suddenly cancelled its incentive plan, and at the same time the fibres division chief claimed that incentive pay simply might be a bad idea, and the incentive plan did not work. However, by analysing the Du Pont incentive plan, Milgrom and Roberts (1992: 388–389) argue that the failure of Du Pont's incentive plan was caused largely by problems with the structure of the plan. Just as Davis (1985: 95) emphasises that 'when a new project overruns its budget, managers should seek causes before remedies.' In Du Pont's incentive plan, what the division chief can do is to find out how the company might design more effective incentive plans, not merely cancel the plan and blame it.

Throughout the above discussion, we argue that incentive plans play an important role in motivating professional employees and this argument is readily accepted by most academics and practitioners (Appelbaum, 1993; Beer, 1993; Bonner and Sprinkle, 2002; Milgrom and Roberts, 1992). However, to provide appropriate incentives to project team-members, project leaders should build up reputations of being respectable and objective. Furthermore, to be most effective, companies should set up performance measures and rewards that motivate capable leaders to build up their credibility.

3.2.2 Teamwork environment: incentive versus performance

Managerial accounting information is used firstly to improve managers' *ex-ante* measurement of the performance in order to improve managerial decisions (Busby, 1999); secondly to facilitate supervisors to motivate their subordinates (Baiman, 1982); and thirdly to help the resources allocation among employees of the risk intrinsic in cooperating in an uncertain business teamwork environment (Davila, 2003). Baiman (1982) argues these motivational and risk-sharing uses of accounting information are interrelated in that team-members' motivations can be influenced by the amount of financial risk imposed on them; also short-term economic incentives (Davila, 2003) motivate higher levels of effort from effort-averse agents, and performance is expected to increase with the steepness of the incentive plan.

Steeper compensation contracts lead to higher effort and also impose more risk on a naturally risk averse manager (Baiman, 1982); conversely, attracting more risk-taking capable managers who have a higher expected pay-off (Beer, 1993; Bonner and Sprinkle, 2002; Davila, 2003; Lebby, 1993). Also, Davila (2003) reveals that a positive relationship is not linear and its intensity (slope) decreases as the percentage of variable salary increased exists between the level of incentives and project performance. However, Jenkins, Gupta, Mitra, and Shaw (1998) conducted a meta-analysis of existing evidence relating to financial incentives performance across different levels of companies and indicated that the relationship is positive for production quantity (productivity) but not for performance quality, which is an essential factor in NPD.

Moreover, speed, flexibility (Imai *et al.*, 1985; Takeuchi and Nonaka, 1986), quality (Clark *et al.*, 1987; Clark and Fujimoto, 1990, 1991; Hayes *et al.*, 1988), and creativity (Hayes *et al.*, 2005; Kohn, 1993) are also supreme and relevant in the NPD and innovation area. Hence,

Davila (2003) critiques that the relationship between financial incentives and performance is not necessarily granted and it may actually be negative, because extrinsic incentives may drive away intrinsic motivation (Amabile, 1993) and appropriate incentive plans for motivating NPD project members may be hard to design, and thus focus NPD project members' attention away from relevant dimensions and discourage risk-taking (Kohn, 1993).

The increasing use of teams for organisational activities such as NPD projects, explicitly, is a move towards less organisational hierarchy and more teamwork (Wolters, 1993). Teamwork environments send a message to employees that fewer promotions are available and integrated cooperation among team-members is essential and necessary. Also, to employers, teamwork implies that maximum flexibility and productivity must be gathered from all professional employees (Cohen and Bailey, 1997). The uses of incentive plans represent one strategy for aligning organisational and individual goals by treating employees as partners in both the risks and the successes of the business (Wolters, 1993).

Literature shows that companies regularly use incentives as a tactic for motivating and improving the performance of employees who use and are influenced by managerial accounting information (Baiman, 1982; Bonner and Sprinkle, 2002; Busby, 1999; Davila, 2003; Lebby, 1993). Further, existing evidence indicates that managers respond to financial incentives and thus the use of monetary incentives in companies is increasing (Davila, 2003; Wall Street Journal, 1999). The following section introduces the purposes, subjects, contexts and impacts of using measurement systems.

3.3 Performance measurement system

The current concern in NPD activities, and more particularly in NPD-related performance measurement, is reflected in research with titles and abstracts featuring words such as: performance (Bonner and Sprinkle, 2002; Busby, 1999; Brown and Eisenhardt, 1995; Rowe, 2004); measurement (Griffin and Page, 1996); performance measurement (Godener and Söderquist, 2004); assessment (Jenkins *et al.*, 1997); evaluation (Ghosh and Lusch, 2000; Milgrom and Roberts, 1992); success (Griffin and Page, 1993); benchmarking (Cooper and Kleinschmidt, 1995); control (Busby, 1999; Kerssens-van Drongelen and Bilderbeek, 1999); monitoring (Kaplan and Norton, 1993; Towry, 2003); auditing and effectiveness (Cohen and Bailey, 1997).

Usually, these words are used interchangeably in NPD literature, but the purposes (uses) and the subjects (e.g. CEO, senior managers, project managers, project team-members, etc) of the measurement efforts, as well as the context for which the proposed concepts are well-matched can be relatively diverse. Thus, Kerssens-van Drongelen and Bilderbeek (1999) recommend that researchers should clarify the purposes, subjects, and contexts of performance measurement efforts before distinguishing the major design parameters of performance measurement systems and discussing the factors that have a supposed impact on these design parameters. In this study, the project team and performance measurement of team and team-members are focal points.

Most managers nowadays, at every level, understand the need to improve NPD measures and recognise the impact that measures have on NPD performance. Further, they are continuously consulted by management experts regarding how to do this (Hayes *et al.*, 2005). Measuring NPD performance is difficult and complicated, because senior managers should consider effective measurement as an indispensable and integral part of the company's organisational structures, management processes, strategies, visions, and resources. However, these managers frequently fail not only to set up new performance measures to monitor new goals and processes but to question whether or not their old measures (e.g. short-term financial indicators like return-on-investment, sales growth, and operating income) are relevant to the new initiatives (Kaplan and Norton, 1993). For example, new process technologies often strengthen the launch of successful new products in many industries and NPD process performance is rooted in specific organisational capabilities and choices (Hayes *et al.*, 2005). Thus, Hayes *et al.* (2005: 217) consider three key drivers of NPD process performance: '1) the integration of product and process development; 2) the timing of technology transfer from development to operations; and 3) the degree of autonomy granted to operating units to develop, change, and improve process technologies.'

3.3.1 Why – Needs of performance measurement

'... [T]eamwork has become a sacred cow to American business. Yet, one survey ... found that only 13 percent of 179 teams received high ratings. ... Teams fail for several reasons including:
- The mental opt-out. Busy managers feel compelled to sit through endless team meetings and frequently "surrender by withholding any real effort." Thus half the decisions reached by teams never get implemented.

- Duelling advice. "Teams start out with everyone very polite. Then they start to storm." Several months can pass before things settle down.
- Old-fashioned pay scales. Often when companies move to teams, they keep individual performance measures and pay systems. Team-based pay systems are not used to reward the entire team for meeting goals. This is an example where two legs of the three-legged stool do not match and the stool thus is not balanced.' (Milgrom and Roberts, 1992: 438)

Milgrom and Roberts (1992) emphasise that performance evaluation provides employees with feedback on job achievement so that employees might improve their performance, as well as provides information in determining rewards. Davila (2003) also argues that NPD performance measures offer feedback regarding the efforts and accomplishments of the project manager and team-members to senior managers for decision-making. For example, senior managers can use this measurement information to design incentive plans as an alternative by performance-contingent incentive (Bonner and Sprinkle, 2002). Thus, it is definite that performance measurement at least provides information for decision-making such as rewards, job assignments, or project go or kill decisions (Cooper and Kleinschmidt, 1990).

Alternatively, Kerssens-van Drongelen and Bilderbeek (1999: 36) define performance measurement 'as the acquisition and analysis of information about the actual attainment of company objectives and plans, and about factors that may influence this attainment.' In addition, they use this concept of performance measurement as part of the broader concept of performance control – feed-forward and feedback control. Feed-forward control is used to ensure that the appropriate organisational resources (e.g. personnel, technology, and capital) (Brown and Eisenhardt, 1995), as well as organisational architecture (Milgrom and Roberts, 1992) are in place to facilitate good performance.

Some companies also use other feed-forward measurement methods such as organisational auditing which compares actual conditions with standards, or benchmarking, both internally and versus other companies, which identifies the critical success factors that set the most successful companies aside from their competitors (Cooper and Kleinschmidt, 1995). The main purpose of these measurement methods is to increase new product success and improve companies' new product efforts overall (company practices, methods, and settings), i.e. the companies' overall new product performance. However, using only feed-forward control of performance cannot guarantee that all companies' new product efforts are effective and efficient (Kerssens-van Drongelen and Bilderbeek, 1999; Kerssens-van Drongelen and Cook, 1997).

Getting feedback via performance measures leads to an improvement in those aspects of performance. That is, feedback is the knowledge of results (Busby, 1999). Feedback control of performance can be considered as decision-making and action, based on the comparison of objectives with measures of actual performance as well as the comparison of these objectives and actual performance with the expected and the actual internal and external conditions (Kerssens-van Drongelen and Bilderbeek, 1999). Explicitly, implementing not only feed-forward but also feedback control of performance is indispensable and essential. Senior managers should take the responsibility for feed-forward control of performance, because only top management has the right to approve a project and form a project team.

Busby (1999) summarises that there are three purposes of feedback control for R&D organisations: correcting errors, obtaining job satisfaction, and learning effective practices and processes. Busby (1999) proposes five reasons why some R&D organisations do not seek feedback. Firstly, generating feedback information needs measurement costs, but the R&D department is eager to keeping down the cost, and focuses on solving current problems, even though seeking feedback might avert future problems. Secondly, some deficiencies were correlated to other departments which would unsurprisingly be difficult for R&D engineers to tackle. Thirdly, to R&D engineers, feedback could express conflicting messages or unachievable goals. Fourthly, some of the feedback was personal and initiated contact with product users or manufacturers. Finally, designers usually are insensitive or oversensitive to the feedback from manufacturing.

However, we disagree with the above reasons. First of all, an R&D engineer's effort is difficult to quantify and monitor, and producing performance information brings measurement costs. But, if paying an R&D engineer on departmental profits motivates more creative effort as well as actions that increase organisational value, then departmental profits would be a productive performance measure, and *vice versa*. That is, what a manager should consider is whether or not this performance measure brings net benefit to the company. Trying to keep down a department's cost does not mean discarding performance measurement or feedback control. If performance measures are necessary and beneficial, what a manager should do is look for new measurement technology to reduce measuring costs of individual performance, rather than ignoring measures altogether.

Second, R&D engineers cannot only produce a new product; consequently a cross-functional project team is needed in an NPD organisation. These team-members come from different functional departments with specific skills, so they can communicate and share information to complete each of their tasks. However, functional differences within a cross-functional project team could also incur problems such as task conflict and/or emotional conflict and cause different results such as functional outcomes and/or dysfunctional outcomes. Triggered by functional diversity, selective perception results in intergroup task conflict, which, sequentially, brings about functional outcomes and tends to improve team effectiveness (Pelled and Adler, 1994). That is, the company should build an environment for technical communication for its cross-functional project teams, rather than ignoring problems.

Third, in some cases, communication between the functions and the cross-functional project team is extremely tortuous, but, facing the truth, it is unavoidable as well. When emotional conflicts are involved in communication about the appropriate testing procedure for a new product between a manufacturing department representative and a R&D engineer, the manufacturing representative would insist the more rigorous tests should be run, and the R&D engineer could report to upper-level managers and complain about the manufacturing representative for using unnecessary tests (Pelled and Adler, 1994). This kind of communication causes emotional conflicts and brings about aggravating reactions, but it should not be a reason for managers to give up feedback information or communication. Again, what managers should do is measuring technical communication between functions and cross-functional project teams.

Finally, based on Busby's (1999) fourth and the fifth reasons, it again shows the significance of cross-functional communication and information transferring within the NPD organisation. Senior management should have the ability and knowledge to communicate and coordinate among different levels of NPD activities in order that cross-functional project teams can enhance team effectiveness and project success. Using innovation performance information, executives can redirect resources (e.g. correcting errors or reassigning staffs) to the new product project, facilitate communication and coordination with other functional departments (e.g. monitored progress and resolved conflicts during implementation), and remove obstacles (e.g. changing unprofessional team-members) to project success (Green, 1995), so performance measurement is helpful and indispensable to companies.

Indeed, Quinn *et al.* (1996) argue that most professional employees want to work with the best, to be evaluated objectively by people at the top of their field, to compete as well as to know they have excelled against their peers. Moreover, numerous empirical studies and review articles have shown that a new product's success depends significantly on its performance and its value delivered to customers (Balachandra and Friar, 1997; Clark and Fujimoto, 1990; Cooper and Kleinschmidt, 1987a, 1987b, 1990, 1993, 1995, 1996; Zirger and Maidique, 1990). For example, these researchers argue that product superiority in terms of unique features, innovativeness, and new product performance is an important element that distinguishes new product winners from losers.

Additionally, management emphasis on ongoing improvement on NPD activities is required for many technology-driven companies. Hayes *et al.* (2005) argue that establishing a common philosophy for achieving improvement efforts from all levels, which legitimises the crossing of functional and geographic boundaries; and a supportive environment, which attempts to involve members throughout the company in the improvement process, is very helpful for NPD ongoing improvement. Also, NPD performance measures provide feedback about the effort and skills of the project manager and team-members (Davila, 2003). Thus, a company which aims to develop a supportive environment should present clear performance measures for tracking desired improvement efforts, making widely known the progress being made, and esteem those responsible for it (Hayes *et al.*, 2005).

3.3.2 What – Areas of performance measurement

Normally, within a company, performance measurement systems are used on at least four different management levels: performance of corporate executives, performance of functional departments and SBUs, performance of teams, and performance of individual employees. Typically, a CEO takes responsibility for managerial decisions (e.g. merger or significant investment decisions) and corporate operations (e.g. net income, net worth, or sales) at transition year. Hence, in this study, how to evaluate a CEO's performance is not considered and our focus is on NPD-related performance measurements.

Griffin and Page (1993) classify 75 success/failure measures into five general categories: measures of firm benefits, program-level measures, product-level measures, measures of financial performance, and measures of customer acceptance. Then relevant measures are categorised into four independent perspectives (see Figure 3.2). Godener and

Customer Acceptance Measures	<ul><li>customer acceptance</li><li>customer satisfaction</li><li>meeting revenue goals</li><li>revenue growth</li><li>meeting market share goals</li><li>meeting unit sales goals</li></ul>
Financial Performance	<ul><li>profitability</li><li>return on R&D investment</li><li>break-even time</li><li>attaining margin goals</li><li>attaining profitability goals</li><li>Internal rate of return (IRR)</li><li>Return on Investment (ROI)</li></ul>
Product-Level Measures	<ul><li>development cost</li><li>lead-time</li><li>launching on time</li><li>product pperformance level</li><li>meeting quality guidelines</li><li>speed to market</li></ul>
Firm-level Measures	<ul><li>strategic fit of new products</li><li>opening of new opportunities stemming from R&D activities</li><li>% of sales by new products</li></ul>

Figure 3.2 'Core' Success or Failure Measures

Söderquist (2004) explain that the product-level measures basically translate NPD process efficiency, and the firm-level measures fundamentally reflect strategic impact of NPD. Derived from the extant literature and case study research, they argue that these four perspectives comprise an appropriate framework for complicated NPD performance metrics.

Godener and Söderquist (2004) examined in depth the different areas of measurement used and developed in the NPD performance measurement literature. They distinguished and identified the most frequently employed measurements in the literature reviewed and found out that studied companies focused on measurements of finances, customer satisfaction, process, and strategic performance, but there was no formal measurement of innovation beyond patent counts, technology, and knowledge management. From the literature on NPD performance measurements, even plentiful studies have investigated how to define new products success or failure, why new products succeed, why others fail, what distinguishes winning new products from losers, and how to evaluate NPD-related activities. These factors and/or measures could be classified in at least seven areas of NPD performance measurement (see Figure 3.3).

3.3.3   How – Use and impact of measurement results

Milgrom and Roberts (1992) use a five-point scale for management team evaluation. Each team-member rates all other team-members on each

Measurements	Objectives/Meanings	Researcher(s)
Financial performance	Definition: Maximising quantitatively measured return on NPD investment. Objective: Maximise the results from each $ spent on NPD thanks to appropriate resource allocation, selection of new financially promising projects or, conversely, cancellation of projects that do not show a satisfactory financial potential. Financial ratios compare budgeted and actual expenditures, and costs and investments relatives to every NPD project are essential to maintain projects on the right financial track.	Brown and Eisenhardt (1995); Cooper (1979a, 1979b); Cooper and Kleinschmidt (1987a, 1987b, 1993, 1995, 1996); Godener and Söderquist (2004); Griffin and Page (1993, 1996); Hayes *et al.* (2005); Kaplan and Norton (1993); Kerssens-van Drongelen and Cook (1997); SAPPHO (Rothwell, 1972; Rothwell *et al.*,1974); Stanford Innovation Project (Maidique and Zirger, 1984, 1985; Zirger and Maidique, 1990); Werner and Souder (1997)
Customer satisfaction	Definition: high performance as exceeding or at least satisfying customer expectations. (1) evaluate market expectations (anticipate success) of a new product (2) evaluate market success after introduction by measuring parameters such as the conformances to specifications, the product's appreciation by customers (add value provided), market share, market penetration, brand image, ... and relate these measures to NPD activities and organisation.	Brown and Eisenhardt (1995); Clark and Fujimoto (1991); Edgett *et al.* (1992); Godener and Söderquist (2004); Griffin and Page (1993, 1996); Kaplan and Norton (1993); Kerssens-van Drongelen and Cook (1997)
Process management	Definition: high performance rhymes with optimising quality, lead-time and cost, and ensuring project process according to process related goals. Measures development lead-time, engineering productivity, total product quality, the effectiveness of communication, and motivational and behavioural factors such as commitment, initiative, and leadership of human resources in the NPD process.	Adler, Mandelbaum, Nguyen, and Schwerer (1995); Brown and Eisenhardt (1995); Eisenhardt and Tabrizi (1995); Godener and Söderquist (2004); Griffin and Page (1993, 1996); Harvard Auto Study (Clark *et al.*, 1987; Clark and Fujimoto, 1991; Hayes *et al.*, 1988); Imai *et al.* (1985); Kaplan and Norton (1993); Kerssens-van Drongelen and Bilderbeek (1999); Takeuchi and Nonaka (1986); Werner and Souder (1997)
Innovation	Definition: high performance as the successful transformation of research efforts into new products – a productive outcome, in the shape of new product concepts and architectures, of the creative application and combination of new and existing knowledge. Focus: outputs such as number of patents generated, the pace of product development and launch, and the percent of new technology content in new products.	Godener and Söderquist (2004) (patents only); Green (1995); Griffin and Page (1993, 1996); Kaplan and Norton (1993); Kerssens-van Drongelen and Cook (1997); Kleinschmidt and Cooper (1991); Werner and Souder (1997)

Figure 3.3   Seven Areas of Performance Measurement

Strategic	Definition: high performance means goal satisfaction, implicitly understanding that goals refer to whatever goals are included in the overall strategic management of the firm before focusing on how NPD contributes to these goals. Metrics: (1) the contribution of NPD to business strategy – they estimate that fit between R&D and business strategy. (2) the ability of NPD to shape and even initiate new strategic orientations – they estimate the number of new business opportunities derived from R&D activities. Contribution: avoid too much of short focus– driven by financial perspective, and too much of good knowledge of direction, but lack of scientific and technical expertise – driven by the customer perspective.	Booz-Allen and Hamilton (1982); Clark and Fujimoto (1991); Cusumano and Nobeoka (1992); Godener and Söderquist (2004); Griffin and Page (1996); Hayes *et al.* (1988, 2005); Werner and Souder (1997)
Technology management	Definition: high performance as the efficient management of product technology for generating a continuous stream of new competitive products. Focus: coupling between product and process technology through the important concept of product platforms. Evaluating economies of scale and scope which are not necessarily related to the degree of innovation in derived products. Purpose: focus management attention to the technical and commercial effectiveness of R&D and NPD on a product family basis, by looking into the dynamics of evolving product lines, the renewal of underlying technical architectures (platforms), and the leverage that platforms provide in generating derivative products and improve manufacturing flexibility	Cusumano and Nobeoka (1992); Hayes *et al.* (2005)
Knowledge management	Definition: high performance as a qualitative return on NPD investment in terms of knowledge creation, knowledge transfer, and knowledge exploitation resulting in enhanced NPD capabilities and intellectual assets. Contribution: a knowledge management model in NPD that provide many inputs to what could be measured – (1) 'brain-ware'(knowledge in the mind of people); (2) 'hardware' (prototypes, products, equipment incorporating knowledge); (3) 'groupware' (unwritten knowledge shared by people, e.g. rules of thumb, procedures, stories); (4) 'documentware' (knowledge stored in paper or e-form); (5) the efficiency of 'search and acquisition of new information', 'search and acquisition of knowledge,' and 'evaluation and application of knowledge and new information.'	Cusumano and Nobeoka (1992); Takeuchi and Nonaka (1986); Wheelwright and Clark (1992)

Figure 3.3   Seven Areas of Performance Measurement – *continued*

of the following ten items: expresses opinions freely, comes to meetings prepared, takes initiative, accepts criticism, listens to others, delegates authority, shares information freely, bases decisions on sound data, values all customers and recognises others' contributions. Subsequently, these individual peer ratings are averaged across the ten items and all team-members to reach an overall peer evaluation for each team-member and the team's overall performance as well as to make pay, promotion, or future team assignments decisions. This five-point scale can be used with autonomous cross-functional project team as well, because these team-members are independent and autonomous.

Werner and Souder (1997) argue that, the effectiveness and efficiency of measurement collection and aggregation of multiple measures, of both quantitative and qualitative nature and joint estimates of NPD performance among functional departments such as R&D, manufacturing, and marketing, are imperative. They also recommend setting comparative performance standards against benchmark quantitative measures.

Kerssens-van Drongelen and Bilderbeek (1999) identify four measurement techniques for NPD performance measurement systems: (1) subjective assessment of superiors (e.g. evaluating of subordinates' performance by their direct supervisor); (2) assessment by an independent third party; (3) feedback from internal or external customers; and (4) objective score on quantitative criteria (e.g. profitability). However, although both subjective and objective measures are used in these evaluations, the subjective evaluations of personnel may be influenced by objective measures of outcomes. In a piece of research concerning the outcome effect of performance evaluations of managers from multi-outlet businesses, Ghosh and Lusch (2000) found out that subjective evaluations of store managers by their supervisors are negatively impacted by unfavourable outcome results. Specifically, if the result of an objective outcome (e.g. profitability) is poor, then the supervisor (subjective measures) feels that the store manager does not perform his job well. More specifically, the drawback in performance measurement or control systems is the outcome effect or bias in which superior evaluators subjectively assess their store managers' performance based on objective outcomes (Hawkins and Hastie, 1990). In this regards, Ghosh and Lusch (2000: 411) commented that 'as expected, outcome determinants over which the managers have control influence their performance evaluations and environmental determinants of outcome over which they have no control do not influence their evaluations.' However, there is an exception – managers have no control in central management determinants of outcome, but it influences their evaluations as well. Actually, the objective outcome could be influenced by many uncontrollable factors (e.g. weather, fire or water damages). So, the key point here is that as long as the store manager made appropriate managerial decisions, then the store manager's performance should be satisfied. Only considering or evaluating by objective outcomes will influence not only the quality of the measurement result but may wrongly reward or punish managers (Hawkins and Hastie, 1990).

In Hayes *et al.*'s (2005) research, Milliken & Co., a winner of the National Baldrige Award, asks each of its departments, from production lines to accounting offices to human resources managers, to select its own performance measures and through large charts on nearby walls to display the improvements achieved in those measures over time. From this measurement approach, it is obvious that Milliken & Co.'s top management is more interested in what they are displaying on the walls for everyone (e.g. the personnel belonging to that department or close departments, and managers or customers who were just passing through) to see that what measures these departments chose, because measures should be the tools for keeping continuous improvement. Hence, as long as these departments felt those measures were helpful and after using them, really improved their departmental performance, then the purpose of performance measurement has been achieved.

From the literature review and analysis, the knowledge regarding why performance measurement is needed, what areas need performance measurement, and how NPD performance measures should be presented, a performance measurement framework can be developed. Loch, Stein, and Terwiesch (1996) argue that the *areas* motivate managers to set specific objectives for the intentional measurement process; the *uses* confine how actually disciplines are utilised in managerial processes and how the results of measurement drive particular actions; finally, the *impacts* echo the resulting outcomes *ex post*. Indeed, when senior managers set some performance measures to evaluate employees in the company, senior managers are supposed to have the ability to foresee what kind of reaction employees may give and to minimise the gap between intention and outcome (Hayes *et al.*, 2005). Loch *et al.* (1996) argue that this is the central practical problem in performance measurement.

In a research regarding the effects of performance-contingent monetary incentives on individual effort and task performance, Bonner and Sprinkle (2002) argue that, generally, clear performance targets, i.e. assigned goals, have positive effects on individual effort and task performance over monetary incentives, thus suggesting that companies should set performance targets with monetary incentives to motivate employees. Uses of performance measurement results can help companies to examine whether employees achieve the assigned goals, whether companies should assign bonuses, and whether employees desire promotions or salary increases. Milgrom and Roberts (1992) also argue that the main purposes of individual performance evaluation are for feedback and rewards.

Millson and Wilemon (2002) argue that NPD managers should measure and document different financial variables during the NPD processes and also the documentation of measures of market success after project completion, because such measures present another area where financial and/or accounting personnel could support NPD efforts. For example, it is necessary to communicate between NPD teams, financial personnel, and senior managers so that unsuccessfully performing projects can be terminated and then senior managers can re-allocate corporate resources to promising projects. Namely, measurement results can be used to assist senior managers for decision-making about resources allocation and communication among NPD-related departments.

In a study of top management support of 213 R&D projects in 21 major companies, Green (1995) examined two diverse perspectives of project performance for project termination and the project to business goals of the company and concluded that the relationship between project termination and business goals is: top management terminated some new product projects, because these projects are much less able to contribute to business goals such as profitability, cost reduction, or market share growth. However, Green (1995) also reveals that controlling project characteristics, measuring project performance, and obtaining top management support, projects were less prone to be terminated. Indeed, project performance could be useful to many measurements such as achievement of commercial goals, technological innovations, NPD process efficiency, team cooperation, and patents (Hayes *et al.*, 2005).

Based on a study of 44 companies, Kerssens-van Drongelen and Bilderbeek (1999) identified uses or purposes of performance measurement results to the organisational levels, namely, where the focus of performance measurement is: individual, team, R&D department and company level. Also, Godener and Söderquist (2004) synthesised five categories from uses or purposes of NPD performance measurement results: communication, control, resources allocation, individual evaluation (not used for all R&D and NPD staff), and continuous improvement. From the NPD

Organisational Levels	Uses/Purposes	Categories	Corresponding Researchers
Kerssens-vanDrongelen and Bilderbeek (1999)	Kerssens-vanDrongelen and Bilderbeek (1999)		
* Individual Bonner and Sprinkle (2002); Milgrom and Roberts (1992); Quinn *et al.* (1996)	• Correction • Decision-making about promotion, and/or salary • Decision-making about project participation • Assignment of bonuses	I. Correction and Control: defining corrective actions based on diagnosis and control.	Busby (1999); Ghosh and Lusch (2000)
		II. Individual Evaluation: deciding on individual promotions, salary increases and other incentives	Bonner and Sprinkle (2002); Brickley *et al.* (2004); Davila (2003); Ghosh and Lusch (2000); Milgrom and Roberts (1992); Quinn *et al.* (1996)
* Team Cohen and Bailey (1997) Milgrom and Roberts (1992); Millson and Wilemon (2002); Rowe (2004)	• Progress control/ correction • Decision-making to dissolve the team • Assignment of new projects • Assignment of bonuses • Learning/continuous improvement	III. Resources Allocation: allocating resources in NPD including forming or dissolving teams and assigning NPD projects – implementing strategy	Davila (2003); Green (1995); Hayes *et al.* (2005); Milgrom and Roberts (1992); Millson and Wilemon (2002)
* Departmental Milgrom and Roberts (1992); Werner and Souder (1997)	• Correction • Assignment of new projects • Assignment of resources • Decision-making about reorganisation • Learning	IV. Communication: communicating objecjective, agreements and rules – quantifying and possibly justifying strategy	Brown and Eisenhardt (1995); Green (1995); Kaplan and Norton (1993); Millson and Wilemon (2002); Pelled and Adler (1994)
* Company Level Cusumano and Nobeoka (1992); Kaplan and Norton (1993); Pande *et al.* (2000)	• Correction • Assignment of resources • Decision-making about reorganisation • Learning	V. Continuous Improvement: NPD process and product innovation	Davila (2003); Hayes *el at.* (2005); Kaplan and Norton (1993)

Figure 3.4   Uses of Measurement Results at Different Organisational Levels

performance measurement literature reviewed and the above analysis we summarise a list of the uses of measurement results, see Figure 3.4.

The company's overall success is not considered in this study. There are too many perspectives such as NPD, significant investment decisions, merger acquisitions, internationalisation, etc., which could affect a company's success. Explicitly, NPD projects may be commercially successful, but the company still fails – from a stock market's standpoint, falling from a public company to delisted company, resulting from reasons other than NPD. Conversely, NPD projects could be financial failures, but the company is still profitable at a transition year, just because the company sold a SBU or made a correct managerial investment decision. Thus, we limit this study within the performance measurement of project team and project team's outcome – new product success.

Usually, a project team is formed from different functions of a company, in case the team has available resources such as professional skills to perform a project. Thus, the relationship between performance measurements of project teams and success of new products as well as the operations, uses, and impacts of measurement results between project teams and functional departments are the central parts in this study. Consequently, the company level measurement is considered in this book.

Godener and Söderquist (2004: 197) argue that the recent NPD performance measurement literature brings few clarifications and examples that would close the loop 'metrics-design-use-impact.' It is important for companies to know what measures need to be used, why to use these measures, who measures it, how data are collected, how to use the measurement results and what influences these measures will bring about (Ghosh and Lusch, 2000; Otley and Fakiolas, 2000). An effective performance measurement system assists top management to achieve business goals, corporate objectives, or the purposes of designing this system. Whether a performance measurement system is effective or ineffective depends on the impacts of measurement results and, certainly, it is management's responsibility to ensure the system is effective.

Milgrom and Roberts (1992) argue for evaluating team performance on team output so that team-members can focus on the common objective and cooperate within the team. Concerning free-rider problems, management can evaluate team-members not only on team output but also on other measures (e.g. peer reviews or a direct supervisor's subjective evaluation) as well. Truly, peer reviews help to evaluate each team-member's performance, but some team-members might downgrade a team-member dishonestly to raise their own grades, especially these team-members who work only for a single project. Fortunately, from literature, there are some suggestions for senior managers to carefully control these dysfunctional incentives before a team is formed (Cohen and Bailey, 1997; Milgrom and Roberts, 1992; Rowe, 2004).

Firstly, the quality of each team-member is the most important element before forming a team. Within a project team, team-members should be capable and understand their own duty for achieving the common objective. Secondly, developing the internal architecture for a project team and deciding how to evaluate the work efforts of team-members before assembling the project team is essential. Namely, decision rights and task assignments must be clear within the project team. Finally, controlling free-rider problems, team-members must decide on the rewards and punishments for members of the project team. Project teams are formed because they are more successful than the over-the-wall approach, but, if these project teams only create pressures, tensions, and loads of unhappiness, then maybe the company should find the causes before dissolving teams.

Kaplan and Norton (1993) emphasise that the balanced scorecard (BSC) – measures that drive performance – provides executives with a comprehensive framework that defines the vision (mission) and then translates a well-defined company's strategic objectives (competitive advantages) into logical performance measures within each of the four perspectives: financial, customer, internal business, and innovation and learning. In Kaplan and Norton's research (1993), this strategic management system helps management, emphasise a process view of operations, motivate its employees, incorporate customer feedback into its operations, adjusting long-term performance, and consolidate strategic information.

Based on a review of general performance management literature, Kerssens-van Drongelen and Bilderbeek (1999) reveal that, coherent with agency theory, NPD performance measurement motivates employees and improves at least those outcomes that are measured. For example, NPD staff increase their responsiveness to improving productivity and reducing NPD time, in addition to alignment with business objectives and decreasing R&D cost. In addition, Kerssens-van Drongelen and Bilderbeek (1999) and Cook (1997) emphasise an important impact of a performance measurement system is to contribute to the justification of the existence, decisions and performance of the manager.

Based on an exploratory case study conducted in three large electronic companies, Godener and Söderquist (2004) concluded that to NPD staff, there was no particular impact on the behaviour of NPD staff as the systems were not feeding back measurement results directly to R&D engineers. However, to project managers, the evaluations on project goals motivate employees and competition for better projects. In addition, although the impact of measurement results is supported by increased motivation of employees, there is no immediate return and by enabling performance benchmarking with other projects, divisions, or companies. Finally, the impact in terms of improved communication between NPD staff and management is found to improve information access and contribute to well-balanced arbitration and decision-making.

Areas	Categories	Impacts	Researcher(s)
1. Individual 2. Team 3. Divisional	1. Individual Evaluation 2. Resource Allocation 3. Control 4. Communication 5. Continuous Improvement	1. Peer pressure and dysfunctional incentives 2. Free-rider Solution 1. Professional employees 2. Internal architecture: Decision rights	Milgrom and Roberts (1992)
Vision + Strategy 1. Financial 2. Customer Satisfaction 3. Internal Business 4. Innovation and Learning	1. Individual Evaluation 2. Resource Allocation 3. Communication 4. Continuous Improvement	1. Operations: process view 2. Motivated employees 3. Feedback: client – operations 4. Adjusting long-term performance 5. Uniting strategic info.	Kaplan and Norton (1993)
1. Financial 2. Customer Satisfaction 3. Process 4. Innovation	1. Personnel Evaluation 2. Resource Allocation 3. Control 4. Continuous Improvement	1. Improvement of those outcomes that measured 2. Increased motivation of the NPD staff 3. Contribution of the justification of the existence, decisions and performance of an agent	Kerssens-van Drongelen and Bilderbeek (1999); Kerssens-van Drongelen and Cook (1997)
1. Financial 2. Customer Satisfaction 3. Process 4. Strategic 5. Innovation (only patent counts)	1. Resource Allocation 2. Correction 3. Communication 4. Continuous Improvement 5. Individual Evaluation (not for all NPD staff	1. No particular impact on behaviour of NPD staff (except project managers: evaluation on project goals motivate competition for better projects) 2. Increased motivation (but no immediate return) 3. improved information access and understanding between the players involved in NPD and well-balanced arbitration and decision-making	Godener and Söderquist (2004)

Figure 3.5 Categorisation of Uses and Impacts of Measurement Results

In Figure 3.5, areas of performance, categories or uses, and impact of performance measurement results are summarised based on literature reviewed in NPD performance measurement. It is obvious that companies really need and already use different measures to motivate, evaluate, reward or punishment, or make managerial decisions on NPD activities.

3.4 Conclusion

This chapter introduced the concepts of organisational architecture and provides an overview of the factors that could be important in determining the finest architecture for a team. The focus in this chapter was to explain the interaction and connection of the three systems; the assignment of decision rights, rewarding and punishing new product project members, and the performance measurement system. Through the assignment of decision rights, the jobs of employees of the team have been decided. The assignment of decision rights to employees of the team is not only the first but important preparation before running a team. Once the tasks are assigned, executives then design the reward systems to encourage members of the team. In addition, the reward systems base their compensations on measurement results produced by the performance measurement systems. The relation of the three systems could be seen as a circle. Once the three systems are well-designed, they will be tightly connect together as well as utilise and support each other. Conversely, once one of the three systems is inappropriately designed, other systems can be influenced and the purposes of designing the three systems could be unachievable.

In social science, human behaviour is complicated and difficult to predict from one single standpoint. Multiple theories are advocated to capture the greater complexity of human behaviour and to address a greater range of the project team's activities. Our conceptual framework is derived from new product success or failure and the organisational architecture literature and is adopted due to its logical position in taking into account the interaction of; incentive, team effort, team effectiveness, team performance, and new product success or failure. Theoretically, the alignment of organisational structures, team incentives, team effort, and team effectiveness does influence team performance which in turn influences new product success or failure. The next chapter provides a detailed discussion of the theoretical framework.

4
Conceptual Framework

4.0 Introduction

This chapter reviews theories and evidence concerning the effects of incentives on team effort, team performance, and team outcome. Previous studies investigated incentive-individual effort and effort-performance relationships but little research has been undertaken to investigate the combined incentive-effort-performance-success relationships have, which is important in explaining the success of NPD. Four theories of agency, stewardship, social identity, and self-categorisation are used to develop a conceptual framework to understand the relationships of incentive-effort, effort-effectiveness, effort-performance, and performance-success.

The remaining of this chapter is organised as follows:

- The economic approach – agency theory
- Sociological and psychological approaches
- Why multiple theories are used in the conceptual framework
- The conceptual framework
- Conclusion

4.1 The economic approach – agency theory

Economic approaches to governance such as agency theory, which emphasises controlling agents through monitoring and incentives aligned with corporate goals, is based on Theory X and the assumption of 'homo-economics, which [describes human beings] as individualistic, opportunistic, and self-serving' (Davis, Schoorman, and Donaldson, 1997: 20), especially, under conditions of internationalisation, diversification, and delegation of authority. Both principals and agents are assumed to be rational actors who seek to gain as much possible utility with the least possible cost, but with divergent interests (Jensen and Meckling, 1976; Tosi, Brownlee, Silva, and Katz, 2003). To counter the divergence of interests, agency theory holds that imposing corporate governance mechanisms (e.g. reporting, auditing, and policies) on the agent is the best way to minimise agency loss (Jensen and Meckling, 1976).

The limits and boundaries of agency theory are restricted by its assumptions (Davis *et al.*, 1997). For example, Perrow (1986) criticises agency theory as extremely narrow, having few testable implications, addressing no clear problem, and being dangerous. Further, he explains the theoretical limits of agency theory, such as not all agents interests are diverged with principals. In addition, Jensen and Meckling (1994) criticise that agency theory contains an economic model of man as being a simplification for mathematical modelling and an impractical description of human behaviour. Likewise, Donaldson (1990) also criticises agency theory as it adopts a narrow model of human behaviour and motivation and neglects a much broader range of human motives such as responsibility and recognition.

Doucouliagos (1994) argues that tagging all human beings as self-interest actors does not explain the complexity of human behaviour. Alternatively, Jensen (1983) argues that agency theory is revolutionary and an influential foundation. Eisenhardt (1989) lies in the middle and argues that agency theory provides a unique, realistic, and empirically testable standpoint on problems of cooperation such as teamwork effort. In addition, Davis *et al.* (1997) argue that agency theory provides a helpful approach to explaining principal-agent relationships and can be brought more into alignment through proper monitoring and a well-designed reward system.

As argued by Eisenhardt (1989), agency theory is most relevant to study new product innovation and settings such as technology-based companies because they combine substantial goal conflict between principals and agents such as professional employees and managers, risks such as sufficient outcome uncertainty, and team-oriented jobs in which performance measurement and contracting problems are difficult. Similarly, Hesterly, Liebeskind, and Zenger (1990) argue that agency theory identifies essential common preconditions for organisations to develop, such as decision rights; monetary incentives; the transportation and communication network; and industrial technology which calls for team production.

From its origins in information economics, the development of agency theory has brought about two almost completely separate research

	Positivist Agency Theory	**Normative Agency Theory**
Mathematical Rigor	Non-mathematical and empirically oriented.	Mathematical and non-empirically oriented.
Dependent Variable	Modelling the effects of additional aspects of the contracting environment and the technology of monitoring and bonding on the form of the contracts and organisations that survive.	• The structure of the preferences of the parties to the contracts; • The nature of uncertainty; • The informational structure in the environment.
Purpose	Purely explanatory	For making prescriptions.
Criticism	• Oversimplification • Unconstrained, tautological and lacking rigor variables	• Tyranny of formalism; • Tractability problem: limits the richness of inputs; • Difficult to analyse the effects of complex equilibrium systems in the contracting milieu.
Argumentation	• Positivist agency theory enriches economics by offering a more complex view of organisations; • A scientific continuing process; • Propositions can be logically rigorous without being mathematical and analysis does not have to take the form of symbols and equations.	• Involvement on careful specification of assumptions, which are followed by logical deduction and mathematical proof; • A broader focus and greater interest and theoretical implications; • More testable implications Focus: Determining the optimal contract, behaviour versus outcome, between the principal and the agent.

Figure 4.1   The Differences between Two Lines of Agency Theory Research

streams; positivist agency theory and normative agency theory. However, both nominally addressed contracting problem between self-interested maximising parties and both use the same agency cost minimising tautology (Eisenhardt, 1989; Jensen, 1983). In Figure 4.1, the differences between the two streams of agency theory are summarised (see for example, Eisenhardt (1989), Hirsch, Michaels, and Friedman (1987), Jensen (1983), Perrow (1986)). Their common assumptions are the unit of analysis, human beings, organisations, and information.

Positivist agency theory helps in understanding the actions of economic agents, such as the selection of accounting procedures, and has influenced the thinking of many economic researchers and some practitioners, on the significant concerns that come up when choosing among accounting alternatives (Kaplan, 1983). The positivist agency theory, with its emphasis on studying and understanding the divergence of interests both internal and external to the company, has a significant role in accounting research (Jensen, 1983). However, Kaplan (1983) comments that the positivist agency theory's assumption – continuous maximising behaviour of informed, rational managers is a tautology in the literature and exists without making explicit tests of this assumption.

Jensen (1983) also argues that using tautologies to develop the positivist agency theory is directly associated with the nature of the scientific continuing process, which involves the use of the agency definitions and the cost-minimising underlying tautology and a subset of the available data, i.e. the observed contract structures to develop propositions about the important aspects and relations of the settings. In addition, if successful, as Jensen argues, the theory provides a theoretical structure that can be manipulated to derive additional non-obvious propositions (i.e. hypotheses), which can also be confronted with previously unknown or unused data to provide a test of the theory. Conversely, if the data are substantially inconsistent with the predictions, the theory is revised or replaced with a new alternative, and the testing process continues.

Kaplan (1983) recommends that before using a particular theory, such as the positivist agency theory for normative studies, researchers need direct evidence on the internal validity and consistency of the assumptions and structure of the model, not just its predictive ability, because other alternative theories would yield consistent predictions of the same observed phenomena. However, as Jensen (1983) argues, the choice among alternative theories will be founded on which is expected to yield the highest value of the objective function when used for decision-making. That is, each theory has its benefits and detriments, if this theory predicts poorly but still better than the best available alternative, it should be valuable, because one can only use a theory to criticise another theory.

'Agency theory, as used in management accounting research, is concerned with contractual relationships between the members [usually focuses on two individuals – the principal (or superior) and the agent (or subordinate)] of a firm.' (Scapens, 1991: 147). '… [T]he objective of agency theory [is] to explain the behaviour of individuals as economic agents …'(Ryan *et al.*, 2002: 75). In addition, Scapens (1991: 5) maintains that '[u]sing agency theory it is possible to demonstrate that some of the observed practices of management accounting could be optimal, despite their lack of conformity with conventional wisdom.' That is, the advantage of using agency theory in management accounting research could offer a way to bridge the gap between the theory and practice of management accounting.

'[The positivist agency theory], generally proceeds as follows (Jensen, 1983 …): decision-makers choose particular courses of action based on their desires, needs, preferences, etc, and these choices are informed by their understanding of how the world works.' (Ryan *et al.*, 2002: 76). Therefore, the positivist agency theory is used in this research to help in understanding observed management accounting practices. In brief, the objective of using positivist agency theory is to explain the observed management accounting practices and then help the decision-makers to understand how the world works. However, there are general limitations and boundaries of the agency model. For example, in management accounting and particular agency theory research, agency theory is still assumed that the owner and decision-maker are rational economic persons intent to maximise their personal utilities, and their actions are set within a system of competitive markets (available for managerial skills and information) (Ryan *et al.*, 2002). In addition, currently agency theory provides few conclusions that can be generalised and empirically tested, because agency theory describes the optimal techniques for particular situations, so most of the results of agency theory are situational specific (Scapens, 1991).

In conclusion, agency theory is an economic theory of interest, of motivation, and of compliance, i.e. concerning how to diminish the conflict of interest between principal and agent (Donaldson, 1990). Firms are conceived as teams that have objectives, strategies, structures, and outputs which relate with the other managerial sys-tems in their environment (Donaldson, 1990; Fama, 1980). The concern for more macroscopic system-level analysis is how to structure the team of willing co-operators to overcome the technical difficulties of achieving adequate integration through optimal corporate strategies, structures, and organisational systems (Donaldson, 1990; Eisenhardt, 1989). Thus, it is essential for organisational economics such as agency theory to be integrated with other psychology, sociology, and politics approaches (Davis *et al.*, 1997; Donaldson, 1990; Eisenhardt, 1989).

4.2   Sociological and psychological approaches

Alternative theories from sociology and psychology treat human motivation, incentive, and compliance as distinct from theories of organisational architecture, strategy, and planning (Donaldson, 1990). An effective project team is a small number of various cross-functional capable team-members who are unselfish; respect each other's particular capabilities; and committed to achieve the team purpose or a common goal through the cognitive, evaluative, and emotional processes to the team (Lembke and Wilson, 1998). Also, psychologists and sociologists emphasise that human behaviour is sometimes produced without deliberate thought, i.e. through personal habit, emotion, taken-for-granted custom, conditioned reflex or unconditioned reflex, and unconscious desires (Donaldson, 1990).

Although the contributions of agency theory are that it offers unique insight into information systems, outcome uncertainty, incentives, and risk; and it is an empirically valid and testable approach, a simplistic model of human motivation such as economic model of man could yield robust predictions and thus be methodically valid (Friedman, 1953), thus using agency theory with complementary theories together are essential (Eisenhardt, 1989). Comprehensive understandings of the characteristics of the manager/agent/steward and of the situation are indispensable to understanding manager-principal interest divergence and convergence. That is, additional theory from psychology and sociology is desirable to explain other types of human behaviour, and it is found in the literature beyond the economic perspective, thus, stewardship theory was used in this study and described below.

4.2.1   Stewardship theory

Stewardship theory, based on Theory Y, has been developed concerning corporate governance (Donaldson and Davis, 1991). It emphasises that stewards will act in the organisation's best interest with few or even without controls under certain conditions, such as higher order needs, intrinsic motivations, identification of high value commitments, and low power distance (Davis *et al.*, 1997; Tosi *et al.*, 2003). Specifically, people under stewardship theory are 'collectivists, pro-organisational, and trustworthy,' because the stewards believe their interests are aligned with that of the company and its owners, as well as aiming to achieve the objectives of the company, so monitoring and incentive costs are diminished and the performance of stewards is affected by whether the empowering governance mechanisms are appropriate (Davis *et al.*, 1997: 20).

Davis *et al.* (1997) differentiate between the assumptions of agency and stewardship theories based on the subordinate's psychological attributes and the organisation's situational characteristics. They argue that people who are motivated by higher order needs and intrinsic motivation, are high in value commitment, are in an involvement-oriented situation, are more prone to use personal power, and have high identification, a collectivist and low power distance culture within the organisation are more likely to become stewards in principal-steward relationships. A comparison and summary of some assumptions of agency and stewardship theories are provided in Figure 4.2

	Agency Theory	**Stewardship Theory**
Presumption	Agents' interests diverge with their principals' interests – Max. individual utility at cost to the principal	Stewards' objectives are aligned with the objectives of their principals – Max. organisational performance
Level or Unit of Analysis	Methodological individualist; Contract between principal and agent	Methodological collectivist; Relationship between principal nad steward
Human Nature Assumptions	• Organisational economics (Theory X) • Economic man: cheating, self-interest, bounded rationality, risk aversion	• Organisational behaviour (Theory Y) • Self-actualising man: pro-organisational behaviour, collective, honest
Organisational Assumptions	• Partial goal conflict and risk preferences among members: compensation, regulation, leadership, vertical integration, whistle-blowing, impression management • Information asymmetry between principal and agent • Monitoring and controlling structures	• A strong relationship between the success of the organisation and the principal's satisfaction through firm performance • The behaviour of stewards is organisationally centred, given potential multiplicity of principal's objectives • Facilitating and empowering structures
Information Assumptions	A commodity which can be purchased	Helpful to confirm the common goal
Psychological Factors Motivation	Extrinsic rewards: Lower order needs – physiological, security, economic	Intrinsic rewards Higher order needs – growth, affiliation, achievement, self-actualisation
Social Comparison	Other agents	Owner
Identification	Low-commitment	High-commitment
Power	Institutional – legitimate, coercive, reward	Personal – expert, referent
Situational Factors	Control oriented	Involvement-oriented
Management Philosophy	Control systems	Trusting relationships
Risk Orientation	Short-term	Long term
Time Frame	Cost control	Performance enhancement
Objective	Individualistic behaviour, High power distance culture	Collective culture: Low power distance culture
Cultural Differences		

Figure 4.2   The Two Theories to Managerial Control in Organisations

(adapted from Davis *et al.* (1997), Donaldson (1990), Eisenhardt (1989), Jensen and Meckling (1976), and Tosi *et al.* (2003)).

4.2.2   Social identity theory and self-categorisation theory

'A team is a collection of individuals who are interdependent in their tasks, who share responsibility for outcomes, who see themselves and who are seen by others as an intact social entity embedded in one or more larger social systems (for example, business unit or the corporation), and who manage their relationships across organizational boundaries.' (Cohen and Bailey, 1997: 241)

Selection of project manager and team-members is very important to ensure the quality of a project team in the first place. Self-categorisation (categorising oneself) is a psychological process that aids judgement about whether or not an individual can be a team-member or a team leader (Turner, 1987). In addition, social identity theory proposes that team cohesion across all individuals relies on the perceived choice of a category (Lembke and Wilson, 1998). However, self-categorisation in a team that is perceived as of low value or low status can bring about identifying with sub-teams within the larger team and disintegration of the team (Turner, 1987). Specifically, categorisation of the social environment causes the judgment of achievable team options for the team identification and category.

Teamwork is the cognitive and emotional process of alignment (Tajfel and Turner, 1986; Turner, 1987) (not the goal of management activity) and differs from project to project in scope and duration, integration into the larger organisational context, intensity of team-member interaction and skill, etc (Lembke and Wilson, 1998). Also, a team has its own attitude and cognition through an emotional attachment to the team which helps effective teamwork (Turner, 1987). Thus, an emotional and cognitive perspective on group behaviour and a theory about the psychological process as involved in teamwork is essential in understanding how teams work. Tajfel and Turner (1986) propose a social identity theory, which emphasises the need to identify the team identity, for the psychological process and its effect on interpersonal dynamics for understanding teamwork in organisations.

In the team management literature, social identity helps an individual to achieve a better understanding of the tasks and behaviour required for the team output and team effectiveness (Lembke and Wilson, 1998). From a social identity perspective, teamwork needs to be motivated by more than individualistic (personal) benefits and is closely linked to the social identity of the team; i.e, team identity (Tajfel and Turner, 1986). Social identification is a transition which is clarified as a reaction to the social context. Further, the individual is important when categorising the self as part of a team, and within the social environment (Hogg and Abrams, 1993; Tajfel and Turner, 1986). When a team identity is adopted, the team becomes the unit of analysis, and then the social environment is clarified with reference to the team, not to individuals (Lembke and Wilson, 1998).

Tajfel and Turner's (1986) teams are concerned with membership itself, but teams with a common purpose are expected to be highly productive because team-members are committed to a common team identity directing behaviour to the reason or purpose for assembling a team. '... team members perceive other team members and themselves as making a valuable contribution, in order to consider the team an effective work arrangement.' (Lembke and Wilson, 1998: 936). Perception and recognition of the team's performance are important to identify effective team purpose and should be measured by measurable standards such as successful completion of their goal so that team-members perceive they can control it.

From the perspective of social identity theory, team-members cannot separate themselves from the team task, the commitment for the team behaviour, and the responsibility for the team output; in addition team-members expect that their behaviour will influence achieving the team purpose. As long as potential team-members have adopted a social identity, and self-categorisation, then these team-members will just contribute themselves to the common goal of the team. Explicitly, social identity theory explains a social psychological process of how managers change the way they present information to potential team-members thus these team-members are motivated to work together and think as a team.

Based on the reasoning of a self-categorisation process, Towry (2003) argues that the effectiveness of incentive systems depends on the level of team identity, namely, a strong team identity leads to greater coordination of a team. Towry (2003) suggests that when the team has achieved a high level of identity, a horizontal incentive system delegating authority for control to team self-management (directly control the actions of each team-member) is the most effective way in the company. Lembke and Wilson (1998: 927) argue that 'social identity theory posits that the motivation for thinking, feeling, and thus working as a cohesive unit is socially constructed.' Alternatively, the effectiveness of a vertical incentive system where team-members report observations of their peers' efforts to management is degraded by a strong team identity.

Based on the above discussion, if team-members have established a strong self-categorisation and social identity of the team (i.e. team identity), the company should allow more peer-based control and empowerment or autonomy to selected team-members so that these team-members can make decisions quickly and concentrate on the goal of the team. That is, team-members do not need to be controlled and they do their jobs properly, so these team-members eventually will improve not only the quantity, such as productivity but also the performance quality, such as speed and creativity. Again, the reasoning is, the right people will do their jobs properly regardless of incentive systems. But, this does not mean the company does not need the incentive plan (Collins, 2001).

4.3   Why multiple theories are used in the conceptual framework

Viewing human behaviour as either completely self-serving or completely self-actualising is not reasonable because human behaviour is more difficult to expect and a contingent mixture of the two. Though it is suitable to monitor progresses in economics, it is more practical to use economics as an extra to a more complicated organisational context. Eisenhardt (1989) recommends that researchers should look beyond the economics literature so that researchers can expand to a richer and more complex range of contexts. Thus, using agency theory with complementary theories such as stewardship theory, social identity theory, and self-categorisation theory all together can capture the greater complexity of human behaviour and a greater range of performance measurement of the cross-functional project team.

Hirsch *et al.* (1987) compare economics with sociology and argue that economics is subjugated by a single paradigm, price theory, and a single economic view of human nature – self-interest, but they agree that the advantages of economics are suspicious development of assumptions and logical propositions. Hence, Hirsch *et al.* (1987) maintain agency theory and yield a more realistic view of organisations. Specifically, agency theory presents a valid but partial view of the world, and also ignores the complexities of organisational life, so exclusive reliance on agency theory is undesirable (Davis *et al.*, 1997; Eisenhardt, 1989). Thus, Doucouliagos (1994) argues that an additional theory such as stewardship theory is needed to explain relationships based on other, non-economic assumptions such as what causes interests to be aligned.

Prior research shows deficiency in clarifying concerns of *how teams work*, and only focus on how teams can be managed effectively or more successfully (Millson and Wilemon, 2002), without describing *what teamwork really is* (Lembke and Wilson, 1998). In addition, teammates' interactions in the team are described, but not from psychological and sociological viewpoints. That is, the emotional and cognitive processes occupied with teamwork are repeatedly neglected. However, '[t]he bundling of tasks into jobs and subunits of the firm is an important policy choice that can affect a firm's productivity dramatically.' (Milgrom and Roberts, 1992: 352). Thus, it is necessary to see what teamwork really is from psychological and sociological perspectives as well.

4.4   The conceptual framework

'Choosing appropriate theories ... lead ... researcher[s] to consider variables either to include or control for in a study because the theories indicate that these variables interact with the variable of interest.' (Bonner, 1999: 385)

Several researchers have developed various conceptual frameworks concerning incentives, effort, performance, individual identity, social identity, internal and external processes communication, group psychosocial traits, environmental factors, organisational context, effectiveness, and so on, from different viewpoints and theories. For example, Bonner and Sprinkle (2002) focused only on whether *monetary* incentive can increase *individual* effort and in turn increase *individual* performance, by review-ing expectancy, agency, goal-setting, and social-cognitive theories. Conversely, Lembke and Wilson (1998) studied how to cohere an understanding of employees of the team to team purpose, by reviewing self-categorisation and social identity theories. In addition, Towry (2003) examined appropriate control systems in a teamwork environment, by reviewing agency theory. However, obviously, these researchers focus only on one-part of organisational architecture rather than a full picture of three-part taxonomy. Therefore, their findings could be incomplete or prejudicial.

Jensen (1983) and Milgrom and Roberts (1992) argue that researchers should consider the three-parts of organisational architecture together so that researchers can get a complete picture of accounting and management control systems. Thus we attempt to get a full picture regarding the structure of project teams and the interaction of teamwork and organisational architecture, which involves the decision allocation, the reward and punishment, and the performance measurement systems.

4.4.1   Incentive – team effort – effectiveness

Bonner and Sprinkle (2002) review expectancy, agency, goal-setting, and social-cognitive theories that suggest mediators of the monetary incentive-individual effort relationship, but the individual effort-task performance relation is not connected to monetary incentives by itself. Bonner and Sprinkle (2002) presume that monetary incentives directly work by increasing effort and then individual effort indirectly leads to increase task performance, and also suggest that understanding these theories is important for determining how to maximise the effectiveness of monetary incentives. Although substantial research has focused on the use of incentives to motivate desired behaviour by individuals, Milgrom and Roberts (1992: 413) argue that 'almost all of the formal theory emphasises incentives for individuals on the grounds that it is individuals who must be motivated to work. Yet the most common explicit incentive contracts are applied across groups of individuals.'

Lembke and Wilson (1998) argue that if individuals are not measured or praised as individuals, and all team-members support the teams final output, team-members for their own good (self-interest) will not separate themselves from the team. Namely, the design of a performance measurement system can help team solidity and cohesion. For teams in organisations, team-members typically work in more than one project team, so team-members need clear direction so as to achieve the fast change of team identities. Tajfel (1982) argues that when team-members work with more than one team, and they are distracted from their team purpose, can weaken their team identity. Also, Lembke and Wilson (1998) and Tajfel and Turner (1986) advise that self-categorisation, team identification, and attraction to the teams should be independent, non-competitive, or ideally co-directed to a common organisational goal.

To achieve the organisational purpose and the goal of the team, Lembke and Wilson (1998) argue that it is necessary for team-members to get more conceptual information to gain understanding of what their contribution to the team is, what the team is trying to achieve, and their relationship with other NPD teams. Moreover, for example, when an autonomous cross-functional project team is entrusted with the breakthrough task in which speed and innovativeness are essential, the project team leader should have the reputation to attract team-members and the rights to defend the necessary corporate resources for the project team (Hayes *et al.*, 2005). Since the form of a cross-functional team is not a panacea, the quality aspects of a cross-functional project team: a capable project leader, team-members and other corporate resources (e.g. budget and technology) are required before forming a team.

Additionally, from a social identity perspective, Lembke and Wilson (1998) discover that project team managers are supposed to spend more time with the whole team in the first place, change the way they provide the conceptual information about the skills needed in the team to team-members in order to achieve optimum team conditions, as well as facilitate the team when team-members have difficulties only if the team has decided to request help. Specifically, the work of project managers is not like the duty of heavyweight leaders in the Harvard Auto Study (Clark *et al.* 1987; Clark and Fujimoto, 1991; Hayes *et al.*, 1988), or case-based pieces of research such as Imai *et al.* (1985), or Takeuchi and Nonaka (1986). For project managers, perhaps it is just a minor adjustment to how they interact and communicate with their team-members, but it is expected to have an important impact on team effectiveness through improved team cognition and unified behaviour by the team (Lembke and Wilson, 1998).

Towry (2003) examines control in a teamwork environment, and experimentally explores the horizontal and vertical incentive systems that both depend on mutual monitoring (i.e. the ability of team-members to observe each other's behaviours). Towry (2003) suggests that the effectiveness of a horizontal incentive system, which directly controls the actions of teammates, rooted in peer-enacted control and team outcome-oriented, is improved by a strong team identity; and then a strong team identity helps teams to reach a cooperative teamwork, as desired by the principal. That is, when a team has achieved a strong identity, it is more effective to delegate responsibility to a self-managed team instead of reporting to management. Towry (2003) argues that by considering the consequences and concepts of team identification from psychology, it is helpful in understanding the causal links among team characteristics, economic incentives addressed by agency theory, and performance.

Based on the above discussion, an incentives-team effort-effectiveness relation is developed (see Figure 4.3).

How a team makes decisions, i.e. empowerment, which is related to, but not the same as autonomy, is one important aspect in understanding teamwork (Levi and Slem, 1995). The basic concept behind empowerment – giving team-members more freedom to make the decisions that influence their jobs and working environments (Hayes *et al.*, 2005) – is helpful for creating a sense of shared responsibility in the team (Levi and Slem, 1995). The degree of empowerment depends on management philosophy: centralisation versus decentralisation (Milgrom and Roberts, 1992), the goal of the team, and the innovation of the project (Hayes *et al.*, 2005).

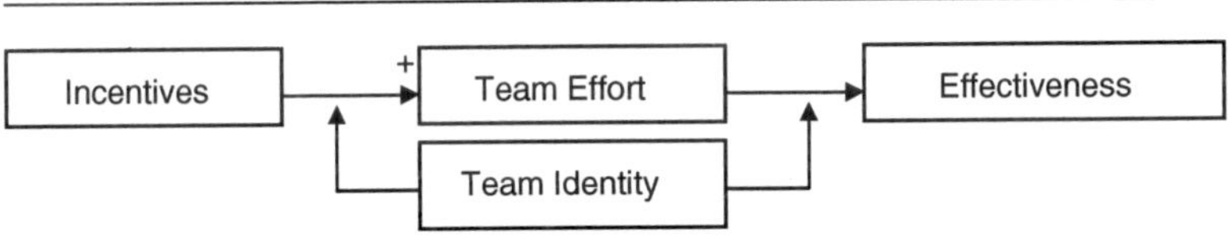

Figure 4.3   The Effects of Incentive on Team Effort and Effectiveness

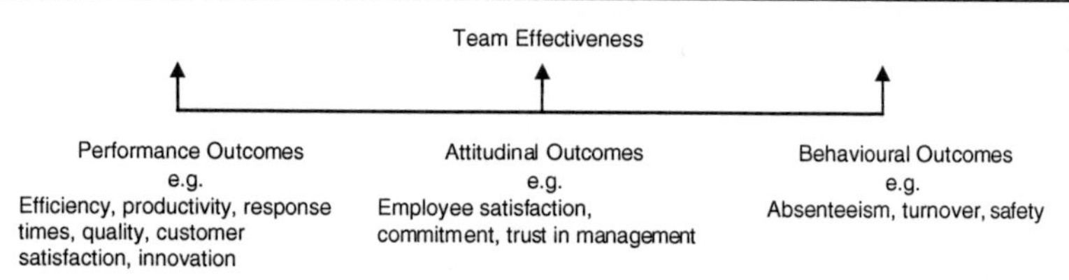

Figure 4.4   Three Dimensions of Team Effectiveness

Highly creative teamwork needs team-members to identify the team as a group and as an attractive work arrangement (Lembke and Wilson, 1998). One of the requisites to studying teamwork is to identify the nature of team effectiveness. As Cohen and Bailey (1997: 260) investigated, managers are frequently required to rate a project team on 'five measures of performance: (1) adherence to budgets, (2) adherence to schedules, (3) innovation, (4) project quality, and (5) overall performance or efficiency.' However, measuring the results of a project team's performance does not totally encapsulate the meaning of team effectiveness. By Cohen and Bailey's (1997) categorisation, team effectiveness should be evaluated by performance, attitudinal, and behavioural effectiveness measures (see Figure 4.4).

Throughout the above discussion, we argue that team identity helps team cohesion, determines the effectiveness of the system of assigning decision rights, the incentive system, the performance measurement system, and also brings out new product success through positive project performance.

4.4.2   Incentive – performance

In an effective environment, performance measurement and reward systems are dependable on the decision rights granted to the SBU manager (Milgrom and Roberts, 1992). In both laboratory studies and field experiments, measurement of performance generally improves performance and decides rewards both of individuals and of teams (Busby, 1999; Milgrom and Roberts, 1992). The external managerial labour market brings pressures for the company to sort and compensate managers according to performance (Fama, 1980; Quinn *et al.*, 1996), although evaluating and rewarding executives' performance is an essential, difficult, and time-consuming job of control in a company (Ghosh and Lusch, 2000).

As argued by Fama (1980), an aggressive ongoing company is always in the managerial labour market for potential new managers who are concerned with the systems by which their performance will be fairly and objectively assessed, and these potential new managers seek information about the responsiveness of the system in rewarding performance. Quinn *et al.* (1996) argue that every company attempts to be the number one in its field, so seeking professional employees is a continuing and important task of the company. Thus, given a competitive managerial labour market, when a company's reward system is not responsive to the manager's performance, the company loses the manager, and the best are the first to leave (Fama, 1980; Milgrom and Roberts, 1992).

Hopwood's (1972) empirical work on the role of accounting data in performance evaluation studied the consequences of evaluating style on managerial behaviour and performance and identified three distinct evaluating styles (see Figure 4.5) used by senior managers such as cost centre managers in holding subordinates accountable for their performance.

More recently, however, Otley and Fakiolas (2000) conclude that the control of manufacturing operations becomes less reliant on budgetary target measures, and the new development of strategic management accounting becomes market oriented, and focuses on customers, competitors, and other external factors rather than a simply internal focus. For example, the focus of cost control changes from real-time operations to product planning and design (Hayes *et al.*, 2005). Therefore, Otley and Fakiolas (2000) argue that the roles of budget-based and accounting-based control techniques, introduced in Hopwood's (1972) research, should be extensively adjusted to response to companies' needs and markets' changes.

The literature of performance measurement mostly concerns detailed descriptions of metrics, of principles for design of performance

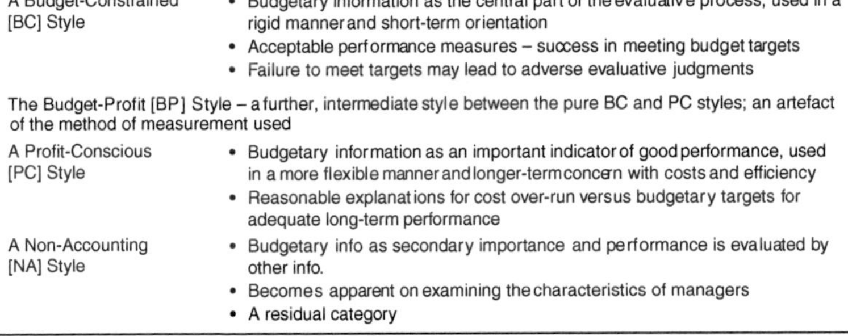

A Budget-Constrained [BC] Style	• Budgetary information as the central part of the evaluative process, used in a rigid manner and short-term orientation
	• Acceptable performance measures – success in meeting budget targets
	• Failure to meet targets may lead to adverse evaluative judgments
The Budget-Profit [BP] Style – a further, intermediate style between the pure BC and PC styles; an artefact of the method of measurement used	
A Profit-Conscious [PC] Style	• Budgetary information as an important indicator of good performance, used in a more flexible manner and longer-term concern with costs and efficiency
	• Reasonable explanations for cost over-run versus budgetary targets for adequate long-term performance
A Non-Accounting [NA] Style	• Budgetary info as secondary importance and performance is evaluated by other info.
	• Becomes apparent on examining the characteristics of managers
	• A residual category

Figure 4.5   Evaluative Styles

measurement systems, and of the for and against of different performance measurement systems, but it has a tendency to disregard the interaction of incentive and performance. In fact, the effect of incentives on motivation and performance is extensively studied in management literature (Lebby, 1993). We attempt to examine the relationship of incentive and performance in practice. Therefore, in the next subsection, we connect the relation of incentive, effort, performance and new product success altogether.

4.4.3 Incentive – effort – performance – success

Many factors that impact new product project team outcomes have been identified in the factors of new product success or failure literature. Cooper and Kleinschmidt (1995) developed a conceptual framework that helps to identify the major constructs, blocks of variables, and individual measures. Their proposition to what should drive positive new product performance includes five blocks of variables. In Figure 4.6, five elements of new product performance and success are combined from NPD literature.

Jensen and Meckling (1976) view the company as a set of contracts covering the way inputs are joined to create outputs and the way receipts from outputs are shared. The three-part taxonomy view of companies concentrates on the nature of the contractual relations among the agents who work together in the company including NPD

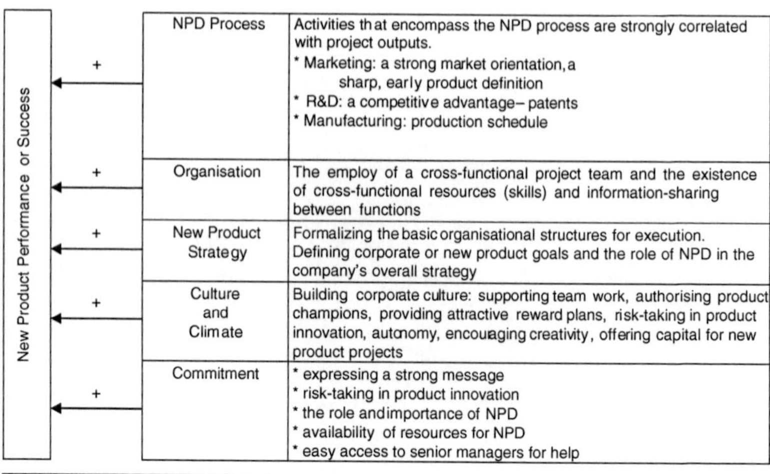

Figure 4.6 Elements of the Company's Overall New Product Success

related participants and provides structure to the notion of the stewardship role of accounting in the company (Jensen, 1983). That is, to order complexity of an organisation for developing cross-functional project team coordination and project performance measurement related topics, three dimensions of organisational architecture need to be considered together: (1) the system for assigning decision rights among NPD participants in the organisation; (2) the reward and punishment system among NPD participants; and (3) the performance measurement system among project teams (Jensen, 1983; Milgrom and Roberts, 1992).

Alternatively, Fama (1980) views the company as a team. Fama (1980) emphasises that members of the team act from self-interest but realise that their futures are influenced to some extent by the success of the team in its struggle with other teams in similar fields. Although Fama (1980) has different viewpoints from Jensen and Meckling (1976) on what the company means, they agree that the function of senior management is to supervise the set of contracts among factors of production and to ensure the survival of the company (Fama, 1980; Fama and Jensen, 1983). Since managers, at different levels, realise that the managerial labour market uses the performance of the firm to determine their future salaries, there is a natural process of monitoring from higher to lower levels of management (Fama, 1980). Further, there should be an understanding regarding a stake in the success of the company. However, agency problems could still arise because contracts are not effectively designed and enforced (Fama and Jensen, 1983; Milgrom and Roberts, 1993).

By focusing on NPD project research, in which all decision rights are concentrated in the project teams, as argued by Fama and Jensen (1983), the way companies allocate the steps of the decision process across NPD participants is significant in studying and explaining the success of new product and controlling agency problems (see Figure 4.7). An effective system of assigning decision rights implies that

Steps	Applications
1. Initiation	Before defining a new product strategy, assigning a project manager to the team, forming a cross-functional project team, management should consider resource utilisation and structuring of contracts
2. Ratification	Making sure every NPD participant knows his or her authority and responsibility
3. Implementation	Executing ratified decisions
4. Monitoring	Measuring the performance of decision-makers and implementation of rewards or punishments

Figure 4.7 Assignments of Decision Rights Process

the control (ratification and monitoring) of decisions should be separated from the management (initiation and implementation) of decisions (Fama and Jensen, 1983). That is, the system of assigning decision rights clarifies the delegation of authority and the obligation of responsibility, so the separation of decision management, decision control, and residual risk bearing is clear and controlling of agency problems is more efficient.

A second significant element of organisational architecture is the reward and punishment system, and as expected, most companies attempt to design attractive reward plans that magnetise and keep professional employees and provide motivations or incentives to these professional employees to exert their efforts and then increase the value of companies. However, there is no magical reward and punishment system which can achieve the *right* behaviour by motivating the *wrong* people (Collins, 2001). If a project manager gets the *wrong* teammates in the team, then the *wrong* teammates are eager to maximise their own interests, not maximise the value of the team. Also, the worst situations, such as incentive related conflicts and free-rider problems among the team-members who are companies' employees, could occur.

In addition, team-members absorb the full costs, such as time and money, of their individual efforts but share the gains such as prize and bonus that accumulate to the team. This agreement inspires the wrong people in the team to free-ride on the efforts of others. Fortunately, free-rider problems can be reduced through designing appropriate reward and performance measurement systems. Unfortunately, however, these designs are costly and hard to oversee. Thus, the usefulness of the reward system and the performance measurement system hinges on the degree to which project team-members have established a strong team identity (Towry, 2003).

Clark and Fujimoto (1991: 169) argue that 'the challenge in *NPD* is not so much unilateral pursuit of organic structure and permissive management style as a subtle balance of control and freedom, precision and flexibility, individualism and *teamwork*' (emphasis added). NPD is not only some functional departments' efforts, but senior management involvement, i.e. NPD is the whole organisation's business. NPD processes are multifunctional, high-risk, but high-profit activities as well; and NPD processes need cross-functional project teams to operate them. Also, NPD processes help cross-functional project teams to produce new products. In a cross-functional project team, R&D engineers may work iteratively with sales engineers to make sure that the designs that are being developed can be accepted by clients or customers; the team's hesitant designs may be reviewed by the R&D and manufacturing functional managers.

Due to the capabilities of accounting systems and the traditional role of management accountants, accounting has been particularly concerned with the standard-setting and performance measurement, but less involved with the development of predictive models of performance and with the generation of apt control actions (Emmanuel *et al.*, 1990). Therefore, based on the literature, the authors, at the beginning of the conceptual framework, illustrated how team identity is the step of primary importance for members to be able to identify with their teammates as a social group. Team identity changes team-members' awareness of performance measurement from 'my task' and 'my responsibility' to 'our task' and 'our responsibility' (Lembke and Wilson, 1998). Because the company is disciplined by competition from other companies, this understanding forces the company to efficiently monitor the performance of the entire team and of its individual members (Fama, 1980).

A conceptual framework is developed (see Figure 4.8). This framework provides an understanding of the incentives-effort-performance-success relationship in several contexts of concern to accounting scholars and concentrates principally on how salient features of accounting

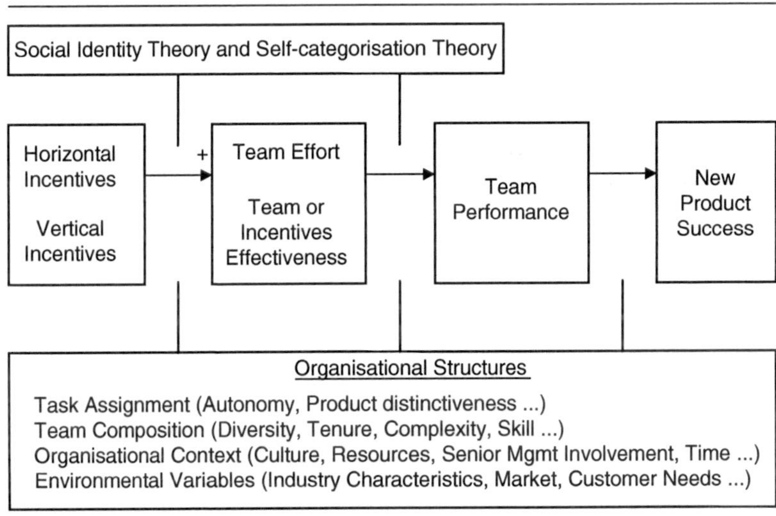

Figure 4.8 Framework for Incentive-Effort-Performance-Success Relations

settings may affect these relationships. The combination and integration of multiple theories and evidence across a broad diversity of disciplines reveals significant implications for accounting research and practice (Bonner and Sprinkle, 2002). We will examine this conceptual framework to find out whether it works. If it works, how it works; if it does not work, why it does not.

As depicted in Figure 4.8, the box of organisational structures presents that a company considers internal (e.g. corporate culture, resources, and product distinctiveness) and external (e.g. industry characteristics, market, and customer needs) variables before forming a project team and also emphasises that initial consideration of internal and external factors might affect the form of management control, team effort or effectiveness, team performance, and in turn new product success or failure. The box of social identity and self-categorisation theories emphasises that becoming a member of the team is a cognitive procedure which helps employees of the team work together to achieve a common team goal. In addition, when a team achieves a strong team identity, a horizontal incentive system would be more effective to management control, and vice versa.

From a psychological viewpoint, a strong team identity helps communication and coordination of each member of the team, i.e. the so-called horizontal (team-member to team-member) communication style. In addition, the effectiveness of a horizontal incentive system is enhanced by a strong team identity. On the other hand, the effectiveness of a vertical incentive system would be improved when a team does not have a strong team identity. A vertical incentive system is just like a vertical communication style, i.e. employees of the team mutually monitor each other's behaviours and directly report to management, i.e. superior managers (team-member to superior manager).

From teamwork literature, executives can utilise horizontal mutual monitoring to enhance the effectiveness of a team which achieves a strong team identity or executives can utilise vertical mutual monitoring to enhance the effectiveness of a team which does not have a strong team identity. The way a company structures a project team is affected by management philosophy and leadership. That is to say, from the literature, the level of team identity does not matter, because executives can choose appropriate control systems to evaluate the employees of the team, to enhance the effectiveness of the teamwork and team effort, improve the performance of the team, and eventually enhance the success of new product, i.e. the output of the team.

From the literature, as long as management appropriately exploits diverse control mechanisms by considering the level of team identity, the effectiveness of team effort and the performance of the team would be improved. Based on this assumption, every team could produce successful outputs and improve its effectiveness and performance all the time. However, in practice, not all teams are successful. We believe that appropriate control mechanisms can help team effort and effectiveness, improve team performance, and in turn enhance new product success.

4.5 Conclusion

Previous research seems to be based on one-best-way thinking: following agency theory is correct and adopting stewardship theory is incorrect or vice versa, as well as simply assuming that all executives are either selfish or self-actualising. However, research is needed that shows where stewardship theory fits in the theoretical setting, corresponding to agency theory, rather than opposing it. In this chapter, we described the differences between assumptions of agency and stewardship theories and introduced self-categorisation and social identity theories to see how organisational structures work together and to explore what teamwork really is. Based on this conceptual framework, this study's objective and research questions, its unit of analysis, the logic linking between incentive-performance, performance-effort, and effort-success relations are systematic and understandable.

In this chapter we reviewed multiple theories related to the teamwork. The focus of the chapter was to develop a conceptual framework in order to examine whether it works or not in practice. In the next chapter, we introduce the research methodology and methods used in this study.

5
Research Methodology and Methods

5.0　Introduction

In this chapter, we explain the overall approach to the research process, from the conceptual underpinning to the collection and analysis of the data. The chapter is organised as follows:

- Alternative paradigms
- Case study research
- Multiple-case study design
- Data collection methods
- Data management
- Conclusion

5.1　Alternative paradigms

There are two main paradigms in social science research: the scientific (positivistic) and the naturalistic (phenomenological) (Collis and Hussey, 2003). Tomkins and Groves (1983a) provide a broad description, similar to Abdel-khalik and Ajinkya (1979), of how scientific researchers undertake investigations of a universal form (see Figure 5.1). Scientific researchers start with a theory formulated in terms of relationships between categories; then establish a model(s), based on the theory, which is transformed into hypotheses and from thence into dependent and independent variables representing the categories involved; and then follow pre-determined procedures for data collection, and then subject the data to mathematical/statistical techniques leading to an almost exclusively quantitative validation of the hypotheses tested.

Hill (1978) condemns that the abstract content of a scientific paradigm has an excessive quantitative bias. Blumer (1978) argues that the conventional scientific analysis is not suitable for the nature of the

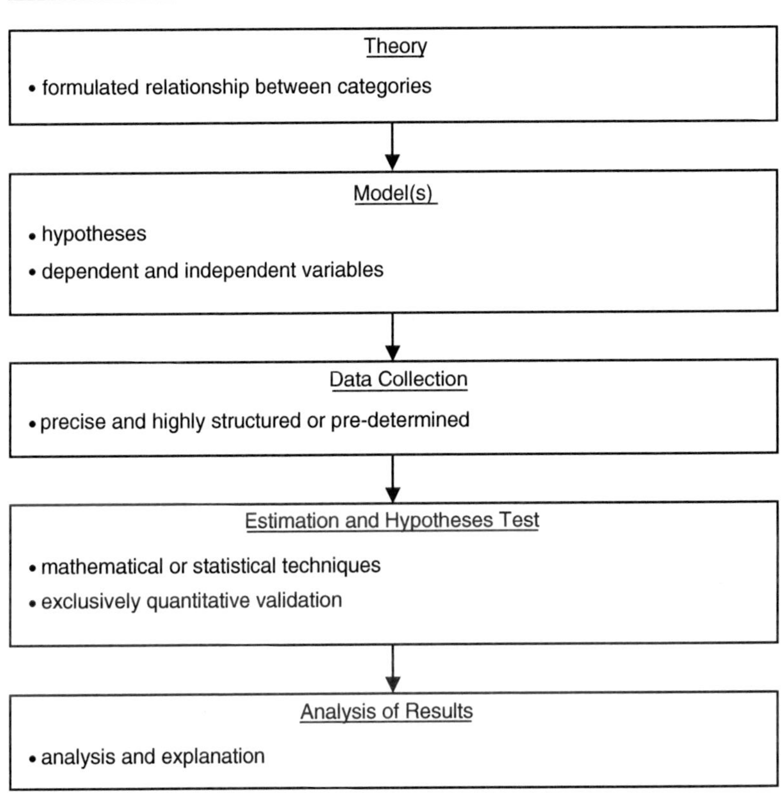

Figure 5.1   A Short-Hand Device for a Scientific Research Paradigm

analytical elements that is needed in direct examination of the empirical social world. Similarly, Tomkins and Groves (1983a, 1983b) argue that such a scientific paradigm has never completely dominated the empirical social research and more naturalistic styles of investigation, involving greater use of qualitative data, i.e. a greater naturalistic contribution to accounting research, are needed. For example, Blumer (1978) argues that adopting a more naturalistic approach, based on exploratory and explanatory study, can lead to an understanding of how to present a fixed and clearly structured problem, what data are relevant to collect and how to identify major lines of relationships for closer inspection.

Tomkins and Groves (1983a) further argue that academic research concerned with studying human behaviour concerning accounting and the value of different accounting procedures does not need to place much emphasis on mathematical analyses and modelling, statistical tests, surveys and laboratory tests. Especially if these are not involved with specific real-world problems, in that they do not concern specific decision contexts. A naturalistic style of enquiry has been developed 'for studying social processes where outcomes result from human intentions, interpretations and meanings.' (Tomkins and Groves, 1983b: 408). Therefore, to the extent that academic accountants are concerned with the use to which accounting reports are put, the influence they have on human behaviour and the human purposes for which they are produced, a naturalistic approach would be appropriate and valuable (Collis and Hussey, 2003; Colville, 1981).

Silverman (2001: 2) argues that 'like theories, methodologies cannot be true or false, only more or less useful.' Tomkins and Groves (1983a, 1983b) argue that if researchers can adequately deduce reality by establishing stable patterns of interactions and stable meanings across people and locations, then researchers can use statistical analysis to test the generality of these patterns and meanings. Alternatively, however, naturalistic approaches must be used for certain types of research problems concerning social behaviour or actions to see whether those patterns and meanings approximate stability (Blumer, 1978; Tomkins and Groves, 1983b). Briefly, the aptness of scientific or naturalistic paradigms and methodologies hinges on the phenomenon being investigated; that is, the type of methodology a researcher chooses should reflect the assumptions of a researcher's research paradigm.

Chua (1986) classifies social science assumptions into the ontology of the social world, epistemology, human nature, and methodology. In addition, Creswell (1998) classifies five philosophical assumptions: ontological, epistemological, axiological, rhetorical, and methodological. Tomkins and Groves (1983a) argue that it is essential for researchers to distinguish evidently the ontological assumptions underlying their research, because different sets of ontological assumptions about the social world imply different epistemologies, different research styles and the research questions pursued and asked.

5.1.1 Ontological assumptions

Morgan and Smircich (1980) have developed a six-way classification of the nature of the reality (see Figure 5.2). Tomkins and Groves (1983a) state that all categories, one to six, may be seen as alternative paradigms thinking of the world in a specified way. Category one assumes that one has readily available, stable, and very simple functions regarding isolated and small subsets of the social world which can be used for

Category	Assumptions or Drawbacks
Scientific Research Approaches – Reality as	
1. a concrete structure	• A strict objectivist view • Social world as a network of determinate relationships much like the physical world • Reality is an external, concrete structure which affects everyone • Drawback: difficult to find readily available, stable, very simple functions
2. a concrete process	• The world is in part what one makes of • The predictable and contingent relationships • Drawback: hardly left the scientific extremity of the spectrum
3. a contextual field of information	• Reality is based on the transmission of information which causes an ever-changing form and activity • Drawback: long periods for the adaptation process; unstable from time to time
Naturalistic Research Approaches – Reality as	
4. symbolic discourse	• Symbolic interactionism: to understand the work situation • Symbolic interactionism: see the world as one in which people from thieir own separate impressions through a process of human interaction and negotiation • The world as one of harmony, with people honestly negotiating with each other • A pattern of symbolic relationships and meanings sustained • Drawback: ignore macro-factors; over-rational model of man ignores the roles of emotion; through the eyes of practitioners
5. social construction	• Social world is created in every encounter; it is fleeting in nature • Drawback: a pure ethnomethodological stance explains all of an individual's behaviour and structural or organisational features enter the explanation to some extent
6. projection of human imagination	• A strict subjectivist view • Reality exists only in the consiousness and in the human imagination; the world of phenomenology in its purest form • Drawback: do not offer as much in relation to empirical accounting research

Figure 5.2 Six Basic Ontological Classifications

accurate predictions, by appropriate observation and measurement scales. Category two, however, argues that it is difficult to find such readily available, stable, and very simple functions, but there are some formulations which describe how things which change are stable and can be used for prediction. Category three assumes human beings are continually processing information, learning, and adapting. Accounting research in categories one, two and three are more objectivist views and used for scientific research approaches.

Alternatively, categories four to six encompass the naturalistic perspectives. Blumer (1978) assumes the world in category four is basically one of harmony, with people honestly negotiating with each other. Tomkins and Groves (1983a) argue that category four seems to divide between the scientific and naturalistic research approaches, since symbolic interactionists attempted to identify the subjective views held by those researched in as an objective (i.e. meaning bias-free) way as possible. In category five, the focus develops deeper into the subjective view of the participant and further from positivistic views. Finally, category six assumes reality only exists in the consciousness.

5.1.2 Epistemological assumptions

'Epistemological assumptions decide what is to count as acceptable truth by specifying the criteria and process of assessing truth claims.' (Chua, 1986: 604). Each different ontological assumption has different epistemological implication (see Figure 5.3).

Category four believes that human behaviour is only possible through exchange of shared interpretations of labels attached to people, events, and situations; and shared meanings are very stable, producing predictable outcomes for interactions within people which specify the observance of clearly established social rules (Tomkins and Groves,

Ontological Category	Epistemological Implication or Assumption
The Nature of Reality	Researchers versus Phenomena Researched Relationship
Category 1 Reality as a concrete structure	To identify the social structure using a positivistic research style emphassing the empirical analysis of concrete structural relationships for producing general disable results
Category 2 Reality as a concrete process	• Still considerable emphasis on measurement and stable statistical functions • Using quantitative measures or standard qualitative classifications • To understand processes of organismic change and the predictable and contingent relationships • The impact of changes in the real-world
Category 3 Reality as a contextual field of information	• The artificial distinction between the subject and the environment • Focus on the whole within probabilistic relations • Research styles using a cybernetic perspective
Category 4 Reality as symbolic discourse	• Start from specific and real-world situations • Broader objectives to discover 'what is going on' in the organisation • Focus on the need for feeling one's way inside the experience of the actor for the research subject's subjective views in specific decision contexts • Focus on how social order is derived
Category 5 Reality as social construction	• To study how individuals make sense of their everyday existence • To show why it is continually central to human existence and not just something one can completely pre-plan • To understand what self-images people hold and especially what underlying assumptions sustain that view in the way each person performs everyday role
Category 6 Reality as projection of human imagination	Researchers employ the form of imagining variations in experience to construct a science of pure possibility

Figure 5.3 Ontological Assumptions versus Epistemological Implications

1983a). However, Mangham (1978) argues that the social world is not in the rules themselves, but rooted in meanings which a group of persons attribute to situations and events; and through different experiences of individuals, meanings can be changed whenever and can produce different interactions which invalidate the earlier apparent social rules. Yet, Denzin (1971) argues that symbolic interactionists focus on how social order is derived as people perceive reality within a basic standpoint of negotiation with each other and develop identical shared meanings, definitions and situations.

In this study there seems to be a particularly extensive range for examining the impressions that cross-functional project team-members have about 'what is going on' (Tomkins and Groves, 1983a: 369) and the part that organisational architectures play in the four cases under study. Obviously, the scientific research approach would not just be difficult to adopt in this research, but it would be inappropriate. Conversely, 'qualitative research is an inquiry process of understanding based on distinct methodological traditions of inquiry that explore a social or human problem.' (Creswell, 1998: 15). Thus, after reviewing the ontological and epistemological assumptions under the two main paradigms, the scientific (positivistic) paradigm as quantitative and the naturalistic (phenomenological) paradigm as qualitative, qualitative or naturalistic assumptions are adopted in this study, thus in the next subsection the focus turns to qualitative or naturalistic perspectives.

5.1.3   Methodological assumptions

'Methodological assumptions indicate the research methods deemed appropriate for the gathering of valid evidence.' (Chua, 1986: 604).

Assumption	Key	Trait	Application
Ontological	The nature of reality	The real-world is subjective and manifold as seen through the eyes of practitioners	Reality is dynamic: The researcher quoted ideas in words of interviewees and provided evidence of different views
Epistemological	The relationship between the phenomenon being researched	Researcher aims to diminish distance between self and that being researched	The researcher spent time in case study sites with interviewees and became an insider (practical working experience)
Methodological	The process of research	Researcher uses inductive logic, studies the topic within its context and uses an emerging design	The researcher described in detail the context of the unit of analysis and continually revised interview questions from experiences in the sites

Figure 5.4   Assumptions under the Qualitative or Naturalistic Approach

Figure 5.4 summarises assumptions under qualitative views to see how the ontological assumption underlines the appropriate epistemological and methodological implications, adapted from Creswell (1998). An inductive logic is adapted to the relationship of the corporate culture, new product strategy, senior management commitment, and organisational structures to the four cross-functional project teams of the four Taiwanese computer companies. The diverse perspective adopted of NPD cross-functional project teams and broad measures for new product performance that the literature indicated companies are applying, suggest that an in-depth case study research is appropriate.

5.2   Case study research

Using case studies in accounting research can be expressive for many different schools of thought in social science (Hägg and Hedlund, 1979). However, case studies are still under-utilised, especially for exploring and extracting agency theories, although Scapens (1990) recommends more use of the case study method for understanding management and accounting practices. The definition of a case study from different views is shown in Figure 5.5 to gain a clear understanding why the case study is adopted in this study.

Researcher(s)	Definition
Hägg and Hedlund (1979: 136–137)	(1) A case is 'what actually exists or happens' (i.e. a case study attempts to get at what really goes on
	(2) One case is different from another case due to differences in surrounding conditions
Stake (1994: 236)	(1) A case study is a choice of object to be studied
	(2) A case study draws attention to the question of what specifically can be learned from the single case
Huberman and Miles (1994: 440)	A 'case' is a phenomenon of some sort occurring in a bounded context – the unit of analysis, in effect
Creswell (1998: 61)	A case study is an exploration of a 'bounded system' or a case (or multiple cases) over time through detailed, in-depth data collection involving multiple sources of information rich in context
Yin (2003: 13–14)	(1) A case study is an empirical inquiry that investigates a contemporary phenomenon within its real-life context, especially when the boundaries between phenomenon and context are not clearly evident
	(2) The case study as a research strategy comprises an all-encompassing method: covering the logic of design, data collection techniques, and specific approaches to data analysis

Figure 5.5   Definition of the Case Study

A case study is a preferred research strategy when *how* or *why* questions are being proposed, when the researcher has little control over events, when the focus is on a contemporary phenomenon within some real-life context, when the boundaries between phenomenon and context are not clearly evident and in which multiple sources of evidence are used (Yin, 2003). 'The case study method is especially appropriate for research in new topic areas and can contribute critical insights as well as identify important factors.' (Montoya-Weiss and Calantone, 1994: 413). Also, 'case studies are more appropriate vehicles for exploring accountability practices in organisations.' (Llewelyn, 2003). Thus, the case study is more useful to this study.

In fact, a postal survey was considered but rejected. A postal survey questionnaire has several limitations, including the possible ambiguity of questions, the lack of control over who actually answers the questionnaire and the potentially low response rates (Collis and Hussey, 2003). Due to the complexity of some of the concepts of NPD activities and more than 70 factors of new product success from the literature, the possibility of ambiguous answers was considered to be high. Also, a survey method cannot conduct an in-depth investigation about the formation of project teams nor does it allow explanations of performance measures on project teams.

A survey method offers no opportunity to clarify questions or to encourage if there is any disinclination to answer particular questions. A postal survey questionnaire could get the wrong impression about performance measures questions and the possibility of non-cooperation in completing it. In addition, a low response rate is another limitation as its complicatedness in adequately establishing causal connections between new product success and performance measures when analysing the collected data.

Furthermore, a survey method just considers particular aspects of respondents' beliefs and actions exclusive of considering the circumstances in which they arise and when ignoring the circumstances it is easy to misinterpret the meaning of behaviours. The most important issue here is that any research must take people's beliefs, goals and the values that motivate behaviour into account when developing and evaluating why people perform and believe as they do. However, a survey method ignores the role of human consciousness, goals, purposes and values as significant sources of people's action (Yin, 2003). Thus, interviews are used as an appropriate way to undertake the problems of non-response and ambiguous answers.

A further reason for employing the case study research is that it may well generate plenty of discussion and politicality which is difficult to acquire through surveys (Hickson, Butler, Cray, Mallory, and Wilson, 1986; Pike, 1988). Although surveys can give practical insights, such methods are to some extent limited regarding the ability to probe into interesting issues that occur during the progression of the research, and the exploration of the inconsistencies that arise between respondents. A strong request of the case study method for this study is the opportunity it affords to examine, in-depth, the links between the decision allocation system, the reward system, the performance measurement system, the cross-functional project team and the new product strategy which, the literature suggests, senior management should support (Hertenstein and Platt, 2000). However, in choosing a case study research under phenomenological methodology, the case study design needs to be carefully constructed to make sure sufficient thoroughness.

Case study research involves an examination of a phenomenon in its natural setting (Veryzer, 1998). Yin (2003: 15) summarises five different applications of case studies. A case study, firstly, can explain the presumed causal links in the real-world. Secondly, a case study can describe an intervention and the real-life context in which it occurred. Thirdly, a case study can illustrate certain topics within an evaluation, again in a descriptive mode. Fourthly, a case study familiarises the researcher with the topic enabling him/her to explore those situations in which the intervention being evaluated has no clear, single set of outcomes. Finally, a case can be an evaluation study. The exact use of case study depends on the nature of the research questions, the epistemological and the methodological assumptions of the topic (Collis and Hussey, 2003; Scapens, 1990; Yin, 2003).

Case studies could offer richer descriptions of management accounting practice (Ryan *et al.*, 2002; Yin, 2003). Ryan *et al.* (2002: 144) argue that exploratory case studies 'can be used to explore the reasons for particular accounting practices' and explanatory case studies are used 'to explain the reasons for observed accounting practices.' In this study, we first generate initial ideas and propositions, which form the basis of an explanation of particular accounting practices and then explain the existing empirical practices in their specific practical context. Further, by using the holistic research method, we provide deep and rich understanding and descriptions of the social nature of the four project teams and their performance measurement systems, as well as locate these empirical practices in their organisational, economic and social contexts.

In summary, this multiple-case study seeks to explore whether there is a connection between the breakthrough product project team performance measurement system and the breakthrough product success in the four Taiwanese breakthrough project teams, and then explain why there is a relationship and what kind of relation between the breakthrough product project team performance measurement system and the success or failure of the output of the project team. Therefore, the nature of this multiple-case study is not only exploratory but also explanatory.

In a review of the NPD literature, Brown and Eisenhardt (1995) reveal that cross-functional project teams enhance new product project success, undoubtedly. However, little research has examined the relationship between the project team and its outcome – the new product. Are there some new concepts or disciplines enhancing new product success? Due to the importance of the project team and neglect of uses and impacts of measurement results to project teams and functional departments in Taiwanese computer companies, an exploratory and explanatory case study is conducted.

5.2.1   Advantages of case study

Case methods could play an important role in accounting research. In an area where there is a lack of theory, real difficulties in defining context, an acknowledged importance of patterns of historical development and continued questioning as to the normative or descriptive basis of the discipline, more explicit consideration needs to be given to the advantages that case approaches to research and inquiry can offer. (Hägg and Hedlund, 1979: 142)

Doing good detailed in-depth case studies, researchers can obtain an interpretation of what is going on more directly, and gain insights into all the relevant views (within relevant frameworks) of the phenomenon being researched by initially not excluding too many variables (i.e. success factors of new product performance) from the list of concerns (Hägg and Hedlund, 1979). Also, case studies can generalise theoretical propositions and the goal of the case researcher is to expand and generalise theories (i.e. the analytic generalisation) (Yin, 2003). Hägg and Hedlund (1979) argue that case studies are appropriate for generating theory but not for testing it, yet, if the observation of the phenomenon being researched needs in-depth investigation, hypothesis testing research can most appropriately be conducted using case studies as well.

5.2.2 Limitations of case study

Although case studies are meaningful in accounting research, in its practical setting, (Nixon, 1998; Hägg and Hedlund, 1979; Yin, 2003) many scholars call for more use of the case study to understand management and accounting practices (Creswell, 1998; Scapens, 1990). Nevertheless, case studies are criticised for not providing any basis for generalisation and under-utilisation especially for exploring and extracting agency theories (Scapens, 1990). Adapted mainly from Hägg and Hedlund (1979) and Yin (2003), four types of limitations of case studies are discussed from different viewpoints of critiques and concepts in Figure 5.6.

From Figure 5.6, it is clear to see that sometimes the so-called limitations could be just incorrect concepts or might be diminished by a valid and high-quality case study design. The case study research is more useful for this research, thus, we attempt to overcome its limitations.

5.2.3 Validity and reliability

McKinnon (1988) generally defines that validity is concerned with the question of whether researchers are studying the phenomena they claim

Limitations	Critiques	Concepts
Little basis for scientific generalisation	• 'How can you generalise from a single case?' • ' A case study is not statistically valid' • It is difficult to generalise from one case to another	• Analytic generalisation: case studies are useful and appropriate for generating theories, hypotheses, or theoretical propositions, but not for testing them • Case studies provide good description: with real-life conditions, it is probably difficult to conduct experiments in the social science • Multiple-case studies
Few rules or systematic procedures to follow	The lack of rigor of case study research	The role of case studies has a view of social reality as dynamic • The case study is a comprehensive research strategy, a plan of research (i.e. the case study itself shows the process of research)
Experienced case researchers required	An inexperienced external person will find it difficult to review the work and understand exactly what has been going on and how valuable might be the research (i.e. replication of case studies is difficult)	• References from experienced case researchers (i.e. textbooks of case study research and articles) • A valid and high-quality case study design
Time-consuming and huge, unreadable documents	Case studies need spend much time and usually get lots of documentation indecipherable	• To relate specific hypotheses to some general framework(s): to prevent blindly following inappropriate paths • Propositions help identify the relevant information (i.e. the more a study contains specific propositions, the more it will stay within feasible limits) • Depends on the topic being researched

Figure 5.6   Limitations versus Critiques versus Concepts of Case Studies

to be studying; that is, when case researchers accidentally design or conduct research covering either more than or less than the phenomena they claimed to be being researched, validity might be impaired. Yin (2003) argues that reliability is related to the question of whether other researchers, doing the same case over again, could reach the same findings and conclusions. Similarly, McKinnon (1988) defines broadly that reliability is concerned with the question of whether researchers are obtaining data on which they can rely. Reliability might be questioned if a later case researcher followed the same procedures as described by an earlier case researcher and conducted the same case study all over again, not by replicating the results of one case but by doing another case study, but the later case researcher cannot get the same findings (Yin, 2003).

For achieving and designing a valid and high-quality multiple-case study, there are four criteria – construct validity, internal validity,

Criteria	Purposes	Threats	Strategies and Tactics
Construct validity	To establish correct operational measures for that being researched	• Data access limitations • Subjective judgements on collecting data • Observer bias • Complexities of the human mind	• Use multiple data collection methods (two or more sources), but approach the same set of facts or findings • Establish a chain of evidence • The draft case study report reviewed by key interviewees
Internal validity	To establish a causal relationship	• Incorrectly conclude that there is a causal relationship between x and y without knowing that some third factor – z • A case study involves an inference but is the inference correct?	• The quality and procedures of data analysis • Use logic models, flowcharts and explanations • Matching empirically observed events to theoretically predicted events • Use convergent evidence • Use Cross-case analysis
External validity	To establish the area a study's findings can be generalised	A study's findings are generalisable beyond the immediate case study	• Use theories in single-case studies • Use replication logic in multiple-case studies
Reliability	To demonstrate the operations of a study can be repeated with the same results	Repeating the data collection procedures cannot arrive at the same results	• Use a case study protocol (see Appendix A) (Yin, 2003) • Develop a case study database

Figure 5.7   Validity and Reliability versus Strategies and Tactics for Case Study
Sources: Adapted from McKinnon (1988) and Yin (2003)

external validity and reliability – which need be considered (Miles and Huberman, 1994; Yin, 2003). This multiple-case study is both exploratory and explanatory in nature; therefore, we considered construct validity, internal validity, external validity, and reliability criterion altogether (see Figure 5.7). The purpose of considering validity and reliability is to minimise the errors and biases during designing and conducting this exploratory and explanatory case study research.

These complaints might be appropriate, given the researcher's experience in doing case studies in the past, but these complaints conversely might be helpful to this multiple-case holistic design at the present and it is not necessarily the fate case studies must suffer in the future. Certainly, to conduct a valid and high-quality case study, as many researchers (Creswell, 1998; Hägg and Hedlund, 1979; Yin, 2003) strongly recommend, case researchers need to be a skilful question-asker and interpreter of extensive data, a confidence builder, a paradigm shifter and a scholar in many different disciplines and capable of the practical aspects of what goes on in the situation being researched. However, before becoming an experienced case researcher, one starts as an inexperienced beginner.

5.2.4   Selection of sample cases[1]

Criterion and replication sample strategies are used for choosing the sample companies for this study. The purpose of using criterion sample strategy (Kuzel, 1992; Miles and Huberman, 1994; Patton, 1990) is to make sure that all cases meet some criteria. We long to confine the core contingency factors, such as type of industry, type of new product, selection of team-member, involvement of senior management level, assignment of decision right, design of reward system, and the strategic control model, recognised in the literature as having an influence on the design, use, and impact of project team performance measurement systems (Cohen and Bailey, 1997; Milgrom and Roberts, 1992). Furthermore, we wanted to ensure that NPD is a strategic activity for the company.

Thus, we set out to identify companies fulfilling the following four criteria: (1) belonging to the same industrial sector; (2) being a Taiwanese brand-name multi-division computer company; (3) having a stra-

---

[1]Each high-technology company is unique and diverse; however, for comparability and examination of the research objective, we selected companies with similar backgrounds to focus on the relation of team performance and new product success/failure.

tegically integrated approach to NPD, accordingly set a New Product Lab for advanced technology and applied research, linked to an NPD organisation; (4) offering corporate resources (budget, technology, personnel) for a breakthrough product project team. We started by investigating the computer companies that have or have had their brand-name breakthrough notebook products in the Taiwan high-technology sector.

Ten multi-division computer companies in the high-technology sector, located in the Taiwan Hsinchu Science-Based Industrial Park and fulfilling the first, the second and the third criteria are approached through academic professors who help in establishing contacts with the presidents and project managers with a proposal to carry out this research. Four companies A, B, C, and D fulfil the above four criteria and agree to participate in this study. The four teams produced breakthrough notebooks, which mean the four notebooks provided not only advanced technological (functions) but enhanced styles (appearances). The CEOs of the four companies allowed access to their breakthrough product project teams and allowed the examination of the documentation of these teams.

5.3   Multiple-case study design

'In some field, multiple-case studies have been considered a different "methodology" from single-case studies.' (Yin, 2003: 46). This section develops a research methodology that investigates the actual performance measures used in four different breakthrough project teams in four different Taiwanese brand-name computer companies. To design and conduct a valid and high-quality comparative multiple-case holistic design, this approach involves four steps:

(1) Preliminary contacts. We contacted the four companies that matched the four criteria for inclusion in the sample. The CEOs of these four computer companies gave authorisation to conduct interviews and held personal conversations with cross-functional project team-members and project managers to understand their thoughts, perceptions and impressions about NPD in their companies or perhaps in Taiwan electronic industry. Their agreements to join were obtained and the project managers responsible for breakthrough product project teams were identified by participating companies. After getting access to these four companies, telephone calls were made to human resource managers and project managers at each company to explain the objective of this research; obtain a basic idea of the role of

project teams in their companies; set dates for visits; and to identify the most suitable informants for data collection.

(2) Case study visits. For each participating company, five-day visits were carried out by one of the researchers to conduct interviews with informants who are familiar or play key roles in new product projects. The researcher went to each case study site roughly 30 minutes earlier before each interview to be familiarised with the atmosphere and working environment, and spent the first few minutes making the interviewee comfortable. Also, the researcher had good opportunities to examine internal documents before interviewing individuals. Multiple sources of data – interviews and documents – were collected in order to maximise construct validity.

(3) Data analysis and post-visit contacts. After each visit, preliminary analysis and data reduction was conducted so that the researcher could get deeper or useful information during the next visit to each case study site. Starting from a within-case analysis, a detailed description of each case and subjects within the case was provided. Following the completion of all four participating companies' visits, a cross-case analysis was performed. During this step, there was also a high degree of involvement of the participating companies for checking case descriptions.

(4) Seminars with participating companies. The final step of this multiple-case study was a one-day seminar held with participating managers from each participating company. This step gave participating informants the opportunity to discuss the results of the within-case analysis and cross-case analysis and best practices with project managers from different new product projects but from the same company. At this seminar, the researcher gained updating and extensive feedback.

Although the conduct of this multiple-case holistic study was time-consuming and needed widespread resources (e.g. money and access to key informants) to conduct, having four cases nevertheless provided stronger effects and became more prevalent, further, the evidence from this study should be considered more convincing, and robust. This multiple-case holistic study follows replication logic to see whether the findings and conclusions could still be duplicated by other case researchers in the future. Each individual case, based on criterion sampling strategy, was carefully selected for a specific purpose within this overall study so that it could predict either similar results or contrasting results but for predictable reasons.

5.4   Data collection methods

We utilised seven processes to this multiple-case holistic study (see Figure 5.8). Initially, we chose interviews, interview-questionnaires, and documents for collecting evidence. However, after preliminary contacts with senior management levels of the participating companies, these practitioners strongly recommend that using interviews and documents would be more convenient and comfortable for them. Thus, we modified the data collection methods in order to get deeper and good quality information from interviewees.

Two methods of data collection were used: interviews and documentation, including those regarding internal records kept by the participant companies such as logs of breakthrough product project teams, history of performance measurements of NPD activities, and publicly available information about these four breakthrough products; each was checked as far as possible with interviewees in the relevant case study. The use of data triangulation, where data is collected from different sources, helped to overcome the potential bias and sterility of a single data method, and enhance construct validity. Although two data collection techniques were used, a series of interviews was

Processes	Applications for this case study
Identify phenomena	• Collecting data on the meaning of phenomena: the organisation of a breakthrough product project team; the interactions of decision allocation, reward and punishment, and performance measurement systems • Qualitative variables: name, job title, employment status • Ordered qualitative variables: social class, qualification, job position
Select samples	• The unit of analysis: the breakthrough product project team • Sample description: one breakthrough project learn/each company: team size; team-members • Purpose: to decide an interviewee list
Select type of data	Qualitative data mostly
Choose collection methods	• Interviews • Interview-questionnaires • Documentation
Conduct this case study	• Preliminary contacts • Discussion of collection methods
Modify collection methods	• Interviews • Documentation
Collect data	There is no exacting timing to collect relevant data

Figure 5.8   Processes of Data Collection

Stages of Data	Collection Methods	Category of Data	Analysis Focused	Related Theories
1. NPD activities	Interviews Documents	• Processes of NPD • Functions • Senior management involvement	• Internal context	• Social identity • Self-categorisation
2. Organisations	Interviews Documents	• Corporate culture • New product strategy • Resources	• Internal context • Policy • Corporate resources	• Agency • Stewardship
3. Breakthrough product project teams	Interviews Documents	• Formation • Communication • Cooperation	• Capability • Experience • Personality	• Agency • Stewardship • Social identity • Self-categorisation
4. Organisational architecture	Interviews Documents	• Reward plans • Authority • Responsibility • Performance measures • Operation, uses and impacts	• Delegation • Measures • Rules • Execution	• Agency • Stewardship • Social identity • Self-categorisation
5. Market, Industry, Government	Interviews Documents	• Technology • Electronic industry • Computer market • Regulations (e.g. patents)	• External context	

Figure 5.9   Five Stages of Data Collection

the principal method. Data were collected in five different stages (see Figure 5.9).

Stage one focused on NPD activities such as processes of NPD, the role of new products, senior management involvement, and functional departments. Data at stage one were collected through interviews with executives and through documents regarding NPD-related documents such as working processes. Stage two focused on organisations regarding corporate culture, new product strategy, and corporate resources to understand whether companies offer an NPD environment. Stage three attempted to get a deeper and clearer understanding about breakthrough product project teams, such as the formation of a team. The information obtained about the new product project related to market research, to *ex ante* and ongoing assessments of the technical problems and the proposals to overcome them, to financial data and, particularly, to the companies' NPD project process.

In stage four, organisational architectures – the system of assigning decision rights, the reward and punishment system, and the performance measurement system – were discussed with presidents, CEOs, human resource managers, and project managers to understand how these three systems operate, how senior management levels use the performance measurement results, and how senior management levels improve or diminish, if possible, the impacts of measurement results between breakthrough product project teams and functions. Finally, in the last stage, we collected data regarding the external business environment to get a full picture about technological and environment aspects.

5.4.1   The primary method – interviews

The sources of data were collected in two stages: the primary and secondary. The primary method involves a series of qualitative in-depth interviews, which focused more on issues regarding project teams and NPD performance measurement systems such as the organisation of breakthrough product project teams, new product strategy and corporate resources for project teams rather than on the wider organisational issues. Issues about NPD were discussed with presidents, CEOs, project managers, and key team informants, such as sales and engineers, who attempt to match customer needs with the company's technical capabilities. Alternatively, issues about the operation of performance measurement systems, the use of the performance measurement results, and the impact of the performance measurement results on breakthrough product project teams and functions were discussed with human resource managers.

NPD-related information such as new product performance measures, the organisation of project teams, and organisational resources is extremely confidential and commercially sensitive. The four participating companies preferred to talk during face-to-face interviews and one-on-one situations, and gladly provided the requested documents after each interview or case study visit. However, these companies did not feel comfortable and were reluctant to participate in a survey or interview-questionnaires. Thus, after considering the practical problem, in-depth face-to-face-interviews were conducted and used as a main source for data collection. Our aim to conduct these interviews was to develop an understanding of NPD process, cooperation and integration of project teams, facts and key informants' perceptions and opinions about the decision allocation, the incentive plans, and performance measures on breakthrough product project teams.

5.4.1.1   Procedures of interviews

The first interviews were conducted in the case study sites between September 2003 and January 2004, and the informants agreed for further e-mail contacts and seminars to review the case study reports accuracy and to update corporate latest policies and procedures of NPD. The second interviews and the seminars were conducted in the four sample companies between September and October 2004. The third seminars

Table 5.1   Sample Interviewees Description

Co./ Team	*Core* *Team* *Size*	Senior Management Levels			
		Functions/Professional employees Represented on Team	Number of Interviewee	Number of Interview	Hour(s) of Each Interview
A/A	15–18	CEO	1	1	×2
		Human resource (HR) manager	1	2	×2
		Project manager (PM)	1	2	×2
		R&D engineer (R&D)	1	1	×1
		Quality assurance person (QA)	1	1	×1
		Sales representative (Sales)	1	1	×1
		Market researcher (MR)	1	1	×1
		Procurement person (Procurement)	1	1	×1
			8	10	15
B/B	12–15	Associate vice president (AVP)	1	1	×1
		HR manager	1	1	×1
		PM	1	1	×1
		R&D technology expert (R&D)	1	1	×1
		QA	1	1	×1
		Sales	1	1	×1
		Marketing business person/ Market researcher (MR)	1	1	×1
		Manufacturing representative	1	1	×1
		Procurement	1	1	×1
			9	9	9
C/C	9–12	CEO	1	1	×1
		HR manager	1	1	×1
		PM	1	1	×1
		R&D	1	1	×1
		QA	1	1	×1
		Manufacturing representative	1	1	×1
		Sales	1	1	×1
		Procurement	1	1	×1
			8	8	8
D/D	9–12	Vice President (VP)	1	1	×1
		HR manager	1	1	×1
		PM	1	1	×1
		R&D (Industrial Design)	1	1	×1
		Sales and marketing	1	1	×1
		Quality technology person (QT)	1	1	×1
		Manufacturing representative	1	1	×1
		Procurement	1	1	×1
			8	8	8

were conducted in the case study sites between February and March 2006. Thus, altogether, this case study conducted over a period of more than seven months on interviewing and 33 informants in total were interviewed (see Table 5.1).

The general agreement in the four participating companies was to involve senior managers such as CEOs to help obtaining the big picture about NPD; project managers to understand the organisation of project teams; human resource managers to review the new product performance measures; and key project team-members to see how they perceive NPD. The reason why these people were involved in interviews is that higher management levels should be knowledgeable about organisational architectures; project managers should be familiar with the formation, cooperation, integration, and communication of project teams; human resource managers are supposed to answer the measures of new product performance; and information from key team-members examines consistency between senior management and employees. As similar and extensive interviews coverage makes replications of these four cases more sufficient.

The interviews (see Table 5.1) were conducted face-to-face with individuals during on-site visits in Taiwan. For example, in Company A these included two interviews, of about two-hours duration, with the project manager (PM), two interviews, of about two-hours duration, with the human resource manager (HR) and one interview about two-hours duration with the CEO. Also, five interviews of about one-hour duration each interview with one R&D engineers, one quality assurance person (QA), one sales representative, one marketing personnel, and one procurement representative who was directly involved with the breakthrough product project. An interview protocol (see Appendix B) was used during interviews, and this recording procedure helped organise thoughts on items such as headings, information about starting the interview, concluding ideas, information on ending the interview, and thanking the interviewee (Creswell, 1998). In total approximately 40 hours of interviews were conducted.

At each participating company, the president or CEO, human resource manager, project manager, and key project team-members were interviewed. At the beginning of each interview, the researcher clarified the purposes of the interview and the objectives of the case study. The intension of the clarification was to eradicate any worries the interviewees might have about the use of interviewing conversations and to guarantee interviewees of the confidentiality of information they provided during interviews. Simultaneously, the researcher made obvious the importance of interviewees' perceptions on teamwork and encouraged interviewees to lead the conversations about their views on new product performance measures. Hence, differences among the perception of interviewees at different levels and differences between the various positions' perception of the process could be examined.

The researcher took every possible precaution to ensure that interview transcripts and information about each participating company's breakthrough product project team and new product performance measures were low in possible bias. Interviews were audio-recorded (and later transcribed) and simultaneously detailed notes were taken during each interview and every interview transcript was cross-checked with and confirmed by each interviewee to ensure accuracy of information. Interview transcripts were organised and footnotes supplemented to clarify any professional and specific terms used by the interviewees. Marginal notes were used to distinguish both main issues and areas where further explanation was required (this was given in the end of interviews). Internal validity was ascertained by asking similar questions of multiple interviewees at conjunction with periodic structure checks.

5.4.2   The secondary method – documentation

As stated earlier, the purposes of documentation were to draw a big picture about participating companies and to cross-check the reliability of the case study interview. Documents relevant to the four cases were collected during on-site visits and after case study interviews. In every case we had access to the log of the NPD project team, internal company reports, and business cases to verify critical events and to confirm and augment information from other sources.

For example, firstly, documentary information was useful in corroborating the correct titles and names of interviewees that might have been mentioned during interviews. Secondly, documents provided inferences for further investigation – for instance, by observing the performance measures for a specific project team, we raised new questions about communication and networking between senior management levels and functions. These documents were combined with interviews data. In the documentation stage, the researcher expected to carry out the last stage of this case study to continuously improve and revise the theoretical framework by using new material available in the area of the research focused. The researcher kept a journal throughout the case study research, developed a master list of types of documentation gathered, prepared four file boxes by masking four companies' names on them and identified related data to specific boxes.

This case study research has taken longer than two years and we needed to review data repeatedly. The first advantage of documentary information is that it is stable and useful to this multiple-case study. Secondly, the existing private and public documents are not created for this case study, so they are inconspicuous and suitable to cross-check the consistency of case study interviews. Thirdly, documents enclose faithful names of key employees, references of organisational structures, and details of NPD activities. These internal reports and information can help the researcher to examine the fitness of academic articles and real accounting practices. Fourthly, private or public documents encompass broad reporting and events. During the data collection period, more and more interesting issues came out and they brought valuable further research directions.

Many people have criticised that some researchers over-rely on documentary information in case study research, because these researchers might mistakenly assume that all kinds of corporate documents contain the unmitigated truth (Yin, 2003). In fact, every internal document is the complete truth, but it was written or created for some specific purpose (e.g. internal decision-making or public reporting) and audience (e.g. senior managers or subordinates) other than for this case study research. We had access to review and copy the internal confidential documents as and when we needed. However, the purpose of each document was discussed with the person who provided the information before using it. Thus, by constantly trying to identify the purposes, the possibility of being misled by documentary information is reduced.

5.5   Data management

The collection, identification, management, analysis, and interpretation of qualitative empirical information should be seen as a systematic, ongoing, and complex process. Before selection of samples, the gathering, identification, reduction, and display of qualitative empirical raw data occurred. During interviews, using audio recorders, note-taking, and margin notes in case study sites, the record, classification, storage, and retrieval of qualitative empirical data have been processed. After collecting data, following data analysis strategies advanced by qualitative researchers, the analysis, interpretation, and presentation of qualitative empirical data is the heart of multiple-case study research.

5.5.1   Management of documents

The key purpose of documentation was to check the accuracy of interviewees' answers. Thus, before conducting interviews, we examined the current available materials and then self-questioned how, why, what questions to check, what other information we should ask for and/or what kind of questions we should ask during interviews. Examining documents that were obtained from public or private sources and self-

Public Domain	Private Domain

1. Mass Media Sources:
  • Newspapers such as Asian Finance, China Times, Taipei Times, U.S. News, and the Wall Street Journal
  • Magazines such as Asia Business, Business Week, the Economist, Far Eastern Economic Review, Fortune, Harvard Business Review, Time, and World Executive's
  • Internet sources (World Wide Web)
  • Television programs such as CNN (Cable News Network)
  • Books written about the participating company or the biography of its CEO published by outside publishers
  • Business school case studies about the participating company
 	
2. Organisational Sources:
Annual reports, mission statements, speeches by chief executives, internally produced publications, advertisements and public relations material about the breakthrough product
	1. Personal Documents:
	  • Log of project team
	  • Diaries of project team manager
	
	2. Organisational: Sources (Confidential materials must obtain directly from the company):
	  • Organisational charts, minutes of meetings, manuals for new recruits, policy statements, and company regulations
	  • Reward and incentive plans
	  • KPI (Key Performance Index) form about individual objectives and performance target
	  • Team performance evaluation related form
	  • Performance improvement form

Who produced the documents? → Why was the document produced? → Was the person or group that produced the document in a position to write authoritatively about the subject or issue? → Is the material genuine? → Did the person or group have an axe to grind and if so can you identify a particular slant? → Is the document typical of its kind and if not is it possible to establish how untypical it is and in what ways? → Is the meaning of the document clear? → Can you corroborate the events or accounts presented in the document? → Are there different interpretations of the document from the one you offer and if so what are they and why have you discounted them?

(*Source*: Adapted from Bryman and Bell, 2003: 419)

1.	Obtaining valuable background information about the company and project team
2.	Using each different source of data as a method of examination against the others
3.	Examining any inconsistent answers in interviews based on printed documents

Figure 5.10   Public versus Private Documents

questioning doubts after studying the available materials were continuous and repetitive processes.

For each case, we identified and collected published data and unpublished confidential materials on the company. During and after data collection, we recorded the name and position of the person who produced the document, the purpose of documents, and then separated the data into public and private materials (see Figure 5.10). These materials, both public and private documents, were all available in elec-

---

Coding Category 1 – Market, Competitor and Industry: 'Uncontrollable External' items such as existing and new technology; competitors versus suppliers; government regulations about patents and R&D of new products.

How does the company face it? Any change to deal with it?

Coding Category 2 – Vision, Core Concept and Corporate Culture: 'Spirit' items such as the company's cultural practices; primary elements of the company's strategy; employee policies; norms; rituals; management versus leadership style; and related items.

How do key executives, CEO, president manage the company? Why? What factors make senior management use different styles? What are the effects of different leadership and management styles?

Coding Category 3 – Organisational Architecture: 'System' items such as owership structure; rewards and incentives; authority versus responsibility; performance evaluation forms.

What is the purpose of organisation structure? How does the company assign the job?
Whether consider authority and responsibility together? Why set these measures?
How to operate it? What results?

Coding Category 4 – New Product: 'Operation' items such as new product strategy; the use of technology; mission; job assignment, and cooperation of functions.

Why set this new product strategy? Who assigns the job? Is job description clear?

Coding Category 5 – Project Team: 'Project' items such as the formation of the team; name, position and experience of project manager and team-members; log of team work.

How to cooperate and communicate within the team? Any free-rider problem? If yes, then how to control or deal with it?

Figure 5.11   Coding Document

tronic form on either the participating company or National Central Library in Taiwan, so we did not spend much time on the collection of relevant documents. Instead, we put much effort into organising and analysing texts of documents in order to tell the story from the complicated but readable data to discover what was going on in the project team.

We followed three steps to manage the data. First, for every case, we developed an index to discover general themes, derived from the research questions. Next, we repetitively examined all of the data that were collected and then grouped them into events. Finally, based on every theme, we systematically coded all relevant data into a coding category, organised according to the categories identified in Figure 5.11, proceeding from broad to narrow aspects of the company. This coding document was the way to draw connections between the ideas and data.

5.5.2   Management of interviews

Before conducting interviews, the researcher considered how to conduct interviews so that the meaning could be analysed in a coherent and creative way (Kvale, 1988). During each interview, the researcher listened, observed, and thought not only what the interviewee really wanted to express but also the way that the interviewee expressed himself or herself. Later, our interpretations of the interviewee's meaning were confirmed with the interviewee (Bryman and Bell, 2003). Thus, the stress was on what the interviewee chose to express about what the researcher wanted to know (Kvale, 1988).

The researcher took notes during the interview, and concentrated on getting down notes on what is said in order to verify any inconsistencies in the interviewee's conversation and to encourage what the interviewee really wanted to say (Bryman and Bell, 2003). Simultaneously, the conversation and talk of interviewing was also audio-recorded in every interview and then transcribed immediately after every interview so that the final detailed analyses could be performed whenever possible. The researcher listened to the audio-tapes closely more than twice initially, and then transcribed only those portions that were useful or relevant to the research questions. Then we employed the concept cards which Prasad (1993) uses in her study to put the written texts into appropriate coding categories – that is, printed documents and interview transcripts both go to related coding categories eventually.

In fact, in the research process, the coding of interview transcripts generally entailed writing marginal notes on them and progressively

Data Source	Interviewee	Incident, Quotation, Opinion, Event
Co. A: Interview No.1	CEO	Describing what is believed in the organisation: ' I always believe that human nature is essentially good ... "Me too" is not my style...'
...	...	...

Figure 5.12   Sample of Concept Card

refining those marginal notes into fitting coding category. Coding was helpful to shape the understanding of the data that was obtained as well as to think about the meaning of the data and then to reduce the mountain of data that the researcher was facing in order to get relevant information related to research questions (Huberman and Miles, 1994). Also, we started to generate some broad theoretical thoughts about the data. By using concept cards, we concentrated on the structure of meanings the interviewee expressed and then identified imperative concepts in the data.

Continuing and keeping the concept cards was an iterative process that began early in the research process. Adapted from Prasad (1993), we accumulated incidents, quotations, opinions, events, or pieces of conversation that related to a specific theme and put them together under a meaningful label on a concept card (see Figure 5.12). As more interviews were conducted and more data were collected, new concepts were generated and further new elements, if any, were added to the concept cards whenever possible. Simultaneously, we considered whether re-coding or re-sorting *old* materials, which no longer belong where they were formerly categorised, was needed.

When sorting written texts into different themes, we did not just summarise interview transcripts but explored some concepts so that all the relevant and useful conversation about a particular theme were in the same place and could be viewed together whenever we needed or updating materials added. Also, reviewing *old* material first before adding together new relevant data (including documents and interview transcripts) by this logically manual method was helpful to organise or confirm where all the data were, so the data did not become lost, miscoded, or misplaced. Concurrently, we expected to see whether there are links between coding categories or themes, and also checked whether the link or the pattern between coding categories was really there.

5.5.3   Data storage and retrieval

The storage and retrieval of relevant materials are important to data management and future academic research, because keeping track of

What to Store	Where Retrieve from
Raw material	Asking and examining: notes (taking in 40 hours of interviews), audiotapes (recording in interviews), printed public and private (confidential) documents
Processed data	Linking ideas together: structured write-ups, interview transcriptions. After interviewing, partially processed write-ups managed from original interview notes.
Coded data	Using categories to code data and then examining each category to see what it is referring to: write-ups with specific coding categories attached, including the coding format in its successive iterations.
Analytic material	Comparing four cases and all ,materials to see how they are different and similar: The researchers' reflections on the conceptual or theoretical meaning and linkages of the data.
Retrieval records	Re-thinking about the data and to see more general shapes in the date: records of links among coding categories.
Data displays	Matrices,charts, or networks used to display retrieved information in a more compressed, organised form, along with the associated analytic text.
Report text	Tracing allinterview answers and related documents for a research question and then searching key conceptual or theoretical ideas expressed in the reponses: successive drafts of what is written on the design, methods, and findings of the study.
Index	A piece of paper that index all the above material.

Figure 5.13　What Is Inside?

reliable data is valuable, as secondary analysis of qualitative data is to be verified and replicated by different researchers in the future. Also, a good storage and retrieval system is useful for the researcher to review all materials that have been organised and insert further relevant information into appropriate types of files. In addition, the researcher cross-referred across different files, defined codes and then arranged relevant data into the best fits place, and finally numbered the longer materials on the outside of the four file folders.

We prepared four file folders for the four cases in the beginning as we intended to compare the four cases in order to find out any differences and connections. In each file folder, we stored similar materials for comparative purpose. Huberman and Miles (1994) and Miles and Huberman (1994), proposed a checklist for data storage and retrieval, as Figure 5.13 shows, which was used in this study to establish what kind of materials would be stored and also where they would be retrieved from. These materials were stored in one place so that they could be reviewed whenever necessary.

Broad ideas and general strategies exist for the analysis of qualitative data by the logically design of qualitative studies. Huberman and Miles (1994) argue that focusing and bounding functions such as choices of theoretical or conceptual framework, of research questions, of sample cases, and of methods all involve preventative data reduction and become indispensable aspects of qualitative data analysis. A good research design is beneficial to not only collecting relevant data but also analysing and interpreting qualitative materials. Therefore, because this study is exploratory and explanatory in nature, we eventually needed to describe and explain a pattern of relationships, which could be done only with a set of theoretically particular analytic coding categories (Miles and Huberman, 1994; Mishler, 1990).

5.5.4   Content analysis method

Content analysis is used as a research method for analysing documents, texts, and newspaper materials and usually involves quantitative content analysis and qualitative content analysis in social science research. On the one hand, quantitative content analysis characteristically counts quantity of occurrence in the text and entails applying predetermined categories to the sources in a systematic and replicable way; on the other hand, qualitative content analysis comprises a way of revealing the underlying themes in the qualitative data that is being analysed (Bryman and Bell, 2003).

Qualitative content analysis can be viewed as a strategy for seeking out themes in the researcher's large amount of data and coding is the most prominent key process that is often employed in the analysis of qualitative data (Bryman and Bell, 2003). In this study, we analysed articles in the popular press about the four cases. Since the four companies are (were) famous in international computer markets, it is very easy to find out related articles about Company (Team) A, B, C, and D (referred to Case A, B, C, and D) from different newspapers, magazines, books, biographies, and business school case studies.

We carried out two analyses of newspapers, magazine articles, and texts about Case A, B, C, and D. The first analysis method followed the traditional content analysis which involved identifying themes based on the research questions and then recording the frequency of their occurrence in texts. This traditional content analysis tried to analyse Case A, B, C, and D's images from the perspectives of readers of the articles. Conversely, the second analysis follows the qualitative content analysis which is more interpretative and involved identification of the metaphors used to describe Case A, B, C, and D over the course of the four breakthrough project teams' history. Conducting this qualitative content analysis aimed to gain impressions from the viewpoint of the writer.

In conducting the traditional analysis method, we acted as a reader of these qualitative materials, many different themes were extracted from the image descriptions of each case and these were dependent on traditional content analysis to establish a pattern of frequency. The traditional content analysis reveals that the themes used to describe each case changed along with the time period in the breakthrough product's history that the articles covered. For example, when the breakthrough product is selling well, Case A is seen as creative, intelligent, and contributing, but when it is going down, it is seen as frustrated, disappointed, and challenging. Alternatively, in the qualitative content analysis, we focused on the writer's descriptions and texts of each case.

5.5.5 Analytic induction

Analytic induction is a very rigorous analysis method, because 'the selection of cases must be sufficiently diverse as to have adequately challenged the theory.' (Bryman and Bell, 2003: 426). In this qualitative research, we attempted to explore something not discovered or even examined before and then describe what is going on in the four cases, based on existing multiple theories, so the inductive approach was helpful for closer examination and to discover what the data really wanted to say and what might be appropriate to the empirical material to be coded. We depicted a flowchart for the process of the inductive method (see Appendix C) to show how we conducted this research.

The inductive analysis method involved an iterative process of collecting data from two sources; interviews and public and private documents, coding, developing, or refining new ideas, relating new ideas to existing theory, and selecting further data or reformulating the hypotheses or research questions for the next phase of analysis (Huberman and Miles, 1994). Data analysis using thematic analysis (Boyatzis, 1998) focuses on understanding why companies set performance measures for project teams, what motivations companies set the measures, and how companies form project teams for breakthrough product projects.

5.6 Conclusion

In this chapter, we explained that the findings could be biased if adopting a survey method in this research. Therefore, although adopting a case study as a research strategy has its limitations, it is consistent with the aim of this study to explore the way and the context of new product performance measures and breakthrough product project teams in the case study organisations. The interview certainly was a principal preference for this research because such work can provide both critical insights and lay a foundation for future research on related topics. By examining previous literature, we developed sharper and more insightful questions about the research topic and many inquisitive follow-up questions were added during the progression of in-depth interviews.

Documentation played an ensuing role in data collection in conducting this case study research, because it provided little insight into issues of *how* and *why*. Therefore, on the one hand we adopted interviews to ask what informants do and what informants perceive; on the other hand, the researcher examined documents in order to see whether what informants perceived was correspondent to what records showed. Following developing a list of themes and coding the data, in the next chapter, we provide detailed descriptions of four breakthrough project teams including the interaction of project teams and NPD processes in the four organisations.

6
Case Study and Interpretation

6.0 Introduction

It was stated in the previous chapter that we used two main methods to collect data; interviews and documents. After managing and organising the raw data, we identified a list of themes in each case. Using these themes, we describe and explain the process of each breakthrough product project team and attempt to understand the causality of the project team performance measurement system and new product success or failure.

This chapter is organised as follows:

– Themes and the code
– Within-case analysis
– Conclusion

6.1 Themes and the code

The texts from the interviews were analysed according to thematic analysis (Boyatzis, 1998), which is a process for encoding qualitative information. That is, we used the data-driven, inductive method to develop a thematic code. There are four cases of which two cases are considered as commercially successful breakthrough project teams (i.e. A and B) and two cases are considered as commercially failed breakthrough project teams (i.e. C and D).[1] The first step of this inductive

---

[1] Interviewees' names have been replaced by their job titles to keep confidentiality, but everything else appears as it did in their original texts of the interview transcripts.

method was to reduce it to a handy size (see Appendices D and E). The purpose of reducing the original data is to get a condensed outline form, which is easier for comparison across the four cross-functional breakthrough product project teams. Next, using the available outlines, we deduce and note potential themes. At this step, we did not provide a detailed, precise description of the themes, but proceeded and recorded

(Potential) Themes	Success		Failure	
	A	B	C	D
Values and Corporate Culture				
Motivation with a slogan or theme for the company	√	√	√	√
Becoming the leader of innovative technology in the industry	√	√	√	√
Decentralised management model				
Human nature is essentially good	√	√	√	N
Human nature is essentially bad	N	√	√	√
Less control (control is not necessary)	√	N	N	N
Much control (control is essential)	N	√	√	√
Management philosophy:				
Equality + Frugality + Involvement	√	N	N	N
Creativity + Autonomy + Supervision + Involvement	N	√	N	N
Command + Supervision + Involvement	N	N	√	√
Management strategy:				
Mutual understanding and trust (I pay, you help)	√	√	√	N
Taking it for granted as a part of job (I pay, you work)	N	√	√	√
Communication, consensus, improvement	√	√	N	N
Communication, agreement (but nothing changed)	N	N	√	√
Thinking and dealing in a human way	√	N	N	√
Creating a teamworking environment	√	√	√	√
Providing the right incentive or motivation	√	√	√	√
Setting competitive but achievable goals	√	√	√	√
Leadership and Vision				
Acceptable technology (one step earlier)	√	√	√	√
Maintaining involvement with NPD	√	√	√	√
Inspiring the diligence of R&D engineers:				
Consulting + Helping	√	√	N	N
Involving + Supporting	N	N	√	√
Considering the challenge of innovative technology	√	√	√	√
Taking the company to the front	√	√	√	√
Teamwork Environment				
The nature of product to be designed:				
Technological	√	√	√	√
Commercial	√	√	√	√
New product strategy:				
Promoting brand image	√	N	N	N
Matching company reputation	N	√	N	N
High value, low risk, user friendly + affordable technology	√	√	√	√
Factors considered:				
Organisational situation	√	√	√	√
Team composition (enough time, people, budget)	√	√	√	√
Environmental variables – e.g. government regulations	√	√	√	√

Figure 6.1   Comparing and Contrasting Themes across Subsets

√: Available in the case
N: Not available in the case.

Corporate resources as requirements	√	√	√	√
Authority versus responsibility for the project	√	√	√	√
The role of project manager:				
Consulting, Reviewing, Helping	√	√	N	N
Supervising, Supporting, Confirming	√	√	√	√
Team identity:				
People in the team feeling pride	√	√	N	N
It is a part of your job	√	√	√	√
Self-categorising as a teammate:				
HR training courses	√	√	√	N
Team meeting	√	√	√	√
The functions represented on this breakthrough project team:				
Project manager – PM Department (PM)	√	√	√	N
Product manager (PM)	N	N	N	√
R&D – Mechanical	√	√	√	√
R&D – Hardware	√	√	√	√
R&D – Software	√	√	√	√
R&D – Firmware	√	√	√	√
QRE (Quality and Reliability Engineering):				
QA – Quality assurance	√	√	√	√
QA – Quality reliability	√	√	N	N
SQE (Software Quality Engineering)	√	√	√	N
Sales (channels)	√	√	√	√
Marketing (market researcher: MR)	√	√	√	√
Procurement	√	√	√	√
Manufacturing – DFX includes: DFA (Design for assembly), DFM (manufacturing), DFT (testing), DFR (reliability)	N	√	√	√
The percentage of time allocated to this breakthrough project team:				
Discussions between PM and Departmental manager	√	√	√	N
Individual KPI (Key Performance Index) setting	√	√	N	√
Performance measurement of the team:				
Individual – KPI as a team-member	√	√	√	√
Individual – improvement form	√	√	N	N
Individual – per year evaluation (Department manager)	√	√	√	√
Individual – cross-functions evaluation (360° evaluation)	N	N	√	√
Team – peer review (every phase)	√	√	N	N
Team – Failure management evaluating analysis (FMEA)	√	√	√	√
Implementing effectively	√	√	N	N
Results in public/returned	√	√	N	N
Outcomes measured:				
→ Objective measure:				
Patents and Reward	√	√	√	√
Sales volumes and amounts	√	√	√	√
Cost: Manufacturing and design costs (adherence to budgets)	√	√	√	√
→ Perceptions measure:				
Quality (project quality)	√	√	√	√
Response (communication, coordination)	√	√	√	N
Delivery (adherence to schedules)	√	√	√	√
Management (overall performance)	√	√	N	√
Continuously improved (each phase)	√	√	N	N
The Meaning of 'Success'				
Teamwork among managers with business sense	√	N	N	N
Commercially succeed (particular project)	√	√	√	√
New technology (patents)	√	√	√	√
The Meaning of 'Failure'				
Cannot change user habits (overall performance)	√	√	√	√
Commercially failed (particular project)	√	√	√	√

Figure 6.1 Comparing and Contrasting Themes across Subsets – *continued*

any reflection of themes or patterns among the two project teams in each subset.[2] At the third stage, we examined the list of themes that have emerged as polar opposites of a trait or may just seem to involve similar phenomena (see Figure 6.1). Also, we placed labels as headings for later considerations.

To begin the fourth step – creating a code – the list of themes that was identified in Figure 6.1 was reviewed; we checked that every theme was present and also reduced the number of themes as much as possible without losing meaningful information. An inductive code is a list of the themes in this case. After reviewing the data and considering the themes, we divided the texts into five themes as shown in Figure 6.1. Validity of the results, reliability of the themes, and quality of the code were further discussed with interviewees by reviewing draft results and the final report.

6.2   Within-case analysis

In this section, we describe and explain the role of agency, stewardship, social identity and self-categorisation theories in each breakthrough product project teams.[3] Furthermore, these theories were used to explain and interpret why some causal relationships do exist in these four organisations based on informants' perceptions and explanations. We used within-case analysis to understand the question of the causality – a plausible mechanism links project team performance measurement system and new product success or failure.

6.2.1   Case A

I.   Background

In 1981, the Taipei-based Company A was established. During the past 24 years, Company A has constantly placed emphasis on NPD which led to the introduction of several profitable breakthrough innovative brand-name products, such as personal computers (PCs) and notebooks for international markets. From the CEO's own commentaries, NPD deployment with technological breakthroughs helps to win media attention and quickly increases the company's reputation as a leading global

---

[2]Cases A and B are considered as the success subset while Cases C and D are considered as the failure subset.
[3]We cannot disclose the details of the breakthrough product due to confidentiality.

high-technology company. Thus, to Company A, constantly developing high quality breakthrough products for international markets is essential not only for the company's profitable growth but also for the company's reputation around the world. For that reason, it is not difficult to imagine why Company A always places emphasis on NPD and requires the full involvement of senior management, especially for breakthrough computer products.

The CEO of Company A, during the past 24 years, has held the belief that 'human nature is essentially good' and greatly invests in employee training courses and exercises less control, because the CEO believes as long as the company provides a good working environment for its employees, then the professional employees will stay and contribute their knowledge to the company. Company A believes that no one likes to be controlled, so the company encourages employees to have a strong 'entrepreneurial spirit' when working as a team in the company. In addition, Company A gives employees of the team much authority and discretion, because the company believes that its employees are self-actualising and pro-organisational stewards. Also, Company A develops a collectivist culture in order to encourage employees to define themselves as members of the company.

The constant objective of Company A is cultivating professional employees, and working as a team is the best way to train employees in cooperation, communication, independence, and responsibility.

> 'Our company always pushes our employees to exploit their greatest potential by setting achievable goals, intrinsic and extrinsic rewards (to breakthrough team-members, the intrinsic motivation is more focused) as well as considering corporate resources,' the HR manager explained.

Thus, before forming a project team, especially for developing a breakthrough product, the company always considers whether it has enough corporate resources to do such a big project. 'When a project team is formed, basic elements such as senior management involvement and support, professional employees, reasonable budgets, approved project plans, appropriate authority delegation, reasonable reward plans, and an open and fair performance measurement system should also be prepared,' the CEO emphasised. 'Then, this project has an opportunity to be successful.'

'As a manager in this company, I very much accept the company's mission, vision, and objectives,' the PM said. 'In this company, managers follow the CEO's directions because managers have a high regard for the CEO, not due to his position in the company. I expect myself to be a person like our CEO.' In addition, even though Company A trusts its employees, the company still designs control mechanisms to make sure that when the employees are given challenges they will self-control their actions. A fair and open performance measurement system acts not only as the intrinsic motivation but also as an intangible stress to employees. Company A trusts its employees, but the company also needs to avoid possible partial goal conflict and risk preferences among employees. 'What the company wants is a long-term performance enhancement objective. We do not care who you are, as long as you are a professional employee, you have a bright future here,' the CEO explained.

Therefore, experienced employees are promoted to be their own bosses in subsidiary companies; on the other hand, employees who under-perform or free-ride are removed by a fair and open performance measurement system. Obviously, Company A creates an easy and fair teamworking environment and develops a collectivist culture to attract self-actualising people and keep professional employees, because it believes that only the professional employees are assets to the company.

As examined in this subsection, the evidence shows that employees in Company A are more likely to become stewards in principal-steward relationships. In addition, the CEO's belief is mostly consistent with the assumptions of stewardship theory (see Figure 4.2).

II.   Structure of Team A

Company A has always practiced a highly decentralised management model so that diverse and creative professional employees have great opportunities to learn how to cooperate and interact with other specialists in a teamwork setting. 'A project team is a collection of individuals who possess specialised skills in their field, who are co-dependent for achieving the team purpose, and who are advantageous for the team,' the PM described. Therefore, although all prerequisites are considered and prepared, the team-based activities could possibly still be ineffective if the company does not set a clear purpose for the team and then select professional employees through a cognitive and self-categorising process. 'Our company adapts a humanised management style. If you really do not want to take this task, just leave it. It is ok, really, no pressure,' all interviewees recalled and agreed. However, if an employee refuses every given challenge and responsibility, this employee's year-end evaluation results could indicate under-performance.

'In fact, the department of human resources provided an introductory course – what is teamwork in Team A – for potential professional employees who either were recommended by their departmental managers or were interested in this project,' the HR manager recalled. After the introductory course, the people should understand the purpose of the team, the requirements of team-members, the degree of the innovative product, the planned timetable, the reward and punishment plans, and the performance measurement system for the team. 'Since it is a big breakthrough product project, it could be an "opportunity" but also more possibly could become a "disaster" for us. Of course, you are the boss to decide whether to take it or leave it,' the MR explained. Apparently, if individuals decided to join the team, it was assumed that they also accepted the tasks, rewards and performance measures; because this information was available to all potential professional employees in the introduction course.

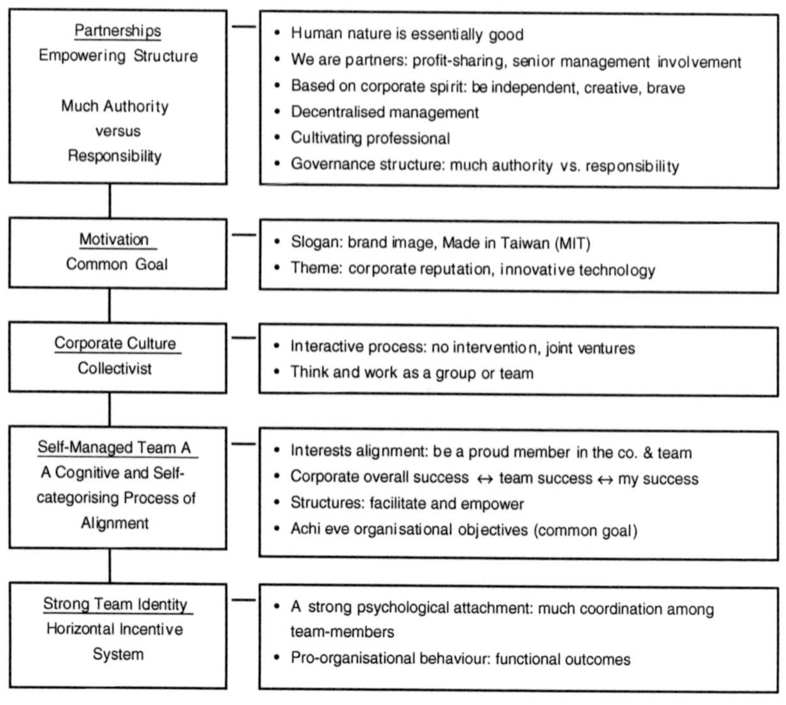

Figure 6.2 What Company A Believes and Employs

Figure 6.2 shows what Company A believes and how it employed its beliefs when it structured Team A. Company A treats professional employees as partners, so it empowers people and places trust in them. Company A believes that management control or administrative orders will only limit imagination and cooperation of members of teams and in turn destroy the teamwork culture, so it gives its employees freedom to join any project team they prefer. Also, executives create slogans and themes (see Figure 6.2) to motivate members of the company to achieve the corporate common goal. In addition, Company A develops a corporate culture which encourages teamwork setting and educates its employees that corporate overall success is derived from each team's success and individual success so that individuals feel pride when he or she contributes his or her maximum level of professional skills for the company.

For Team A, the PM selected a diverse set of professional employees, who have unique skills for different functions, to work as a team. It is logical that these team-members felt proud when they were selected to join Team A, and believed that they could create valuable contributions to what the team symbolises, i.e. its purpose. In fact, most of the members of Team A volunteered to join it. They compared Team A with other teams in the company and felt pride and defined themselves as a part of Team A. During the training courses, members of Team A realised that they cannot walk away from the team tasks and their responsibility for the team output. Members of Team A expected that their performance will affect the team purpose. 'Members of Team A felt that "we are important to the company" and recognised that they should stick together so that they can efficiently achieve the team purpose,' (the HR manager).

Members of Team A treated the formation of the team as a cognitive and self-categorising process of alignment, and the goal of Team A was to achieve the organisational objective, i.e. friendly new technology. This categorisation process is consistent with self-categorisation and social identity theories. In addition, according to social identity and teamwork literature, the evidence shows that members of Team A have established a strong psychological attachment, i.e. Team A has achieved a high level of team identity. With a strong team identity, Company A empowers the PM, delegates much authority to its members, lets them directly control the actions of their teammates (i.e. adopting a horizontal incentive system), and plays an encouraging, supporting and consulting role. This is consistent with Towry's (2003) research and the conceptual framework in Figure 4.8 (see Chapter 4).

III.   Interaction of NPD process and Team A

The PM of Team A was the person who initiated the Notebook A Project. The PM proposed and discussed the 'preliminary Notebook A development plan' with the manager of the PM department. The PM department approved and proposed the preliminary plan to the CEO. The CEO gave the PM of Team A one month to propose a formal and detailed Notebook A development plan. Therefore, the PM was working with the marketing researcher and sales person to investigate the potential market opportunity, and confirming production capability and suppliers with the manufacturing department and procurement people. Finally, the PM, who was in charge of the Notebook A project, held an initiation meeting and proposed the detailed plan to the CEO. The CEO considered corporate resources and then approved the Notebook A development plan. Thereafter, the PM and the project management manager decided a set of NPD processes and discussed the related duties of each member of Team A.

Figure 6.3 presents a set of Notebook A development processes. For example, it includes 'initiation,' 'preliminary formation,' 'prototype design,' 'testing,' and 'finalisation,' as well as the duties of each function in the Team A. Within each process, Team A had considerable autonomy to design and arrange detailed job descriptions for members of the team, but the Notebook A project could not move to the subsequent process until it had been examined through a 'formal process review meeting.' In Figure 6.3, the Notebook A development process is sequential, but it is an overlapping procedure as well; although each process must be confirmed by a formal process review meeting, it does not mean that every member of Team A has to wait for each other before moving to the following process.

- Initiation

This stage is the critical foundation for the breakthrough product development project, because the PM has to provide supportive evidence (e.g. the results of market research and cross-departmental meetings, mission descriptions, limitations, etc.) and convince the CEO to invest corporate resources into the Notebook A project. In this pre-activity stage, the CEO considered the corporate common goal, resource evaluations, corporate reputation and imagination, new product strategy, and also evaluated technology development and the market objective to decide whether it was a promising project. 'Approval to begin Notebook A project' is the review result of this stage.

Process	Senior Management Involvement (e.g. CEO, HR, PM department) (Providing resource)				
Team	Initiation	Preliminary Formation	Prototype Design	Testing	Finalisation
Marketing researcher (M)	* Market research * Market opportunity	* Customer needs identification ($\leftrightarrow$S)	* Series product development plan * Marketing plan	* Meeting with sales person	* Market readiness * Market introduction
Sales person(S)	* Potential distributors	* Identify end-user * Competitive product (Marketing)	* Confirm distributors	* Customer sample test * Sales plan * Promotion	* Accept customer orders ($\leftrightarrow$Mfg.) * Credit evaluation
R&D engineer	* Product architecture * State-of-the-art tech. * Detailed specs	* Hand-made 15 prototypes * Feasibility test	* Hand-made 200 working models * Decide materials	* Reliability, battery life, function test * Design revised	* Pre-sale meeting with customer service, Mfg., QA, P
Manufacturing representative (Mfg.)	* Production limitations	* Estimate Mfg. cost * Manufacturability ($\leftrightarrow$R&D)	* Final components * Factory trail (few units) production	* Pilot-run * Revise production process	* Ramp up production * Commercial rollout * Mass production
Procurement representative (P)	* Supply chain strategy	* Timetable ($\leftrightarrow$Mfg.)	* Prepare detailed bill of materials	* Prepare pilot-run materials	* Pre-sale meeting * Mfg. timetable
Quality Assurance person (QA)	* QA procedures	* Degree of quality test ($\leftrightarrow$R&D)	* Evaluate prototype and Set quality	* Revise QA procedure ($\leftrightarrow$Mfg. R&D)	* Production QA check
• Finance expert	* Project objective		* Make-or-buy ($\leftrightarrow$Mfg.)	* Budget review	* Pricing ($\leftrightarrow$Mgmt)
• Law consultant		* Patent	* Copyright law	* Regulations ($\leftrightarrow$R&D)	
• Customer Service			* Service item ($\leftrightarrow$Sales)	* Customer support	* Pre-sale meeting ($\leftrightarrow$S)

Figure 6.3   Breakthrough Notebook A Process and Duty of Team A

- Preliminary formation

At this stage, to begin with, market researchers and sales representatives identified the customer needs. Thereafter R&D engineers developed and evaluated some possible product concepts; and also they hand-made 15 original prototypes for feasibility testing so that R&D engineers can convince manufacturing department representatives that this product concept is achievable. Simultaneously, the manufacturing department representatives estimated manufacturing costs for the finance department and evaluated manufacturability for the QA person and R&D engineers. Law consultants investigated patent related regulations (e.g. patent law and legal decisions, design law and legal decisions, etc.) and prepared the necessary documents to apply for a patent both in Taiwan and abroad.[4]

- Prototype design

This stage includes preliminary and detailed prototype designs. This stage in Case A is a challenging part especially for R&D engineers, because the Notebook A product was an intangible idea and it needed to be created by state-of-the-art technology. R&D engineers, for example, mechanical, software, firmware, and hardware professional employees, usually worked together in a particular laboratory so that they could understand the situation quickly and easily. Market researchers at this stage began market planning and evaluated the series product – for example, the same appearance, the same weight, the same functions, but different hard disk drives (HDD), development plan. Sales representatives confirmed suitable distributors for Notebook A after discussion with market researchers. The manufacturing department produced few units for factory trail production and discussed production procedures with the procurement people in order to improve production efficiency, and also discussed make-or-buy decisions with the finance department.

- Testing

The purpose of the testing stage is to confirm the reliability and quality of Notebook A. Usually, sales representatives found some potential cus-

---

[4]Taiwan is not a member of the United Nations due to its sensitive political position. Therefore, it is better for Taiwan's high-technology companies to apply for a patent in any other country, as long as there are business branches or customer services there.

tomers to test sample models of Notebook A. R&D engineers, having considered the end-users' opinions, revised and tested the components and functions of original Notebook A model, e.g. battery life, wireless, etc. After this, the manufacturing department started a pilot run for several hundred units and attempted to speed-up production efficiency with procurement representatives. Also, the QA representatives worked with manufacturing and procurement people and attempted to control the quality of production at this stage.

- Finalisation

In this stage, the marketing and sales representatives launched commercial Notebook A products to the public. Sales representatives checked 'supplier credit records' before accepting customer orders. Thereafter, the manufacturing, procurement and QA departments worked together in order to meet the deadline of Notebook A delivery. One of the competitive advantages of Company A is customer service ability, e.g. speed, quality, attitude, etc. All NPD related departments (see Figure 6.3), after the commercial products is launched to the market, held a FMEA meeting for feedback and learning purposes.

In Figure 6.3, it is clear to see that Company A has a matrix organisational structure. According to the organisational literature, the potential drawback of the matrix organisational structures of companies is that every team-member is reporting to two managers, i.e. their own departmental managers and the PMs of the project teams. However, in Company A, members of Team A did not treat it as a drawback, because team-members shared the information (e.g. NPD process related documents) with each other and kept updating their progress to their supervisors in case they immediately needed extra resources or help.

IV. *Performance measurement of Team A*

From the generated idea to the final successful market launch, Team A spent about one full year developing the breakthrough Notebook A. From go-to-market to leave the market, Notebook A not only won international media attention concerning innovative technology and many quality rewards but it was also a money-making product for the company for about one and half years. 'Team A's success depended on teamwork between managers and team-members with high coordination, direct communication, fast decision-making, and a reliable corporate governance structure,' the PM observed. What does 'success' mean to Company A? 'It depends on what the team's purpose was,' the

CEO explained. 'Making-money is not a big deal; it is the basic requirement for any company, because it is the "company" that is established to make money. For going concerns, we want and need more.'

The purposes of Team A were to develop a potential market – no matter how small the market could be; to register valuable patents, i.e. innovative technologies; and to replace current technology, i.e. changing customers' habits. 'Centrino technology which is designed to extend battery life for notebooks as well as wireless networking to support thinner and lighter notebooks has successfully replaced the Pentium 4 Processor,' R&D explained. 'Most notebooks install Centrino now. However, two years after launching Notebook A, it seems it did not make a big bang on new technology.' However, indisputably, Notebook A is a commercially successful breakthrough product; has won global media attention; and was applied for novelty patents. 'We got reasonable bonuses and enjoyed working as a team due to this project ... We are looking forward to co-working again ... Yes, I personally agreed that it was successful,' a sales representative confirmed.

Most people may think that the success of Notebook A was expected, since the company had considered and organised corporate resources for the team. However, as the CEO emphasised, although corporate resources were appropriately arranged, Team A could still have failed. Although 'planning' is always perfect, the most difficult part is 'implementing.' The job of the capable PM of Team A is to identify the right people for a role and use these employees' specialised skills effectively. That is, the role of the PM is to inspire every team-member to excel in his or her way and adequately coordinate the events. 'A transparent and efficient performance measurement system is the most promising motivation for employees to devote themselves to the team and company,' the HR manager strongly concluded.

In 1995, for developing an important NPD project, Company A provided compensation contracts and provisions that were much higher than benchmarking companies, but the project still failed. 'After each project is completed, we always call for a review meeting – FMEA to assess compensation and responsibility,' the PM recalled. 'We are curious, because we cannot imagine why such high pay cannot inspire our people.' At that FMEA meeting, the company attempts to find out 'causes' so that the company can provide appropriate 'remedies.' After interviewing some key employees who worked in that failed team, the company noticed free-riding and discriminatory evaluation problems. 'If we cannot "cure" these "diseases," it will destroy our corporate reputation and upset our employees,' the CEO warned.

Then what should the company *do*? 'We reformed the compensation structure and openly discussed pay with employees. We made accessible the individual key performance index (KPI) so that everyone knows what his or her responsibility is and returned the results of performance measurement back to employees as a feedback,' the HR manager explained. 'There are no rumours or dark secrets in our company.' The new compensation structure of Company A is divided into two parts: base-pay (fairly modest wages for basic living expenses) and pay-for-performance (an extremely high and attractive bonus). Every three months, individuals discuss with their direct supervisor the past three-months performance and the next three-month individual objectives. If any employee fails to achieve his or her KPI, then this under-performing employee needs to fill in an improvement form and set an improvement goal with his or her direct supervisor. After another three months, if this under-performing employee does not improve his or her performance, then he or she will quit or be dismissed.

'Pay-for-performance is not a way to control people, although some people think it is another way to downsize or save money for the company,' the HR manager explained. 'Pay-for-performance is a sign to show that "we only keep the right people in our company." That is, if people left the company, the key reason would be under-performance, since the company practices pay-for-performance and requires open, non-discriminatory evaluation and communication. 'Challenging one person to do three-person jobs and then paying twice the salary,' the R&D engineer happily clarified. 'I would like to work twenty-four hours per day for you but please let me feel it is worthwhile.' A professional employee has no fear of being evaluated, what he or she wants is to be evaluated by a fair and open performance measurement system.

V.   What motivates Team A?

Figure 6.4 elaborates and explains the way the CEO approved the Notebook A project, the way the PM formed Team A, the way departmental managers set individual KPI for each team-member, the way the person in charge of the PM department set PM KPI for the PM of Team A, and also the way executives measured employees. As depicted in Figure 6.4, in the prerequisites box, the senior management evaluated internal (e.g. corporate resources, collectivist cultures, etc.) and external (e.g. market opportunity, customer needs and acceptance, etc.) conditions before approving the Notebook A project and before structuring Team A. 'Our company is eager to explore employees' potentials, not abuse them to act out Mission Impossible,' the CEO

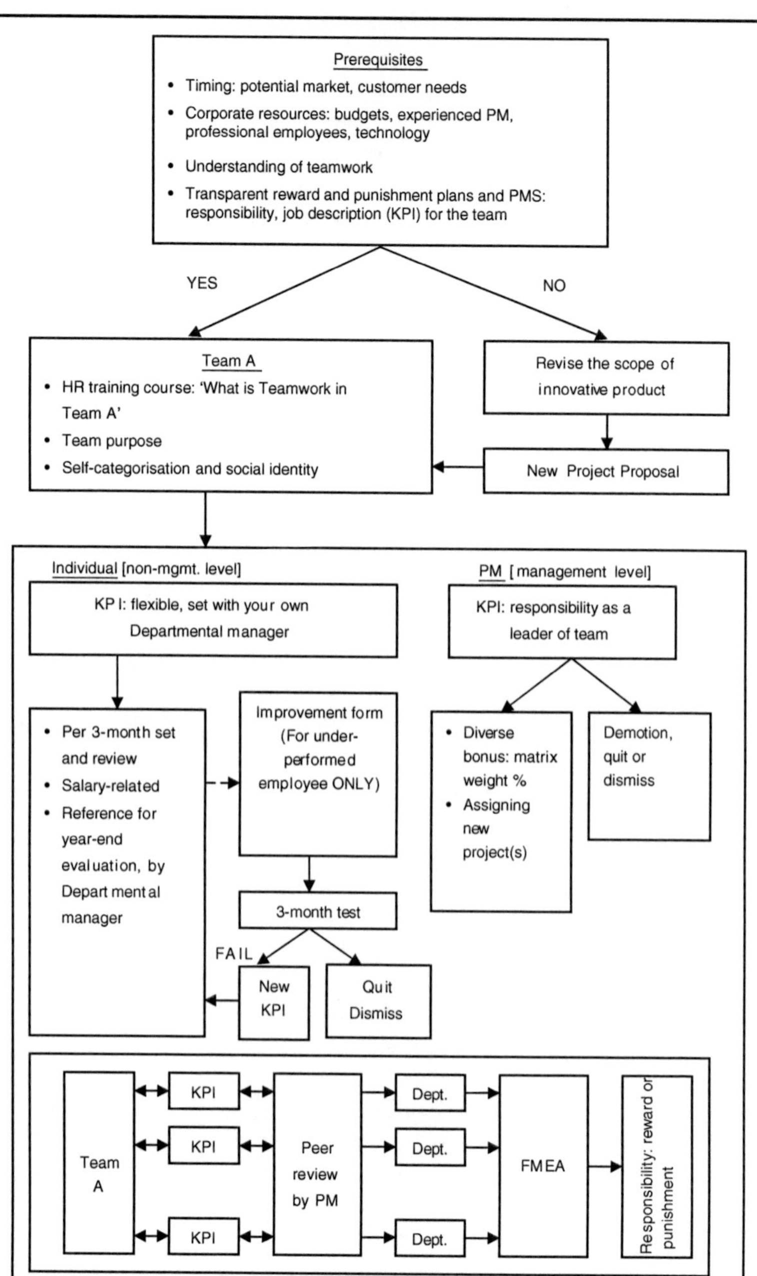

Figure 6.4 Explanation of Self-Managed Project Team A

laughed. 'If you are going to conquer a mountain; the more you are prepared before you start it, greater the possibility of you reaching the top of the mountain within the given time.'

'As I emphasised earlier, if the timing is not right, e.g. customers are not ready to accept this kind of technology, I will suggest that the PM changes the scope of innovative product development and proposes a new project proposal again,' the CEO explained. In Case A, the CEO was satisfied with the Notebook A development plan and empowered the PM to structure Team A. 'The way Team A was structured (e.g. the introduction course for Team A) aligned members of the team,' (the HR manager). 'Every member of the team perceives that he is unique and important. Everyone has his job and nobody can do it for you. No one wants to delay others or be the one who has made no contribution to the team.' Members of Team A do not feel shame to ask for other members' help; conversely, they feel ashamed if they pretend they can handle it but the results show that they cannot.

Working in Team A, market researchers and sales representatives do not like to be scheduled. 'I know what I should do and I will not delay others, so I do not need my supervisor to remind me,' a sales representative explained. Conversely, one of the QA representatives and the software R&D engineer wished the PM could remind them or develop a detailed job list and timetable. 'I prefer to work alone. I do not like getting along with people,' the software R&D engineer answered. 'As an experienced PM, I can tell every member's personality and talents,' the PM emphasised. 'However, I cannot please everyone, and I am not going to do this.' When these professional employees joined Team A, they recognised the team purpose and their departmental managers set individual KPI with them (see Figure 6.4). 'Even if I am a manager, I still have my KPI,' the PM laughed. 'My KPI is simple – making dreams come true, i.e. producing a successful Notebook A product.'

'Individual KPI is set and updated with each departmental manager every three months. Individuals will be evaluated by his or her departmental manager four times per year, i.e. every three months,' the HR manager explained. 'Our company also lists "performance factors" in individuals KPI form. Every departmental manager usually marks either "Meets/Exceeds Acceptable Level of Performance," "Improvement Required," or "Unacceptable" with explanations.' Employees who meet or exceed acceptable levels of performance evaluation will get a pay-for-performance bonus and set another three-month individual KPI with departmental managers. Employees who are required to improve will fill in an improvement form and get another three months to improve their performance. However, if employees' performances are unacceptable, Company A will suggest to them to find other suitable jobs (see Figure 6.4).

Company A obviously exploits diverse performance measurement systems to motivate employees and align employees' interests with shareholders' interests. To some members of Team A, they volunteered to join it due to the year-end evaluation (twelve-month performance). 'Our company gives you space to think, make decisions, and evaluate yourself before you join any team,' the CEO said. 'If you do not join the team and you do not make contributions to any project, during twelve months, you just get base-pay. It is your choice.' 'At the end of a year, your departmental manager will evaluate your twelve-month per-formance. If you only get twelve-month base-pay, well, I am sorry that you must leave,' the HR manager explained. 'That is why people con-tribute their maximum potentials to our company. They do not want to leave our company, unless they are underperforming.'

To the PM of Team A, his performance factors are quite objective. In fact, the computer markets are regarded as evaluators by the PM of Team A. However, the PM cannot control or change markets, i.e. some-times, a new product failing is just bad luck, so Company A adopts diverse bonus and a matrix weight system for the PM. 'Our company creates a win-win situation to employees of the company. You get what you want; the company gets what it wants as well,' the CEO said. 'You show your ability and become rich and famous. The company keeps good employees and makes much money.' 'Performance mea-surement systems tell you that as long as you have ability, you do not have to worry about your background,' (a sales representative). 'People respect you because of your ability, not your position.' 'Our company does not cheat; conversely, it makes everything open,' the firmware R&D engineer said. 'I know my responsibility, performance factors, base-pay and bonus, and the results of measurement. The fair and open measurement keeps me here.'

6.2.2   Case B

I.   Background

Company B, a Taipei-based technology-oriented corporation with com-petent R&D teams and with emphasis placed on NPD, was established in 1990. Although Company B is still new, during the past 15 years, it has won lots of rewards in high-quality innovation and successfully attracted global media interest in the unique appearance and technological function of its products. 'Technology is our heart; professional employees are our hands; long-lasting NPD is our base,' the AVP explained. 'I believe that human nature is essentially good, but I also believe that no one likes to make money for others.' According to the AVP, employees understand that their future salary is based on current performance; and for their own good, they work hard to improve their performance. Therefore, Company B uses 'quality, speed, and *partnerships*' as slogans, but the principle-agent relationship is in operation. The company's mission statements show *partnerships*. However, it is not matched by what the AVP believes.

'Our company does believe human nature is good,' the HR manager explained. '… the premise is there are no goal and interest conflicts among employees and the company. However, usually there are many conflicts.' Therefore, Company B believes that delegating authority with control and monitoring structures, as well as attractive intrinsic and extrinsic returns, are combined to reach employees' highest talents. 'Delegating authority to "employees" of Team B, not to individuals is the first important step,' the PM said. 'I usually compare myself to other managers in the company or even other companies in the high-technology sector. I expect an "acceptable" relationship between our company and me.' Company B treats Notebook B project as a short-term cost and productivity objective more than a long-term performance enhancement. 'Long-term objectives are also important to the company. However, the goals of Team B are to produce a breakthrough new product and win more media attention and make more money,' a sales representative noted.

Senior management treats a breakthrough product project as a huge investment to the company, so senior managers pay much attention on the progress and the output of Notebook B project by supporting and controlling every phase of NPD and Team B. 'Although my engineering teacher said: NPD is everybody's business. But I really think "everybody's business is nobody's business" in the end,' a manufacturing representative commented. 'We have clear teammates' job descriptions so that I can get involved in all tasks and know who should take responsibility for it.' Company B develops an individualistic culture for individuals; but, on the other hand, the company encourages collectivism for teamwork. 'There is no conflict. Everybody should have the ability to achieve his own jobs. But, if you work with your teammates, you can help as long as you are happy and you wish the tasks could be done earlier,' the MR explained. 'However, because everyone is busy at his tasks, the management expects you to have the ability to take care of yourself or maybe you are not suitable to work here.'

It is clear that the concepts and beliefs in Company B are more consistent with the assumptions of agency theory that assumes principal-agent interests divergence. However, this does not mean that in Company B employees are all lazy and selfish. Conversely, the AVP argues that the nature of man could be both essentially good and self-serving. The AVP believes that there is no conflict between principals and agents, as long as the company can develop an open and non-discriminatory performance measurement system. 'Then, we can create a win-win situation,' the AVP commented.

II.   Structure of Team B

A breakthrough product project definitely needs diverse professional employees who possess specialised skills and require cooperation and coordination of each division. That is why most of the high-technology companies that want to be world-class innovative leaders emphasise teamwork. 'Working alone is unproductive and inadequate in our company,' the HR manager emphasised. 'We have training courses to educate and gradually influence our people that teamwork is necessary and the reason why it is necessary.' That is, unless employees have better suggestions for successfully developing a new product project, working as a team should be the best valuable choice in the company. 'Members of Team B do not waste time on complaining about their teammates,' the PM believed. 'They find a way to comfort themselves and still offer valuable contributions to achieve the team's purpose.' Members of Team B realised that their jobs is to produce a successful breakthrough product, so team-members, if necessary, should get involved in all tasks and cover for their teammates.

Figure 6.5 shows the procedures of structuring Team B. A breakthrough product project is just like a high-risk, high-return investment plan to the company. Before the company invests in a project, it definitely will consider the possibility of success and the rate of return-on-investment (ROI) by reviewing the budgeting of each division. However, no matter how comprehensive the project proposal is, there are still many unanticipated variables that the team and the company need to face and solve. 'The only thing that will not change is that everything is changing every second,' the AVP commented. Thus, 'once you have got an idea, just try it,' the PM suggested. 'The best way to learn how to perform a project is to perform a project in practice. The company is always eager to train and motivate its employees to run an independent project in their own way, of course, within reasonable budgets and time.'

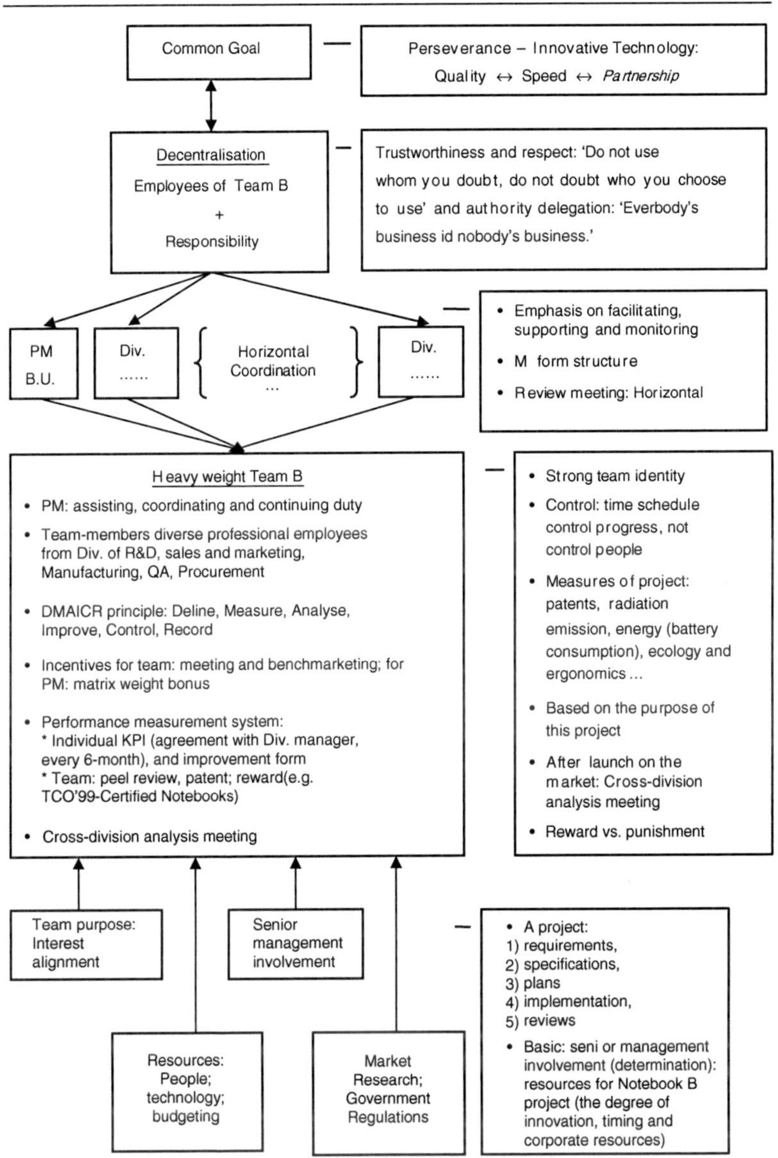

Figure 6.5 Corporate Governance Structures for Team B

Company B treats professional employees as corporate assets and promising projects as investments. 'Senior managers who were decision-makers on the Notebook B project were held responsible for their strategic decisions,' the HR manager recalled. Before the Notebook B project is formally started, a review meeting is held and every divisional manager attends to evaluate the project and to decide whether the company should form a team to put this project into practice. Although a few people disagreed at that review meeting, the majority of managers agreed and that is why the project was begun. Thus, senior management should involve and support the team so that all team-members have a common team purpose to achieve. Thus, in Company B, senior management takes responsibility for the failure of any new product project. Specifically, the responsibility of members of Team B is to excel to their highest potential and that is the only thing they need to do.

As depicted in Figure 6.5, during the review meeting, the PM discussed with divisional managers the nature and qualification of the Notebook B project and then found out suitable employees from each division to structure Team B. 'Although we were selected by the PM and our divisional managers, we categorised ourselves as a part of Team B,' an R&D technology expert explained, and the procurement representative agreed. 'Because we realised that our behaviours will affect the output and purpose of Team B.' The PM posted clear job descriptions on the wall of the meeting room so that the team-members can check the progress of Team B and NPD process. In addition, senior management assigned necessary resources to Team B and cared about the output of it. 'If your supervisor walks in the meeting room and asks: how is it going? every day, you know he really cares,' the QA person said.

Company B is well-known as 'prudence' in the Taiwan high-technology industry. Generally speaking, employees of Company B are very attentive to their jobs. Being divisional managers of Company B, they are experienced and realise their people's skills and talents. When divisional managers recommended their people to join Team B, managers considered their people's qualifications for the Notebook B project, rather than just finding 'whoever' to fill the places in Team B. That is, before starting the Notebook B project and structuring Team B, executives evaluated corporate resources and external factors (see Figure 6.5) to see whether Company B has the probability to make this breakthrough product project successful.

To sum up, members of Team B were assigned to work on Notebook B project and they understood what their tasks and responsibilities were. Also, members of Team B realised what Company B wants and what the team needs to produce, which is a successful breakthrough product. They understood their goal and if necessary they would cover for their teammates. 'The show must go on,' a manufacturing representative emphasised. 'The job must be done. What can you say?' Therefore, Team B has achieved a high level of identity and the management adopted a horizontal incentive system for it. This concurs with teamwork literature.

III.   Interaction of NPD process and Team B

Company B is organised into geographic organisations and then divided into divisions (business units (BU)) (see Figure 6.5). That is, divisional managers and the PM of Team B have identical institutional power in the company. The industrial manager discussed with the PM of Team B, structured the flow of Notebook B project tasks and activities, and then decided upon a Planning and Preparation, Design, Testing and Modification, and Commercialisation (PDTC) approach. 'NPD projects, especially breakthrough product projects, usually involve many different tasks and activities, which are performed by many different groups of people in our company,' the PM observed. 'With the intention of facilitating integration and tracking progress, it is important to organise the tasks and activities of NPD into a logical structure.' In fact, although the Notebook B project was a breakthrough product project, the differences from other NPD projects in Company B are the planning and preparation stage and design stage. Each stage is discussed below.

- Planning and preparation

In this case company, the PM and sales representatives directly co-proposed the Notebook B proposal to the AVP. After reviewing it, the AVP was interested and encouraged the PM and the sales representatives to make a detailed proposal to all divisional managers. The PM and sales representatives asked the MR to help. After three weeks, at the review meeting, the PM, the sales representatives and the MR proposed a detailed Notebook B project, involving market research results, budgets, people, and the extent of innovation. 'In our company we do not waste time on waiting, estimating or thinking,' the AVP emphasised. 'If you do not try it, how do you know you cannot do it? People who work in our company will not give up when they encounter problems; they overcome them.' 'I believe that the executives have considered internal and external environments before they make any decisions or set goals for employees,' an R&D engineer noted. 'Since executives have decided to execute Notebook B project, what I should do is to complete it.' Similarly, since the CEO and president approved the Notebook B project, senior managers supported it and became fully involved in this project.

The planning and preparation stage mainly included idea development, market research, resource evaluation, division budgets, concept development, and related internal, i.e. corporate and external factors. In order to shorten Notebook B project's timeline, to speed-up PDTC progress, and to overlap several subsequent phases, in planning and preparation stage, divisions of HR, finance, law, PM, R&D, representatives of sales and marketing, manufacturing, procurement, QA, and after-sale service were all involved. The HR division prepared training courses on NPD-related expertise. The finance division monitored project budgets and costs during each stage. The law division focused on regulations on defence and design patents. The PM division drew up a plan and coordinated NPD-related divisions for the Notebook B project. The R&D division played an important role in concept development and shared work progress with divisions of manufacturing, procurement, and after-sale service. The sales and marketing division analysed customer needs, acceptance and the variability of the market.

Each division of Company B and each member of Team B realised their jobs and implemented them. The purpose of the planning and preparation stage is to avoid termination of the project and to increase the probability of the Notebook B project's success and Notebook B's competitive advantages in the international market. The performance of planning and preparation stage is determined by the effectiveness of coordination, cooperation and communication of the various divisions. The HR division set DMAICR principle (see Figure 6.5) to evaluate each task and activity. The PM followed this principle to record Team B's log. Also, in the beginning of the planning and preparation stage, each team-member's KPI, the rules and results of performance measurement, and benchmarking from competitive companies were available and clear.

- Design

The idea of the product (Notebook B) is highly innovative, i.e. the functions and the appearance of Notebook B are new to the world and therefore both its operation is unproven and current customers are unfamiliar with it. Therefore, R&D technology experts pay much attention to 'concept development' (planning and preparation stage) and 'detailed design' (design stage) phases. Design stage mainly includes preliminary design, detailed design, and formative prototype. R&D technology professional employees, for example, mechanical, software, hardware, and firmware experts played important roles in detailed designs and prototyping. 'It is not difficult to put a new function into the notebook, but it could be difficult to find someone to offer the service,' an R&D technology expert explained. 'For an example, there is a TV connection function in your notebook, but no TV stations in Taiwan offer this service.'

In the design stage, the R&D technology expert designed the prototype of Notebook B; together, the PM contacted government authorities. Also, R&D technology experts discussed with manufacturing, procurement, sales and marketing, HR, and after-sale service representatives to see whether the manufacturing division can improve its production skills and procedures, whether the procurement division can find suitable suppliers, whether the sales and marketing division can find suitable distributors, and also informed HR and after-sale service divisions about the new technology service so that the HR division can offer helpful courses to technicians. These tasks and activities are overlapped, i.e. manufacturing division does not have to wait until the R&D division delivers the prototype. What these divisions need to do is to keep in touch, share timely information and communicate with each other.

- Testing and modification

The testing and modification stage mainly includes user acceptance tests, safety and compatibility tests, e.g. crash-test, battery-test, waterproof-test, compatibility test, hardware torture tests. Failure to perform in any one of the safety and compatibility tests means that improvements and modifications are required. In fact, the items and procedures of notebook tests are similar to other NPD projects, so it did not take too much time at this stage. 'All test rules and standards are referenced by USA standards and approved by the AVP,' the QA person explained. 'That is, it is achievable. R&D technology experts are professional employees and they do not argue with QA standards; conversely, they achieve them.' 'Giving up is the easiest thing in the world,' an R&D technology expert said. 'We are making an impact on the world, so we do not expect everything to go smoothly. Our company turned us into professional employees in our fields and offered the tools to us. The company did its job, now it is our turn.'

At this stage, the sales representatives started to check client background with the finance division, take client orders and then inform manufacturing and procurement divisions. The manufacturing division produced one hundred units for trial and attempted to improve the production process. The procurement division conferred with material suppliers and set a timetable to ensure delivery on time. The sales and marketing and after-sale service division also attended the testing meeting to understand Notebook B's possible defects and competitive advantages. At the testing and modification stage, all divisions are involved and cooperate with other each other. 'We have a common and clear goal and we are excited to complete it,' a procurement representative explained. 'We are in the same boat, we should make it float.'

- Commercialisation

The commercialisation stage mainly includes mass production, serial Notebook B promotion, customer service, and the cross-division analysis meeting. In the commercialisation stage, the manufacturing division played an important role in mass production. The procurement division communicated with the manufacturing division and ensured that the materials were delivered on time for production. The sales representatives conferred with the manufacturing and procurement divisions whether to accept client orders. The MR and R&D technology experts discussed whether serial Notebook B is possible. Three months after the day Company B launched Notebook B on the market, the PM of Team B held the cross-division analysis meeting in order to get feedback and experience from the Notebook B project to each division. Notebook B project took 15 months to launch. The sale life of Notebook B is about one year.

IV. *Performance measurement of Team B*

The PM of Team B, who belongs to the senior management, has ten years of related work experience and a high reputation in the electronics industry, so it is helpful and easier for him to value his team-members' unique personalities and integrate them into a coordinated way of working as a team. A team meeting is held by the PM to establish the purpose of the team; introducing the position and responsibility, i.e. KPI of each team-member; dealing with the pay arrangements and performance measurement methods; and then setting a timetable for project progress. 'It is not good to pretend that people are not interested in comparing each others' salaries,' the PM implied. 'The more everything is under the sun, the less interest there is in gossip.' Company B has always pursued fairness and non-discrimination of employees and the best way is publicising the compensation structure and results of performance measurement.

A question was raised, 'will not employees feel uncomfortable when the company publicises such private matters?' 'Not unless you are an unprofessional employee or a free-rider,' the HR manager answered. 'The purpose of "teamwork" is to find out differences among team-members. It is a great opportunity, for capable employees, to show their best; for the PM and the company, to value and cultivate the right people.' The duty of the PM of Team B was to observe, communicate, and encourage team-members and their divisional managers to work together and achieve the common goal of the team, i.e. to find out who is valuable and who is free-riding. 'I am rich enough, so what I want is fair and worth it,' an R&D technology expert emphasised. 'Most of high-tech companies provide pretty high pay for experts and teams, so what? Everybody got the same pay … A performance measurement system is just like a black box. Can you see-through the black box?' All interviewees of Company B supported the pay structure and results of performance measurement to be made public.

However, undeniably, measuring performance costs money and time, and the company stresses the cost-effective principle. 'Since we use corporate resources to do measurement, we want something back,' the HR manager emphasised. 'Whatever you do, you must have a purpose. We measure, because we need information to make decisions, e.g. replacing underperforming team-members.' An open and non-discriminatory performance measurement system should govern the design of reasonable measures, their operation, uses, and expected impacts. For Team B, the company empowered divisional managers to set individual KPI for their subordinates for authority delegation and clear job descriptions; empowered the PM to arrange the project progress and evaluated team-members every phase by team peer review. Divisional managers would mark their divisional employees; the PM of Team B could provide his opinions as references.

For an individual in team B, everyone has his or her own KPI. Each team-member sets his or her individual six-month objectives and measuring performance targets by communicating with his or her direct supervisor, i.e. the divisional manager and the PM of Team B; both the team-member and the direct supervisor need to sign the agreement.

After six months, the direct supervisor will assess the employee, provide comments and give another six-month KPI if the employee is substandard. On the other hand, if the direct supervisor agrees with the PM's comments that the employee is underperforming, the supervisor needs to explain the reasons and report to the discipline committee. Usually, when the underperforming employee is a manager, he or she needs to improve his or her performance within three months; whereas when the substandard employee is a subordinate employee, he or she has two months to improve his or her performance. After the improvement period, if there is still underperformance, then the underperforming person is required to leave the company.

For the whole team, the company sets team peer reviews after each phase of the project. The purpose of peer review for Team B is to discover free-riders, or whether there were people who were bad at working with others. 'Only free-riders feel the pressure,' the HR manager explained. 'We are not going to make it a competition here. Peer review is a way to "re-choose" your team-members.' The company provided a way for employees of Team B to decide whether to reveal free-riders or not. 'Ace speaks,' the QA person observed. 'It is your call. If you keep silent, do not complain in the future.' After assessing the results of peer review, the PM can exercise his rights to express his opinions and communicate with related divisional managers regarding whether to replace any team-members. 'Replacing anyone in the team does not mean he is an unprofessional employee or a free-rider. Could be that he is just not suitable for this project,' the PM emphasised. 'So I need to explain why "we" (including teammates) want to replace this person.'

For the PM of Team B, the company prepared a different manager level pay structure and performance measures. The PM also had an individual KPI, reported the team's progress, and communicated any dilemmas the team faced to his director. 'Frankly, I do not need to "hide" any bad news or problems. It will not make things better; it just delays failure,' the PM observed. 'You can conceal others, but do not do it to yourself.' Company B always develops an easy communication environment for its employees. That is, the company encourages employees to raise their ideas, needs, and even difficulties and consult with their supervisors. As the AVP emphasised, 'NPD is not an easy job. Without the senior managers' support and involvement, the possibility of success would be lower.'

V.   *What motivates Team B?*

It is easy for high-technology companies to design reasonable performance measures for their employees, i.e. reasonable and acceptable to them. However, not every company can efficiently put these measures into operation, use the results of the performance measurement to achieve their purpose, and persuade employees to trust the senior management to implement a fair and open performance measurement system. After every new product project ends, no matter whether it is a successful or a failed project, Company B always holds an analysis meeting to get feedback for other project teams. Thus, although Team B has generated a lot of profit, registered patents, and won rewards and global media attention, the company still holds a meeting to find out 'why it was successful.' At Team B's analysis meeting, senior managers discussed the purposes of the team and the performance measurement system for it.

In fact, not all of the new product projects are successful in Company B. As the Chinese saying goes, 'failure is the mother of success.' Company B exploits failure as a stepping stone. Through each analysis meeting, the company explores the reasons why some project teams were commercially successful but others failed. This provides valuable information for diverse project teams in the future. Company B discovered that the most difficult part when developing new products is to appropriately motivate and measure team-members of project teams. 'You just cannot find a perfect way to satisfy everyone,' the HR manager sorrowfully said. 'Not everyone can be motivated by money; besides, some people can be bought by money, but they are not worth it.' Then what should the company do to be worthwhile? 'Think logically,' the AVP responded.

Company B believes that the attitude of the senior management and the environment of the company create slackers or diligent people. 'What do self-actualising employees want?' the HR manager asked and continued '... in a speech, I asked them: "do you want high pay every month or an easy working environment?" Both, most replied. If you can only choose one? I said, narrowing down the options. They laughingly answered, "an easy working environment." ...' The company designs the corporate governance structure, and the governance structure to cultivate employees. Working in a fair and transparent corporate environment, which provides a reasonable pay structure and an open and fair performance measurement system, is the best way to attract and keep diligent professional employees, because all that a self-actualising person wants is fairness.

Company B arranged the performance-incentive pay structure to serve shareholders' interests and simultaneously motivate diligent employees to devote themselves to the company. The AVP emphasised that the success of Team B is based on the other teams' failures. The key success factor of Team B was to successfully motivate team-members by a transparent and fair performance measurement system.

6.2.3   Case C

I.   Background

Company C is a Taipei-based technology corporation striving to be innovative and responsive to customer needs. It was founded at the end of 1979 and went public in 1991. Company C merged with Company L in the middle of 1999.[5] Company C was a conservative, traditional, and financially successful brand-name notebook computer developer and manufacturer with a fine reputation in the international market. The company has achieved several honours for innovations and won press attention in computer product evaluations conducted all over the world. 'I supposed that this company should have a promising future in its own way,' the CEO sighed. 'If this company can keep valuable professional employees, only the right people, in-house experts are assets of the company.' According to the CEO, Company C believed that employees usually will not work hard for their employers; employees work hard for higher performance and eventually for themselves. 'It is a principle and agent link in the company. This company believed that people will work hard when they get adequate returns,' the HR manager commented.

Company C believed that the governance structure, such as delegating authority, well-designed compensation contracts, and a non-discriminatory performance measurement system, can align interests of shareholders and employees and then motivate employees to achieve the corporate common goal. Thus, Company C placed emphasis on the design of compensation arrangements and performance measures for the individual, team, and functions. 'Management has the institutional power to delegate authority, and then it should have ability to control unfair conflict and risk preferences among employees,' the PM said. 'It

---

[5]Company C is now a subsidiary of Company L. All interviewees were working in Company C and currently they work in Company L.

does not matter whether human nature is good or bad; people always think about themselves first and then others.' The sales representative also commented that 'usually people think only about themselves but do not care about others. It is not wrong, as long as you do not hurt others.'

Company C had rigorously implemented and used the results of measurement for employee decision-making, and returned them back to the employees as feedback for improvement. 'I do not mind that our company is control-oriented. Control mechanisms could be helpful to employees as long as they work,' the QA person commented. 'You should ask yourself why you design this mechanism, and then examine whether you achieve the purpose.' Finally, the HR manager reviewed the impact of decision-making to employees in order to improve the measures. 'I wake up, and just cannot wait to start to work, because I perceived I got what I desired,' an R&D engineer recalled. '... both intrinsic and extrinsic rewards and returns were used in the company ... more focus on extrinsic returns.' 'I have a doctor of philosophy degree in engineering. But in the end my purpose is to get a good job,' the PM admitted. 'I do not really agree with this company's mission and vision but it is not my concern. Once my team produced a profitable product, the honour belongs to me and my people as well.'

Company C evidently believed that human nature is selfish and self-serving; assumed that employees will not sacrifice their own interests if it conflicts with those of shareholders'. It adopted delegating authority and control mechanisms, focused more on extrinsic returns, and pursued short-term cost controls and profitability. Therefore, Company C was more likely to apply the agency theory.

According to many media sources, such as newspapers, and organisational sources, such as annual reports, Company C had definitely successfully developed some products or new technology with market potential and was a profitable company. However, Company C's reputation and operations were going down after 1994. Some senior managers not only left the company but took its main clients and professional employees. In 1998, Company C changed its policy and was planning to merge with Company L. The purpose of Team C was to win a reputation and make money for the company. Management paid attention to the progress and the output of Team C. However, Team C failed to achieve its team goal and purpose. We attempted to find out what was going on in the company, by reviewing the structure of Team C, interaction of NPD process and Team C, and performance measurement of Team C.

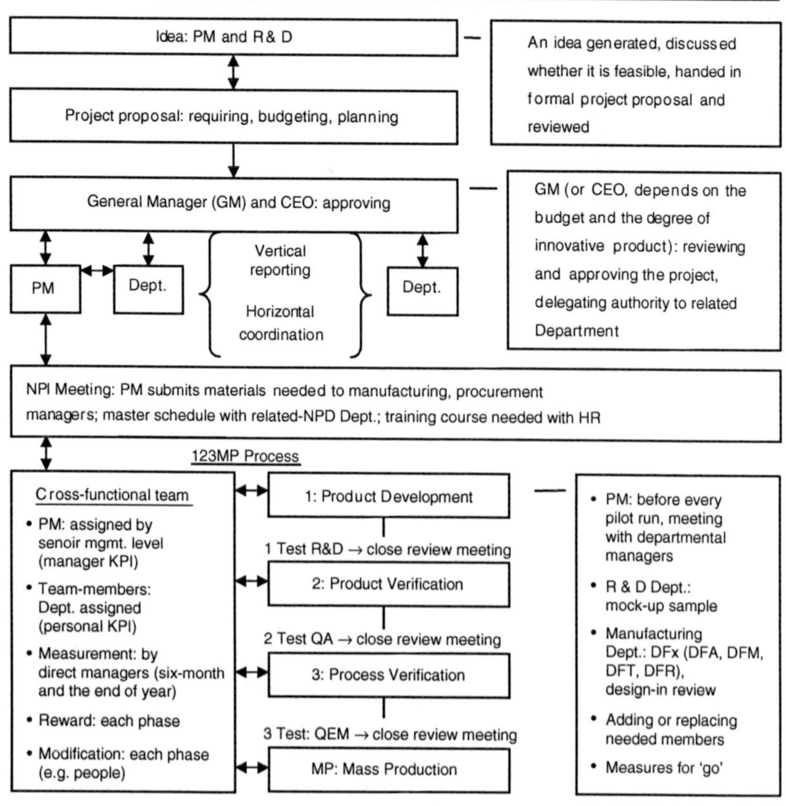

Figure 6.6   Coordination of Project Team C and NPD Process

II.   Structure of Team C

'Trust your instincts and try it, of course, within reasonable budgets,' the PM stated. The company holds a 'New Product Initiation' (NPI) meeting to assess the current environment and project achievability, i.e. corporate resources and acceptable risk. At Notebook C NPI meeting, functional managers recommended suitable people to join Team C, and discussed Notebook C's NPD process and team progress with the industrial manager and the PM of Team C. Members of Team C were assigned by their functional managers (see Figure 6.6 – vertical style), because functional managers were familiar with their talents and timetable. 'There is no best way to structure a team,' an R&D engineer said. 'I do not mind to be assigned, as long as my team-members are professional employees.'

The HR manager supported each department when functional managers or the PM of Team C required training courses.

Members of Team C understand their jobs, because the PM and the industrial manager develop clear job descriptions and flowcharts for each NPD process. 'You will get your own job descriptions and also can check team-members' tasks through computer files (you must log in), in case you need help or find someone to take responsibility for,' a manufacturing representative indicated. Although senior management claimed that they were involved and paid much attention to team-work, the PM, sales and procurement representatives did not agree with the management's arguments. 'If the management exercised due professional care, it should understand that what team-members want is feedback and fairness,' the PM explained. 'Professional team-members did not feel they belonged to Team C. They [professional members] felt shame working at Team C, because they perceived that evaluation is just a procedure, and they did not think it is fair to them.'

Therefore, professional members of Team C took responsibility only for their own tasks. 'I do not know the results of the evaluation, but I know someone always asks teammates to cover for him,' an R&D engineer said. 'However, this free-rider also got a bonus. Then, why should I do his job for him? No one will see.' Also, professional members of Team C started comparing their own tasks with that of other team-members. 'Everyone got the same pay, why I do more jobs?' a sales representative asked. 'As you can image, members of Team C disagreed with the argument about "our task" and "our team purpose."' Based on this description, members of Team C do not have a strong team self-categorisation and team identification. Due to unavailable measurement results, members of Team C turned themselves into 'spies,' i.e. team-members observed each other's actions and then compared, complained and reported to the management. This is consistent with teamwork literature.

III.   Interaction of NPD process and Team C

There is an official procedure, called '123MP Process'[6] (see Figure 6.6), for all NPD projects in Company C. Functional departments coordinate and share information with each other. In addition, each department can directly report to the management. The design of a matrix organisational structure helps to structure the cross-functional project teams.

---

[6]Company C exploited 123MP process for any NPD projects; however, the tasks and activities in 123 phases would be totally different. They depend on the degree of technology and product innovation.

The R&D department is responsible for phase one and during this phase, R&D experts transform ideas into 'mock-up samples.' Also, for manufacturability, the manufacturing department assigned 'DFx experts,' including DFA (design for assembly), DFM (design for manufacturing), DFT (design for testing), and DFR (design for reliability) to assess whether the mock-up sample is practicable, i.e. so-called 'design-in review.' At the end of phase one, R&D experts are in charge of testing the sample and its so-called 'engineering variation test, EVT.' After reviewing and communicating by R&D experts and manufacturing DFx people, DFx experts sent a needed component form to the procurement department.

During phase two, the team holds a meeting for all NPD-related departments to discuss *product issues* and produces a few samples for sales representatives to verify with potential customers. Obviously, the purpose of the phase two meeting is to find out the problems of the sample product according to all NPD departments. The QA department is responsible for phase two and its so-called 'design variation test, DVT.' At phase three, the QA department sends experts for quality engineering management (QEM) and its so-called 'product variation test, PVT.' At the end of phases one, two, and three, managers always hold a closed review meeting to decide whether this project can 'go' to the next phase. Indeed, there are some 'subjective' measures such as lower X percentage defective rate and the degree of product innovation, solved for each phase, and the departments who are in charge to ensure each phase was completed before moving on. 'The company measures what it thought was important,' the HR manager implied. 'Thus, team-members just focused on these measures, and there was nothing wrong with it.'

'When the company approved phases one, two, and three, no matter what the product looks like, it will go to the MP phase and then go to the regional office (RO),' the manufacturing representative explained. 'At the MP phase, the departments of manufacturing, procurement and sales representatives have the main roles.' After launching Notebook C on the market, an evaluation team (ET) was formed to appraise and inspect the tasks and activities of the 123MP process and Team C. Finally, Notebook C's ET leader proposed his investigation to the president and the CEO. 'ET is an extraordinary management procedure. It does not happen often,' the PM said. 'Unless the situation is really bad.'

IV. *Performance measurement of Team C*

Teamwork in Company C is an opportunity for innovative employees to try out their ideas and learn how to coordinate and communicate with other experts. 'It took a bushel of energy, but I really enjoyed it and had fun,' an R&D expert, who has nine years experience in Company C, recalled. 'I mean working with other teams … oh, nope, not including Team C.' Company C set personal KPI and every six months the company truthfully implemented evaluation. Usually the HR manager returns the results of evaluation to employees. Also, the company gives bonuses after every NPD phase to project teams and decides on the individuals' salaries based on the results of their performance measurement. Therefore, team-members believe in 'efforts with returns.' 'In my own opinion, I think it has nothing to do with measurement,' the HR manager argued. 'People want to be measured fairly, and they are eager to know whether compared with their peers inside the company they are being paid fairly.'

Individual members of Team C were evaluated every six months, based on personal KPI, which was discussed with the relevant functional manager and the PM of Team C, by their functional managers. The PM is evaluated by perception measures, such as planning and organisation, judgement, initiative, flexibility, and by objective measures e.g. cost and schedule control. The whole team performance is evaluated when each phase of the 123 Process is examined at closed review meetings (see Figure 6.6). 'Team-member peer review is used, too,' a procurement person said. 'During closed review meetings, the PM of Team C collects peer review results and discusses it at meetings.' Company C believes that increasing the degree and frequency of management control could help members of Team C to get feedback and change their behaviour in time. Therefore, Company C sets detailed tasks and activities for phases one, two and three and reviews each task and activity using established standards.

V.   What ruined Team C?

'Company C assigned another person to measure the performance of members of Team C,' the HR manager recalled. 'Management did not explain why the old person was replaced by a new person. This new person never returned the results of the performance measurements back to the employees of the Team C, but "everyone" got his/her "bonuses" [pay-for-performance part]. The fact that everyone got bonuses does not mean that "everyone was happy about it."' For example, in a breakthrough product project team, the team needs R&D experts at least in mechanical, hardware, software, and firmware fields. Different R&D experts have diverse jobs. Thus, supposedly, they should get different bonuses due to different results of performance measurement. 'If everyone was working hard, I would have felt better,' an R&D expert complained. 'But the truth is that we (including other R&D experts) all felt "someone" was slothful and he got a bonus, too.' At that time, these diligent R&D experts started to consider that maybe they should accept other companies' offers or start their own businesses.

R&D experts reported to senior managers about unfair evaluation and under the table performance feedback. 'We are waiting for the company to improve this situation,' an R&D expert explained. After each phase of NPD, Company C grants the bonus to the whole Team C. Again, however, everyone equally shares the bonus. Obviously, the company disappoints its professional employees. Although eventually Notebook C was launched on the market, its functionality and appearance were nevertheless not good. 'Even though I work very hard, I still had to share my efforts with some lazy people,' a sales representative disappointedly noted. 'There is no fair evaluation ... I want a bonus, but I also want "fair" salary that compares with my peers.' At this time, some professional employees had exploited corporate resources to start their own businesses and some have found other jobs.

'Find the key cause of the problem, before you try to solve the problem,' the CEO recommended. As an old Chinese saying goes, 'the trouble has been brewing for quite some time.' The failure of Team C was the effect of ineffectively implementing and reviewing the performance measurement system. Even if R&D engineers can design a breakthrough Notebook with a new appearance, of high quality, and with advanced functionality, it still needs to be promoted by sales representatives, served by customer support engineers, and, most importantly, be supported by senior management by their commitment, attitude, and determination, as well as the provision of the necessary advertising budget. 'The birth of the Notebook C showed the result of *teamwork*,' the PM clarified. 'The company sets a time-to-market, the team absolutely will catch the deadline ... However, R&D experts of R&D experts are gone; you can image the quality of the product.'

A breakthrough product project needs a mass of capital, a lot of time, a mountain of related-materials, and a ton of energy to achieve the basic purpose of producing a commercially successful breakthrough product. Expectantly, the breakthrough product project team needs to be properly motivated by adequate compensation arrangements and evaluated by non-discriminatory responsible people. As the CEO concluded, the most difficult part of developing brand-name new products is 'corporate internal management.' 'Developing an authoritative performance measurement system is the duty of the senior management,' the CEO admitted. '... a fair and open performance measurement system that works with an attractive compensation structure is what we are pursuing.'

6.2.4 Case D

I. Background

Company D is a Taipei-based high-technology corporation. It places emphasis on product R&D, manufacturing, and distribution channels. It was founded in 1979, went public in 1989, and was delisted from the Taiwan stock market in 2004. According to media sources, in its early years, Company D continuously placed emphasis on NPD, which led to the introduction of many innovative and profitable products, and 1979 – 1990 were its growth years. Also, some outstanding Taiwan universities even used Company D as a successful case study for their business students. However, after 1998, profitability began to decline and after 2000, key professional employees in NPD project teams started to quit. In August 2004, Company D left the market, but it did not go out of business. Conversely, the company is trying to re-engineer its organisation by improving its governance structure and recruiting professional employees and becomes a publicly listed company again.

Company D was an organisation with empowering structures. Decentralised management structure was adopted, since the company believed that human nature is essentially good and the employees' objective is aligned with the company's objective, because employees perceive that if the company went bust they would be unemployed. Therefore, management is more likely to delegate much authority to their subordinates and respect their decisions. 'People in our company are selected by careful interview panels,' the HR manager explained. 'Since we hire employees, we should give them opportunity and responsibility to learn and grow.' As the VP described, 'the link of the company and employees is built more on trustworthiness rather than contracts. However, a contractual relationship is also needed because management should prevent partial goal conflicts among employees, as well as to protect corporate assets and other employees.'

Based on both trust and contractual relationships, the company has 'hard cultures,' such as organisational structure (e.g. empowering structure), systems (e.g. performance measurement system), corporate policies and procedures (e.g. resource conservation), rewards (e.g. intrinsic and extrinsic) and layoffs (e.g. measures); and 'soft cultures,' such as corporate educational practices (e.g. long-term performance enhancement), norms (e.g. vision), slogans (e.g. enjoy your technology life!), and management style (e.g. involvement oriented). 'The company is well-organised, so if you give good performance, you have a bright future here,' the VP expressed. 'Our company focuses more on such intrinsic rewards as self-actualisation, affiliation, etc. Professional employees accept this model of motivation because they perceive that there is hope (vision) in our company.' Therefore, although 'Pay? Silence!' is the 'red code' of the company; professional employees still believe that the management will be fair and honest to them.

In addition, as the VP explained, 'we create a collectivist culture. ... I personally will not force my people by using my institutional power. Actually, I never heard employees complaining that someone forced them to do things they did not want to do.' Company D cares about the managers' personality and morals, because the management wishes a supervisor to be a mentor to his employees.

Based on the above description, people who work in Company D are more likely to become stewards in principal-steward relationships, because employees have high identification with the organisation (by accepting its mission and vision, as well as producing a satisfying relationship), as well as are more motivated by intrinsic rewards.

II. Structure of Team D

Before forming a project team, senior managers consider five perspectives (see Figure 6.7) to examine whether the project is promising and is worth further investigation. 'Unless senior managers do not want the

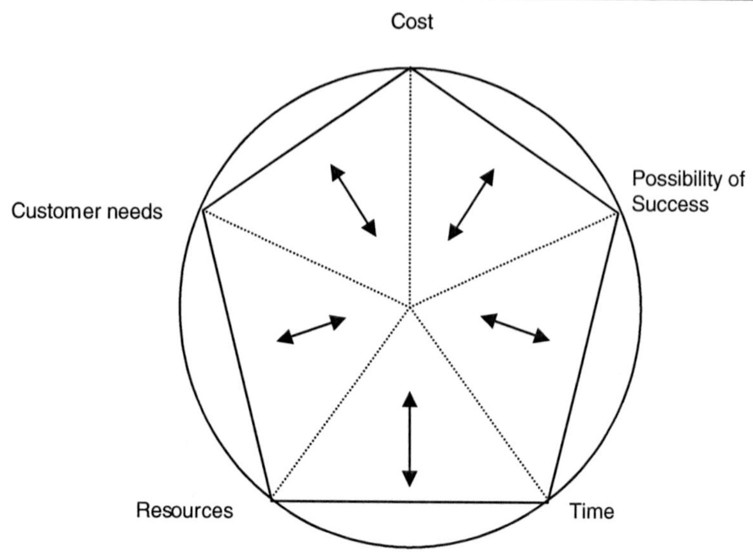

Figure 6.7   NPD Project 'Round' Consideration

project to succeed,' the PM believed. 'Even an experienced capable PM could lose control on a breakthrough product project. Senior managers only can ask the PM to effectively use resources, not to "find" resources for the team.' The purpose of Team D is to produce a profitable and breakthrough product.

All departmental managers attended the Notebook D meeting, and the review Project Plan (PP) included each department's budgeting and allocation of time to the team. After this meeting, the chair of the meeting submitted the PP to the general manager and the CEO. The CEO approved the Notebook D project, and then the managers of the various departments gave recommendations about suitable people to the PM of Team D. The PM reviewed potential candidates' profiles, interviewed them, and then decided on the team-members. Similarly, individuals in the company have individual KPI that were discussed and set with his or her direct supervisor. 'When you joined a team, you must show your KPI to your team-members so that everyone in the team knew *what is your*

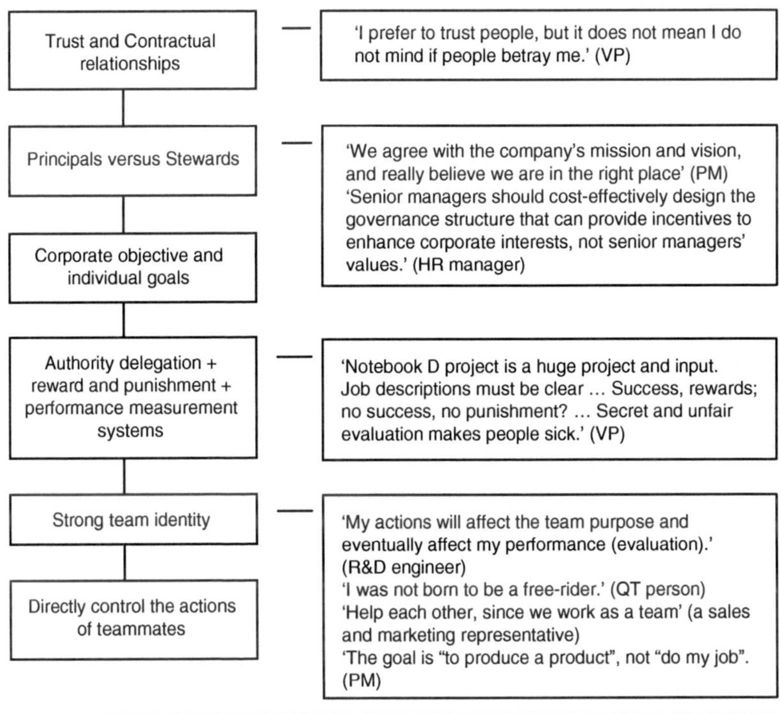

Figure 6.8   Implications of the Teamwork Setting

responsibility and field,' the PM explained. Figure 6.8 connects corporate culture and the structure of Team D.

Although members of Team D were selected and assigned by their departmental managers and the PM of Team D, team-members did not feel unhappy or refused the given challenges and responsibilities. The R&D engineer, QT person and the sales and marketing representative all understood that their jobs are to achieve the team purpose (see Figure 6.8). Also, the job descriptions were clearly given and the PM had a meeting with members of Team D and made sure the descriptions are understandable. 'I would be happy to help my teammates as long as they are not free-riders and as long as I have done my tasks,' an R&D engineer said. 'Every employee in this company was hired to do something. I cannot accept free-riders in our team. ... what if it really happened, I guess I will feel upset and wish I am not in the same team with him.'

Based on the above discussion, Team D had achieved a high level of team identity, i.e. members of Team D had a strong self-categorisation and team identity. Therefore, team-members chose to directly control each other's behaviour rather than report to management. This is consistent with Towry's (2003) research.

III.   Interaction of NPD process and Team D

'A "NPD process" is seen as an *information processing path,*' the PM stated. 'For the Notebook D project, the industrial manager set Concept, Development, Modification, and Mass Production as a series of NPD stages.' The four NPD phases were named by the main purpose of each phase. Also, at each phase, the PM listed detailed job descriptions, checking points, and recorded the results of evaluation of tasks. 'A fulfilled job list and evaluation result is valuable for improvement and management control,' the HR manager explained. 'R&D tasks cannot be listed in detail; however, the manufacturing department needed detailed factory production procedures.' As the QT person said, 'a good interaction between process professional employees and members of Team D is based on trust and understanding.'

An independent business unit called PM department evaluated the performance of the PM and the team. To Team D, the company set three phases to evaluate whether the team was worth keeping investing in. Also, the company set a 'three-phase team bonus' for the whole team if the team passed the first phase review, then the team won the first phase bonus, and so on. However, the team will not get the bonus until Notebook D is launched on the market (the goal of the second phase). 'It is an accumulating motivation concept. Every time team-members see the progress, they are motivated,' the PM explained. 'Because the second phase bonus is much higher than first phase bonus, team-members definitely want to get it, and they can get it [market launch is an achievable goal].' Obviously, the goal of every NPD phase is reasonable and possible. Also, interviewees of Company D all agreed that the bonus, after passing the phase review, was attractive.

- Concept

The concept stage mainly included a series of pre-activity evaluations, e.g. resources evaluation, feasibility evaluation, financial forecast, etc. 'Why did we call it the "concept" stage? … it's easier to get success if you make decisions based on correct concepts,' the VP explained. 'We were investing, not gambling.' The PM department proposed the Notebook D project to the VP; after project reviewing, the VP called an initiation meeting for departmental managers of R&D, sales and marketing, manufacturing, procurement and QT people to confirm whether the Notebook D project is possible to be achieved within reasonable corporate resources. In the initiation meeting, managers from diverse departments recommended suitable people to work in Team D for the Notebook D project. The PM interviewed them and ensured that these professional employees are willing to join Team D and perceived themselves as members of it.

After interviewing potential candidates, the PM selected twelve diverse professional employees to structure Team D. Also, the PM discussed with these members their tasks and duties in Team D. The assignment of tasks was done openly. 'We posted detailed task descriptions, measurement indicators, and team bonuses of each NPD phase on the wall of the Notebook D project room,' the PM explained. 'There is a permanent project room for Team D to use. … yes, we can use the room until Notebook D project is completed.' All of the interviewees accepted this 'posting on the wall' method and treated it as a reminder. 'If something goes wrong, at least I know who I should talk to,' the QT person explained. At the beginning of this stage, the market researcher focused on customer needs identification; in the middle of this stage, the PM department held a concept review meeting to monitor Team D's progress; at the end of this stage, the PM department held a feasibility review meeting before going to the next stage.

- Development

The development stage mainly included preliminary design, detailed design and prototyping. 'The purpose of the "development" stage is to "develop" the concept stage,' the PM indicated. 'That is why we named it the development stage.' The R&D engineers and manufacturing representatives were fully involved from the beginning to the end of this stage. In the middle of this stage, the QT person held a preliminary design review meeting and communicated with the R&D engineers and manufacturing department representatives about production procedures and how to achieve the established standards. At the end of this stage, the QT person held a final review meeting to ensure the prototype concurred with the established standards. Procurement department representatives contacted suppliers and prepared materials for the Notebook D prototype. A patent attorney was hired to deal with the related patent application. At review meetings of each stage, finance experts reported the expenses of each activity and discussed the budget.

- Modification

The modification stage mainly included end-user testing, design modification and product improvement. 'The purpose of modification is not to make a perfect product,' the R&D engineer and the market researcher both claimed. 'What we chase is to produce a "saleable" product and to attract "profitable" customers.' Before going to the mass production stage, the PM held three review meetings to monitor the project's progress. First of all, the manufacturing and procurement representatives are responsible for the critical product review meeting. Secondly, the sales and marketing and R&D representatives are in charge of the end-user testing review meeting. Finally, the manufacturing and procurement representatives are accountable for the manufacturing feasibility review meeting.

- Mass production

The mass production stage mainly included pre-production, mass production, post-production, launch on the market and an aftermarket evaluation meeting for executives. The sales representatives confirmed with distributors about outright purchases or sales and/or consignment methods. 'After production, Notebook D has been sold, partly through outright sales, and partly by the way of consignment,' the sales representative explained. The customer service centre provides comprehensive service for its customers. In the middle of the production stage, a market readiness review meeting was held. Also, at the conclusions of production, a market introduction meeting was held.

IV. *Performance measurement of Team D*

Performance of individuals of Team D is measured by their own direct supervisors every four months. The measurement indicators are emphasised on 'job competence and achievement,' 'professional skills,' 'job quality,' and 'teamwork.' The individual had his 'performance evaluation and development plan' which showed employee's date of hire, personal responsibilities and measurement items. The employee, his direct manager and the reviewing manager signed the form. However, the HR manager did not publicise and return the results of the performance evaluation and development plan back to members of Team D. The bonus is granted to whole team and the PM discusses with team-members how to divide the bonus. 'I felt that the performance measurement is just a routine procedure, because we did not get feedback. Since we do not get results back, there is no improvement form for underperformance use,' the R&D engineer explained. 'At the end of year, a one-year evaluation is held to measure each employee of Company D and departmental managers mark it.'

For the PM of Team D, the measurement indicators are focused on 'leadership ability,' 'planning and organisation ability,' and 'coordination ability.' The indicators are subjective and flexible. 'Everybody is the same. Performance is measured twice per year, i.e. six-month and one-year evaluations,' the PM said. To Team D, team performance is evaluated based on the whole team. Whole team performance was evaluated at each review meeting, and the performance indicators focused on stage target achieved, within budgets, and relations with departments. 'Stage bonuses for Team D were attractive,' the manufacturing and procurement representatives answered. 'However, the way the PM divided the bonus is disputable.' At each review meeting, members of Team D, departmental managers, and the PM department manager all attended and they co-evaluated the team performance.

V. *What ruined Team D?*

After discussing with the VP, we used the causal chain mode to describe and explain the cause-effect linkage of the performance measurement system and Notebook D's commercial failure (see Figure 6.9). Company D abided with the long-established tradition of privacy since 1979. However, the company ignored external environment variables. Many Taiwanese go abroad and study in Western countries such as the USA, so the concepts and management modes have been transformed into American styles. Many Taiwanese high-technology

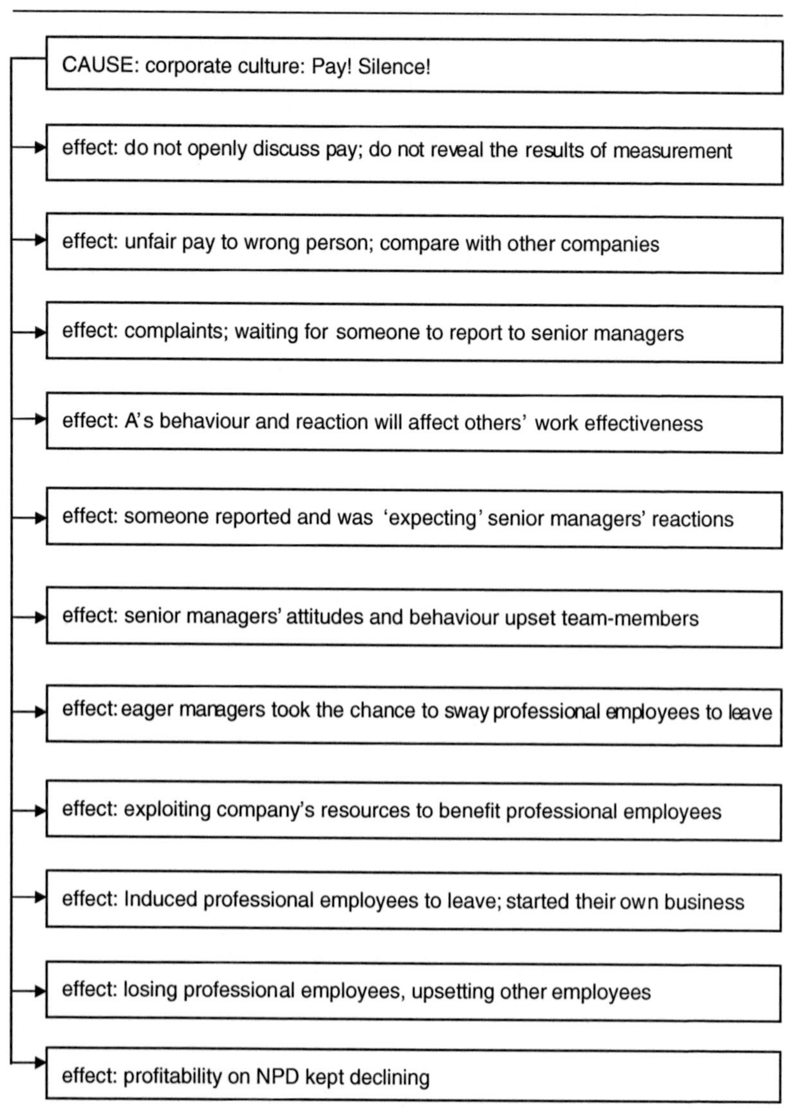

Figure 6.9　The Causal Chain of Team D[7]

---

[7]A cause provides an effect which will turn into another cause for another effect. A good manager, as a good doctor, will find the main cause before trying to give remedies.

companies, but not Company D, have already changed themselves to a humanised management style – openly discussing pay and KPI, considering the purpose before designing the measures, and returning and making public the results of measurement.

'Just because nobody asks does not mean that nobody is interested in the pay structure,' the HR manager emphasised. 'People have friends who work in other high-technology companies in the same field or position, and they can and will compare and chat about their pay.' Especially, when professional employees hear of underperforming colleagues who are in the same field and get the same or even more pay than professional employees here, they feel upset, make complaints, and wait for someone to report to higher managers. A dissatisfied professional employee will influence others' work effectiveness. 'If you do not do your job properly, I must cover it for you. Why? The job must be done,' the PM complained. For example, it was lunch time, and the whole team was waiting for lunch. The dissatisfied employee was the one who was supposed to buy lunch for the team-members, but the person said that he did not want to go out, because outside was too hot and he will get sick. This dissatisfied employee's behaviour had adversely affected other employees and their job schedules.

Further, someone went to the general manager (GM) and reported the unprofessional behaviour of the employee and the performance measurer. 'If the GM's attitude is affirmative and he starts to investigate what was wrong with the system, I guess things may be different,' the PM sadly explained. Together, eager managers who are keen to start their own businesses exploit this opportunity to convince and attract the professional employees to leave the company. These managers automatically got bonuses or higher pay from higher managers for the dissatisfied professional employees and encouraged them to start their own businesses. The progress of Team D was seriously delayed and the costs of Team D were overrun. However, nobody reported to the GM any more: 'Why bother? His response only makes things worse,' the VP commented. Later, these professional employees left the company and started their own businesses.

'Professional employees will not leave the company just because "somebody" is lazy or unreasonable,' the HR manager believed. 'Because they know in every company, the free-riding problem always exists.' Certainly, employees leave because of many reasons, but there should be a decisive key reason why they finally decided to leave. 'Will you kill yourself if your accounting course failed? Nope,' the PM continued. 'But if simultaneously your boyfriend dumps you, you are bankrupted, it is as if God totally forgot you ... Now, will you commit suicide?' Although Company D re-assigned some new members to solve the 'lacking people crisis,' and eventually Notebook D was launched on the market, but it was too late. Overrun budgets and unfamiliar product characteristics made sales and marketing people panic.

In this case, at first Team D had achieved a high level of identity and team-members realised that their job is to cover for each other and eventually produce a successful breakthrough product. However, some professional team-members could not tolerate underperforming unprofessional members, and also the management's attitude made them lose patience; in turn they did not treat themselves as a part of the team. That is, in this case, members of Team D transformed themselves from members of Team D into employees of Team D. Once professional employees have started to question the management's commitment, they do not believe management any more and also worry about their future if they keep staying in Company D. Case D shows that team-members at first strongly stick together (a strong team identity); however, before the team output is achieved, team-members could change their attitudes and become individualistic.

6.3 Conclusion

The above four cases show that vision, management philosophy, leadership, corporate resources and culture influenced the degree of innovation and the way of structuring project teams. In addition, all companies agreed that only professional employees are assets to the company. Companies A and D applied stewardship theory; Team A produced a successful breakthrough product, but Team D failed to achieve its purpose, i.e. a profitable product. Alternatively, the concepts and beliefs of Companies B and C are consistent with the assumptions of agency theory. However, Team B was successful, but Team C failed. Therefore, based on the findings of the four cases, we argue that researchers should focus on integrating the limits and boundaries of agency and stewardship theories, rather than dispute either agency theory or stewardship theory as a one-best-way to corporate governance.

Furthermore, evidence shows that Teams C and D, both commercially failed breakthrough product project teams, failed because Companies C and D kept losing their valuable assets, i.e. professional employees. The reason why Companies C and D could not keep professional employees was their lack of an open and non-discriminatory performance measurement system. How to attract, cultivate, motivate, and make professional employees contribute their talents is the main issue in the four companies, especially, after Taiwan's government announced a new pension plan, which came into force from July 1, 2005. In the next chapter, we compare the four cases and attempts to develop an empirical model based on the finding of the four cases.

7
Cross Case-Studies Analysis

7.0   Introduction

In Chapter 6, we provided a comprehensive overview of each case study including a background of each company case, the structure of the team under study, the interaction of the NPD process and the breakthrough product project team, the performance measurement system adopted in each company case to evaluate the project team, and finally what motivates each team. Within-case analysis was based on a series of themes, which look directly at the causal relationship of team performance measurement systems and new product success or failure. Cross-case analysis places emphasis on what motivates employees and what causes new product success or failure in the four cases. The purpose of case-oriented and cross-case analysis is to preserve the uniqueness of each case and also to make comparisons across cases to see replication logic.

This chapter is organised as follows:

- Introduction
- Internal and external factors
- The organisational architecture
- Agents or stewards?
- The level of self-categorisation and team identification
- Developing an empirical framework
- Conclusion

7.1   Internal and external factors

In the four companies, we found out that before the approval of any new product projects, especially breakthrough product projects, and structuring a breakthrough product project team, the senior management considers many internal and external variables because running a breakthrough product project needs a huge investment in time and money. The management sets the project purpose and new product strategy, evaluates corporate culture and resources, as well as considers the potential market, technology and external environment so that it has relevant information to make informed decisions, e.g. whether to approve the project and structuring a project teams. Figure 7.1

Factor \ Company	A	B	C	D
INTERNAL				
1. Objective	Market share and profits	Reputation and profits	Reputation and profits	Competitive advantage and profits
2. Culture	Collectivism	Individualism	Individualism	Collectivism
3. New Product Strategy	Diversification (new product and new market)	Diversification (growth strategy)	Diversification (n product to new market)	Product Development (existing market)
Basic project definition	Exploratory broader concept	High-risk and high-reputation	Long-term involvement	Exploratory and high risk
4. Resources				
• Staff	Experienced professional employees	Experienced professional employees	Experienced professional employees	Experienced professional employees
• Skills	Diverse specialis	Specialists with diverse talents	Departmental specialists	Departmental specialists
• Budget	Budget control	Budgeting	Monitoring	Controlling
5. Organisation				
• Structure	Matrix	M form	Matrix	Matrix
• Management involvement	Full-involvement	Supporting and monitoring	Controlling and involvement	Supporting and observing
• NPD Process	Initiation; Preliminary Formation; Prototype Design; Testing and Finalisations.	PDTC Approach	123MP Process	Concept; Development; Modification; Mass production
EXTERNAL				
1. Market				
• Customers	Involved	Ignored but tested	Forecasts from market research	Market research
• Competitors	Considered	Considered	Considered	Considered
• Suppliers	Fully involved	Good interaction	Good contact	Coordinating
2. Technology	One step earlier new; acceptable, easy, human technology	Innovative technology for high-revenue level	New to the world	Market potential
3. Environment	Taiwan is a supporting environment for innovative technology	Government encourages high-tech firms to develop new technology	Government helps and supports Taiwanese firms to produce new technology	New technology is one of the competitive advantages of Taiwan
Type of Team (see Figure 3.1)	Self-managed	Heavyweight	Heavyweight	Heavyweight

Figure 7.1   Preparation for a Breakthrough Product Project Team

summarises the internal and external variables that Companies A, B, C, and D had considered before structuring Teams A, B, C, and D.

7.2 The organisational architecture

Figure 7.2 gives a description of the organisational architecture of Companies A, B, C, and D to see how the four companies delegate authority, set incentive plans and measures to each team-member, the PM, and the team. Figure 7.2 shows that management delegated authority to the leader and members of the team. Correspondingly, the four companies used individual and manager KPI to set individual tasks and define responsibilities. Also, the four companies released team-identifications (i.e. credentials) to each member of the team so that team-members can legally check relevant records and/or team progress from the company's data stream. In addition, the team-leader and team-members have the rights to use with authorisation, corporate resources such as the library, seminar room, etc. It can be seen from Figure 7.2 panel I, the assignment of decision rights is similar in the four teams.

Figure 7.2 panel II lists the four companies' reward and punishment plans to members and the leader of the team and the team itself. It is understandable that in practice the pay structure is comparable in similar fields. For example, KFC and Burger King both pay similar amount of money per hour for part-time staff, although the individuals' tasks maybe different. Similarly, in the Taiwan high-technology sector, companies usually set X percentage[1] base pay and Y percentage performance-related bonuses to reward and motivate employees or managers. Companies A, B, and C used peer-review and NPD phase evaluation to evaluate the communication and coordination of team-members and NPD staff (see Figure 7.2, panel II (1)). Although Company D did not use peer-review to evaluate team performance, Company D did measure each NPD phase's performance. In addition, team-members and the team-leader understand that if they fail to achieve the team purpose, their company could dismiss or sell the whole team (see Figure 7.2, panel II (2)).

From the interviews and the official records of team log in the four teams, the crux of four companies is the performance measurement system of new product project teams. As shown in Figure 7.2 panel III, the areas of measurement are similar in the four teams and concur with

---

[1]The percentage of base pay and performance-related bonus is floated and affected by the company's policy. In addition, employees (not management level) and managers (management level) have a different percentage level.

the literature, but differ from the literature on the priorities in the performance measurement areas. From the interviews, we found out the priorities of measurement areas were affected by the corporate culture, reputation and imagination. For example, Company A emphasised

System \ Team	A	B	C	D
Panel I. Assignment of Decision Rights				
• **Member of Team**	1. Clear job descriptions from individual KPI; set, agreed and assigned together by employee, PM, departmental manager 2. Freely use corporate resources, e.g. common room, exercise room, corporate library, etc. for team work (log in required)	1. Clear job descriptions from individual KPI; set, agreed and assigned together by employee, PM, divisional manager 2. Self-disciplining for using corporate resources 3. Employee identification for data stream and computer use	1. Clear job descriptions from personal KPI; set, agreed and assigned together by employee, PM, departmental manager 2. Using and arranging corporate resources (recording and signed) 3. Employee I.D. for team use	1. Clear job descriptions from individual KPI; set, agreed and assigned together by employee, PM, direct supervisor 2. Self-disciplining for using corporate resources 3. Team I.D. for team (access to database)
• **Project Manager**	1. To produce a successful output (broader concept) 2. Supporting to and consulting with teammates, NPD staff	1. Resource checking and requiring 2. Facilitating and observing teammates 3. Broader authority	1. Coordinating, passing info. to NPD-related departments 2. Meeting with team-members 3. To achieve the team goal	1. To d develop an innovative technology and achieve team purpose 2. Broader empowering
Panel II. (1) Reward and (2) Punishment				
• **Member of Team**	(1) Base pay + three-month bonus (measured and given every three-months) and one-year end evaluation (measured end of every year) (2) Improvement form (three-month test; pass set new KPI; fail: quit/dismiss)	(1) Base pay + three-month bonus (measured and given every six-months) and end of one year evaluation (2) Improvement form (six-month test; pass: set new KPI; fail: replace, quit/dismiss)	(1) Base pay + three-month bonus (measured and given every six-months) and end of one year evaluation; measures based on personal KPI (2) transfer; replace	(1) Base pay + four-month bonus (measured and given every four-months) and end of one year evaluation; measured based on personal KPI (2) transfer; replace
• **Project Manager**	(1) Diverse bonus: matrix weight %; promotion; prize; honour (measured every six-months) (2) Improvement form (six-month test); demotion, quit or dismiss	(1) Matrix bonus on each NPD phase; promotion; reputation, prize (measured every six-months) (2) Improvement form (four-month test); transfer, dismiss	(1) Manager bonus given after closed review meeting (2) Assigned to next project; demotion	(1) Mixed pay structure (base pay + phase bonus) (2) Transferred or assigned to next project; demotion
• **Team**	(1) Peer-review; after each NPD phase; FMEA after launch (2) Dismiss or sell whole team	(1) Peer-review; reviewing end of each phase; Cross-division Analysis Meeting (2) Dismiss	(1) Peer-review (at end of every NPD stage; closed review meetings) (2) Dismiss or sell	(1) Three-phase evaluation and bonus (2) Dismiss or sell

Figure 7.2 Three-Part Taxonomy (Organisational Architecture) of the Four Cases

Panel III. Performance Measurement				
• **Areas (ranked according to the importance)**	1. Customer satisfaction 2. Innovation 3. Strategic 4. Process management 5. Financial performance	1. Innovation 2. Process management 3. Customer satisfaction 4. Financial performance 5. Strategic	1. Financial performance 2. Process management 3. Strategic 4. Innovation 5. Technology management 6. Customer satisfaction	1. Process management 2. Innovation 3. Strategic 4. Customer satisfaction 5. Financial performance
• **Uses or purposes**	1. Continuous improvement 2. Individual evaluation 3. Communication 4. Resource allocation (Managerial decision-making) 5. Control	1. Communication 2. Control 3. Resource allocation (Managerial decision-making) 4. Individual evaluation 5. Continuous improvement	1. Control 2. Individual evaluation 3. Resource allocation (Managerial decision-making) 4. Continuous improvement	1. Process management 2. Resource allocation 3. Individual evaluation 4. Control 5. Continuous improvement
• **Impacts**	1. The results (feedback) of measurement motivated professional employees 2. Improved info. access and understanding of teammates and Dept. staff who involved in NPD activities 3. Adjusting and improving long-term performance	1. Openness of measurement results made members feel much pressure and motivated 2. Nobody likes to be treated as a free-rider or underperformed 3. Improving performance and adjusting timetable	1. Under the table and black box measurement results 2. Due to management's attitude, professional employees do not trust management any more 3. 'Adjusting' actions to other cases or preparing to leave	1. No feedback (no return of measurement results) 2. Professional employees feel unfairly treated and uncomfortable 3. Comparing tasks and actions with other members 4. 'Adjusting' behaviour to 'completing my own job' and finding new jobs
Result	Financially Successful	Financially Successful	Financially Failed	Financially Failed

Figure 7.2   Three-Part Taxonomy (Organisational Architecture) of the Four Cases – *continued*

'service attitude and speed' and pursued 'high customer satisfaction,' so the management took 'customer satisfaction' measures as the first consideration. Contrary, Company B pursued 'media attention and reputation,' so the management focused more on 'innovation and process management' measures. Company C was eager to make profits, so the management concentrated more on financial performance. Company D was eager to develop a competitive advantage, so the management emphasised process management and innovation-related measures.

As shown in Figure 7.2 panel III, the uses or purposes of measurement results are also similar in the four teams and concur with the literature; the divergence from the literature is the priorities of using the performance measurement results. From the interviews, the priorities of using the performance measurement results are affected by corporate policy and management philosophy. For example, Company A utilised measurement results mainly on continuous improvement, because the management expected Team A could be an idol for the other teams. Company B utilised the performance measurement results mainly on communication, because the management believed increasing coordination between team-members and NPD staff will be much helpful to the team purpose. Company C was focused on control, because the management believed that control will be helpful to enhance team-members and NPD staff's performance. Company D utilised the performance measurement results mainly on process management, because the management was focused on product and process innovation and it believed that process management will be helpful in achieving the team purpose.

The impact of using the performance measurement results is obviously the main difference between successful and failed teams. Company A made available the performance measurement results to the individuals. The results motivated professional employees to keep contributing to the team and forced underperforming employees to improve their behaviour. Also, the results improved communication between team-mates and NPD staff. Company A achieved the purpose of designing the project team performance measurement system and successfully motivated team-members to contribute, adjust and improve their behaviour and in turned achieved the team purpose. Similarly, to Team B, the openness of the performance measurement results made team-members feel much pressure, but also motivated them to achieve the team's purpose. Due to openness and peer-pressure, nobody likes to be treated as a free-rider or underperforming member in Team B, so team-members adjusted their timetables and devoted more time to the team.

Contrarily, Company C merely set measures and did the paperwork for performance measurement, but the evaluators did not return the results to the employees and failed to achieve the purpose of the performance measurement system. Under the table and black box measurement results made employees lazy and careless. In addition, due to the management's attitude, professional employees did not trust management any more and then adjusted their actions to those of the other teams or planed to leave the company. Similarly, Company D did not return the measurement results to individuals, so professional employees felt unfairly treated and uncomfortable. The professional team-members compared their tasks and contributions with other members of Team C and then adjusted their behaviour to 'completing my own job' and started to find new jobs.

7.3 Agents or stewards?

Figure 7.3 compares Companies A, B, C, and D's presumption, level, assumptions of human nature, organisation, and information, as well as psychological and situational factors to see which of the four companies were more inclined to agency theory and which more inclined to stewardship theory. That is, Figure 7.3 shows that although Companies A, B, C, and D all decentralise and delegate authority to their teams (i.e. project managers and team-members), the two groups (Cases A and D belong to stewardship theory group; Cases B and C belong to agency theory group) are based on two contrasting assumptions of human natures.

The agency theory group delegates authority to members of the new product project team to achieve the team purpose (e.g. increasing team

Company	A	B	C	D
Presumption	Providing a good working environment, professional employees will stay and contribute their knowledge to the company.	Employees understand that their future salary is decided by current performance For their own good, they will work hard.	No one will work hard for others. Employees work hard for higher performance and eventually for themselves. Every man for himself and the devil takes the hindmost.	Employees' objective is aligned with the company's objective, because they know if the company shutdown, they have no income.
Level	Principal-Steward	Principal-Agent	Principal-Agent	Principal-Steward
Human Nature Assumptions	Self-actualising; human nature is essentially good	Self-serving; human nature is good when there are no intere conflicts.	Selfish and self-serving; human nature is essentially bad.	Self-actualising objective; human nature is essentially good.
Organisational Assumptions	Empowering structure; much authority	Controlling struct Delegating authority	Controlling and monitoring; Delegating authority	Much delegation of authority
Information Assumptions	Resource (more)	Resource (more)	Commodity (more)	Resource (more)
Psychological Factors				
Motivation	Intrinsic (more)	Extrinsic (more)	Extrinsic (more)	Intrinsic (more)
Social Comparison	Principal	Other managers	Other managers	Principal
Identification	Higher value commitment	Higher value commitment	Lower value commitment	Higher value commitment
Power	Personal power (more)	Institutional power (more)	Institutional power (more)	Both personal and institutional power
Situational Factors				
Management Philosophy	Involvement-oriented	Control-and involvement-oriented	Control-oriented	Control- and involvement-oriented
Risk Orientation	Trust and control mechanisms	Control mechanisms and trust	Control mechanisms	Trust and control mechanisms
Time Frame	Long-term	Short-term	Short-term	Long-term
Objective	Performance enhancement	Cost control and performance enhancement	Cost control	Performance enhancement and Cost control
Cultural Difference	Collectivism; Lower power distance	Individualism; higher power distance	Individualism; Higher power distance	Collectivism; Lower power distance
Implication	Stewardship Theory	Agency Theory	Stewardship Theory	Agency Theory

Figure 7.3   Agency Theory or Stewardship Theory?

performance, which in turn produces a successful new product) and believes that members of the team need to be controlled by management in order to prevent opportunism. Alternatively, the stewardship theory group argues that the task of management is to arrange the teamwork environment and empower the employees of the team so that professional employees can contribute their talents and individual KPI by directing their own efforts toward the team purpose.

From the interviews, we found out that Company A believes that human nature is essentially good and Company A's employees are self-actualising, so the management's responsibility is to provide a friendly working environment and much delegation of authority and encourages employees to self-evaluate and then volunteer to join any teams which are suitable to them. To Team A, Company A offered more intrinsic than extrinsic motivations. For example, joining Team A was a 'the best of the best' signal; conversely, monetary incentive is not that important to members of Team A. Team-members treat principals as idols for learning and agree with the company's vision and action. In addition, members of Team A follow the management's direction due to the management's reputation, not its authority. The management got fully involved and assisted the leader and members of Team A when the team-members asked for help.

Although the management trusts employees and believes they are self-actualising, the management still adopted control mechanisms, such as performance measurement systems. The management sets the project team performance measurement system for on-time decision-making and on-time improvement (see Figure 7.2 panel III uses or purposes). The management believes employees are self-actualising, but it does not mean it believes in whatever employees do is correct or matches the company's imagination. Therefore, trust and control co-existed. To Team A, the management pursued long-term performance enhancement and expected Team A could become a 'successful model' for other teams. Based on this discussion, Company A was more inclined to stewardship theory and adopted stewardship theory to Team A.

Company B believes that human nature is good, but no one likes to make money for others. According to corporate documents, Company B's vision is to 'empower' employees and pursue 'partnership.' However, the interviewees in Team B felt that the management merely delegates authority and treats professional employees as assets, not as partners. To Team B, Company B offered more extrinsic than intrinsic rewards. For example, monetary incentive is the dominant offer to members of Team B. Team-members treat other managers as 'bench-markers' and agree with the company's vision. In addition, members of Team B followed the management's direction more due to the management's authority. For example, even if the PM is not consistent with the CEO's decision, the PM will take the orders due to respect and institutional power.

The management got fully involved and assisted the leader and members of Team B when they asked for help. The management set the project team performance measurement system for on-time decision-making and NPD process control (see Figure 7.2 panel III uses or purposes). To Team B, the management pursued cost control and performance enhancement and expected that the output of Team B would bring media attention.

To sum up, Company B was more inclined to agency theory and adopted it to Team B. Similarly, as can be seen from Figure 7.3 Company C was more inclined to agency theory and adopted it to Team C. Contrarily; Company D was more inclined to stewardship theory and adopted it to Team D.

7.4   The level of self-categorisation and team identification

Figure 7.4 presents the level of self-categorisation and team identity of team-members and Teams A, B, C, and D. For example, our interviews indicated that members of Team A realised that they cannot be separated from the team task and responsibility for the output of Team A. Also, the members of Team A compared their team with other teams in their company and in other companies. In addition, the team-members expected that their performance will lead to achieving their team's purpose. Based on this self-categorisation, members of Team A had achieved strong team identity. That is, each member of Team A treated self as 'a part of team.'

Members of Team A understood that whatever their tasks are, the only output that the management wanted was a successful Note-book A. Also, the management paid much attention to the progress of NPD and the output of the team. For example, because senior managers go to 'Notebook A research room' and frequently ask about team progress, members of Team A felt that the management really cared about this project. As members of Team A voluntarily joined it and felt pride in being a part of the team, Team A had achieved a strong team identity. Figure 7.4 further explains why Team B had achieved a strong team identity and why this is not the case of Team C. Due to the level of self-categorisation and team identity, Team C adopted a vertical incentive system for controlling the employees of the teams. Contrarily,

	Team A	Team B	Team C	Team D
Self-categorisation Theory	1. Members realised that they cannot be separated from the team task and responsibility for the team output. 2. Members compared Team A with other teams. 3. Members expected that their performance will lead to achieving the team purpose.	1. Members involved in all tasks and cover teammates and realised: there is only one job – a successful product. 2. Members categorised themselves as a part of the team. 3. Members realised their performance will affect the team output and purpose.	1. Members took responsibility only for their own tasks. 2. Members compared own tasks with that of other team-members. 3. Members disagreed with the argument about 'our purpose' and 'our task.'	1. Members at first categorised themselves as a part of team and obligated to achieve 'our job' … then felt shame and turned into 'my job.' 2. Members compared themselves at first with other team-members then turned into Team D members.
Findings	Stronger 'A part of team'	Stronger 'A part of team'	'My job, my responsibility'	Stronger → Weaker
Social Identity Theory	1. Members understood their interdependent tasks and involved in all tasks. 2. Management fully involved on the team, paid attention to the progress and output of the team. 3. Members voluntarily joined Team A and felt pride in being a part of team	1. Members working on Team B with clear job descriptions. 2. Management assigned necessary resources to the team and cared about the team output. 3. Members were chosen to join the team and take pride to in being a part of the team.	1. Members knew their jobs by given clear job descriptions. 2. Members did not fe management was involved in teamwork. 3. Members were selected from different department and treated it as 'jobs.'	1. Members understood each other's tasks. 2. Members felt MGMT did not respect and care about the team due to management's attitude. 3. Eventually members of Team D spent time on looking for the next job.
Findings	Strong team identity	Strong team identity	Weak team identity	Strong → Weak identity

Figure 7.4   The Level of Self-Categorisation and Team Identity

Teams A and B used horizontal incentive systems. This is consistent with the literature.

The level of identity of Team D is an interesting case within the four teams. At first, members of Team D categorised themselves as a part of the team and obligated to achieve 'our job.' However, due to the free-riding problem and the management's attitude, professional members felt ashamed of being a part of the team and just focused on 'my job' rule. That is, after re-evaluation, members of Team D turned themselves into self-serving persons and Team D had a weak identity.

7.5 Developing an empirical framework

In this section we develop an empirical framework based on the findings of the four cases, see Figure 7.5. This framework explores the interactions of the project team measurement systems and the success/ failure of breakthrough products. Figure 7.5 identifies the structure of the team, organisational architecture, efforts, effectiveness, performance system, and the effect on the team output. The diagram in Figures 7.5 summarises how a project team is presumed to form and work. Although the boxes of the framework are shown in a linear way, the relationships among the boxes are expected to be complex, interactive, and recursive over time.

Milgrom and Roberts (1992) argue that three determinants of a company's external business environment – technology, markets, and regulation – will affect the company's strategy, which in turn helps to determine the organisational architecture. Further, Cohen and Bailey (1997) develop a framework that considers external environment factors, task design variables, team composition variables, organisational context variables, group processes, and group psychosocial traits for analysing the effectiveness of the teams. Lembke and Wilson (1998) argue that potential team-members are viewed only as individuals until they adopt a social identity and self-categorisation process. That is, social identity and self-categorisation theories describe a social contextual process of how individuals perceive the team and are motivated to work as a team.

From the findings of within-case and cross-case analyses (see Figure 7.1), before forming the breakthrough project teams, all four companies considered their internal corporate resources and external business environment first, and then determined their new product strategies to help to determine decentralised decision rights, compensation, and measures used to evaluate performance of the team-members and the team . That is, before forming Teams A, B, C, and D, Companies A, B, C, and D all

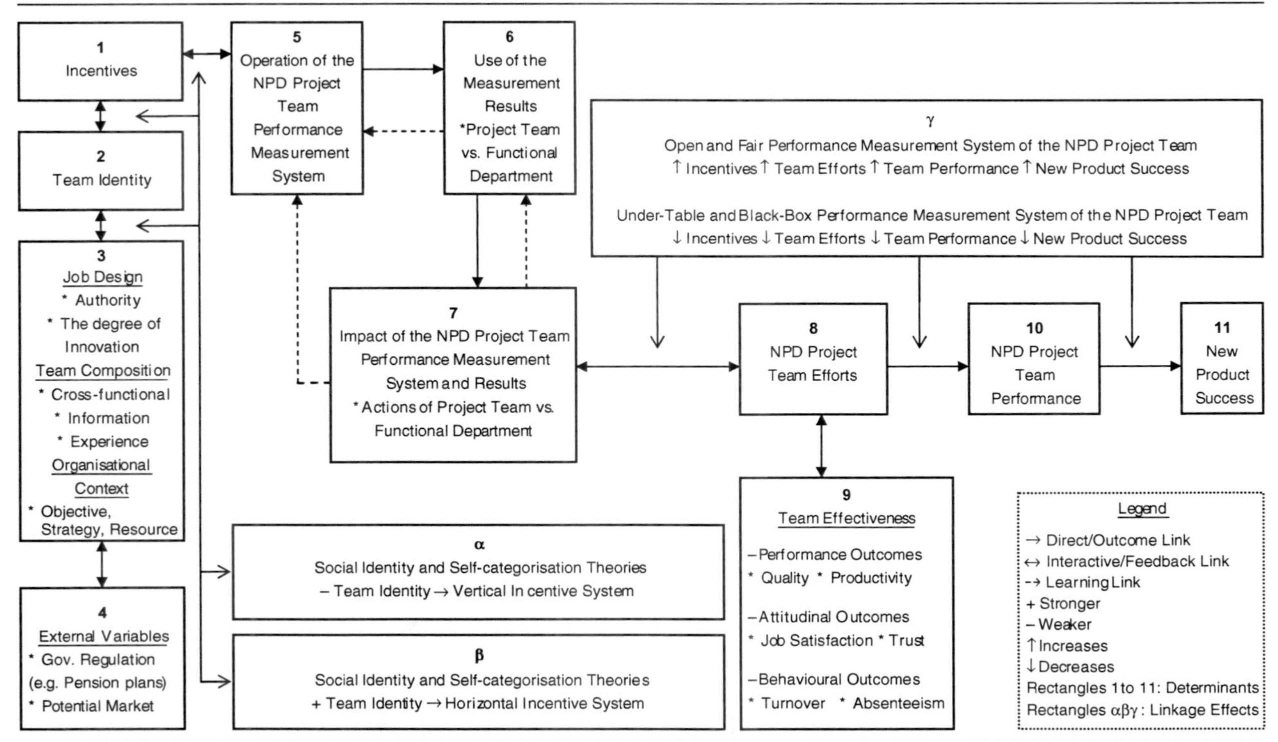

Figure 7.5 Empirical Framework for Studying the Team Measurement System

considered the factors in Figure 7.5, boxes 1 to 7. As such, our findings are consistent with the management literature.

Members of Teams A, B, C, and D have different levels of identity (see Figure 7.4) due to different reasons, such as corporate culture, management philosophy, etc. However, when joining a 'particular' team, individuals will categorise themselves and turn self into either 'a part of the team' or 'an employee of the team' as well as perceive their performance as 'my job' or 'our job.' That is, self-categorisation and social identity is a psychological process when joining a team and the members' perceptions of identification or performance could be changed or affected during the teamwork (e.g. members of Team D). In Figure 7.5, boxes α and β therefore show that the level of identity could be affected by the way a team is formed and the way the management deals with the members of the team. Two-way arrows show the interactive effects.

Towry (2003) suggests that when the team-members have established a strong team identity, delegating authority for control to the self-managed team and the team-members directly to control each others' actions (i.e. horizontal incentive system) is the most effective way for the company and the team. Alternatively, the team-members report observations of their peers' efforts to the senior management through reporting mechanisms (i.e. vertical incentive system) if the team has a low level of identity. That is, the strength of team identity helps to determine the effectiveness of the reporting mechanisms. This has been confirmed by our finding related to Team A. Team A has achieved a high level of identity and the team-members directly control each others' actions and the efforts and effectiveness (see Figure 7.5, boxes 8 and 9) of Team A are improved and the outcome (box 8, 10, and 11) of the teamwork is successful.

However, the findings related to Teams B and C on the reporting mechanisms showed that although both Companies B and C apply agency theory, any particular team may have its own way to run. Team B has achieved a high level of identity and team-members have delegated authority for mutual monitoring of each others' actions. The efforts and effectiveness (see Figure 7.5, boxes 8 and 9) of Team B with a strong team identity increased performance of Team B (box 10) and in turn increased (box γ) the success (box 11) of the team output. Conversely, Team C has not achieved a strong team identity and team-members mutual observation of each other's behaviour and reporting them to the management. However, the findings show that although Team C used the vertical incentive system for weak identity of Team C, the efforts and effectiveness of Team C have not improved and the performance of Team C has decreased and the team output failed financially.

Godener and Söderquist (2004) create a propositional framework, developed from the literature and the findings of their empirical study. They used the propositional framework to study, in particular, the operation of performance measurement system, as well as the use (and impact) of performance measurement results in (on) project teams and functions. Godener and Söderquist (2004) also suggest that a further study of the rational links of the three core elements of the framework: the operation of the measurement system, the use of the measurement results, and the impacts on the actions of the team-members help to gain a better understanding of the relationships of a complete performance measurement system. Our framework responds to this call for further study.

As depicted in Figure 7.5, boxes 1 to 7, α, and β help to address the first research question by examining how the company considers its internal and external business environment, determines the new product strategy, structures the new product project team, motivates and delegates authority to the employees of the team, and evaluates the actions of the team-members. Box 5 helps to address the second research question by studying what measures of performance the company uses for its breakthrough product project team and the team-members and why the company sets these measures. Boxes 5 to 11 help to address the third research question by examining how the company uses the results of the performance measurement and what impact it has on the actions of the project team and functions. The boxes 3, 5, 6 and 7 help to address the final research question by examining who evaluates the performance of the team-members.

Literature suggests that when analysing the effectiveness of a team, researchers need to consider internal corporate environment factors related to job design, team composition, and organisational context variables, as well as external business environment variables, such as technology, regulation, and markets. Business environment helps to determine new product strategy, such as the degree of innovation. In practice, as shown in Figure 7.5, our findings show that both business environment and new product strategy will affect organisational architecture (i.e. decision allocation, incentive and punishment, and performance measurement systems). Both the level of team identity and the results of performance measurement help to determine the effectiveness of incentive system. Two-way arrows connect the boxes to show the interactive effects.

The operation of the performance measurement system provides information to the management regarding the actions of the employees. The management uses the results of the performance measurement system for decision-making on compensation plans, investing or cancelling new product projects, replacing underperforming team-members, and so on. Further, when the management sets measures of performance for the team, team-members and their functions, the management should consider the impact of the actions of the employees. Since the team-members come from different departments within the company, the person who measures the performance of each team-member will affect the actions of all team-members.

The literature suggests that departmental managers measure their subordinates' performance and project managers just give suggestions about team-members' behaviour. That is, team-members could face a trade-off conflict between their functions and the project teams.

Obviously, when researchers study performance measurement systems of new product project teams, it will be helpful if they can integrate the operation of the performance measurement system, the uses of its results, and the impact on the behaviour of team-members and their functions. In our framework, a direct link one-way arrow connects the box for the operation of the performance measurement system to the next box concerning the use of the performance measurement results by the management. Relatively, a learning link one-way arrow connects the box concerning the use of the performance measurement results to the box concerning the operation of the performance measurement system for feedback and the use of its results. That is, management can learn and improve by getting feedback from their earlier decisions.

In theory, attractive incentives will increase team efforts and *vice versa*. However, in practice, simply increasing team efforts does not mean enhancing team effectiveness. Therefore, in Figure 7.5, the box for team efforts (i.e. box 8) interactively connects with the box for team effectiveness (i.e. box 9) to show that team efforts should be effective and measurable to the management. The last two boxes (i.e. 10 and 11) of this framework are outcomes of studying the performance measurement system of a new product project team. Furthermore, theoretically, incentives work by increasing team effort, which, in turn, leads to increase team performance and subsequently enhances new product success. In practice, an open and fair performance measurement system (see box γ) itself is an incentive to motivate the members of the team and then increase team effort, which, in turn, leads to increase team performance and subsequently enhances new product success.

A direct link one-way arrow connects the outcomes to the ultimate goal – new product success. These groupings show the practical relationships with each piece of the empirical framework with which they are connected and which they influence or be influenced by.

From the findings of cross-case analysis, the empirical framework shows that both Teams A and B follow the flows of the framework (boxes 1 to 11 and β) and gain the positive (increase) effects of box γ. However, Teams C and D follow the flows of the framework (boxes 1 to 5 and α) and achieve the reverse (decrease) effects of box γ. Accordingly, our analysis shows that an open and fair performance measurement system is the main difference between success and failure. From the interviews and documentary evidence, Companies A and B's open and fair project team performance measurement systems had successfully motivated the members of Teams A and B, provided feedback for the senior managers and the team-members, as well as signified that 'only the professional employees are an asset to the company.'

7.6   Conclusion

In this chapter, we first compared the internal and external environment of the four companies. The four companies considered internal and external variables before approving their breakthrough projects and forming breakthrough project teams. Then, we introduced the organisational architecture of the four companies. The assignment of decision rights and the reward and punishment system are similar in the four cases. All of the four companies set different performance measurement systems for individual project teams. The main divergence is that Companies A and B have similar open and fair project team performance measurement systems, but Companies C and D do not.

Further, we compared the four companies' presumption, level, assumptions of human nature, organisation, and information, and psychological and situational factors. Companies A and C are more likely to become stewards in principal-steward relationships. Conversely, Companies B and D are more likely to become agents in principal-agent relationships. Subsequently, we analysed the level of self-categorisation and team identity of team-members in the four cases. Teams A and B have achieved a strong team identity. Conversely, Teams C and D failed to achieve a strong team identity. Finally, we developed an empirical framework based on our findings. In the next chapter, we will discuss the overall results of the empirical study.

8
Discussion

8.0　Introduction

In Chapter 7, we undertook a cross-case analysis that has helped in developing an empirical framework. The events were staged in repeated cause-effect-cause-effect patterns to give general explanation that fits each of the individual cases, although the individual cases might vary or differ in their details. In this chapter, we further discuss issues related to this study in the following four sections.

This chapter is organised as follows:

- Validity and reliability
- The role of management accounting and management accountants
- Agents versus stewards
- The gap between theory and practice in management accounting
- Conclusion

8.1　Validity and reliability

In designing and conducting this multiple-case study, the construct validity, internal validity, external validity, and reliability of the research study have been considered and assessed. For construct validity, during the data collection research phase, the researcher first uses more than one source of evidence (i.e. interview and documentary evidence). In this case study, the validity of particular sources of evidence (i.e. the contexts of the interviews) was assessed by collecting supporting evidence (i.e. documentation) about these sources. That is, the validity of each piece of interview context evidence was assessed by comparing it with documentary evidence on the same topic. Next, we created a case study database and also established a chain of evidence to increase the reliability of the information in this empirical case study. Finally, the draft case study report was reviewed by key informants (e.g. the PMs and HR managers) during seminars, which were held after conducting all the interviews.

Once the construct validity of the research study had been assessed, the second test was to consider the internal validity. Internal validity is only a concern for an explanatory case study. As discussed in Chapter 5, this multiple-case study is not only exploratory but also explanatory. Therefore, we attempted to determine whether there is a causal relationship between project team performance measurement systems and new product success. However, because some events cannot be directly observed, we should infer that the particular events resulted from some earlier occurrence, based on interviews and documentary evidence collected as part of this empirical case study. For example, we cannot directly observe how the four companies propose, evaluate, and approve their breakthrough product projects. However, based on the documentary evidence and the logical analysis, we can infer that the four companies have similar evaluation procedures and considerations.

The interview context was not the only source of evidence. The National Central Library in Taiwan has many reference sources regarding the four sample companies and the four breakthrough products. In addition, the four sample companies allowed us to cross-check their relevant documentary information. Therefore, we were able to cross-check the context of interviews and the internal and external documentary evidence to see whether the documentary evidence is consistent with the context of the interviews. Fortunately, we obtained the same evidence from alternate sources (i.e. internal documents from private sources as well as external documents from public sources) and found the data supporting the original evidence (i.e. the context of interviews). Based on cross-checking results, we believe that the interview context and documents are trustworthy and convergent. That is, the same evidence comes from different sources and consequently it is sufficiently reliable.

Furthermore, our intention was to determine whether breakthrough product project team performance measurement systems led to breakthrough product success. If we incorrectly infer a causal relationship between the breakthrough product project team performance measurement system and breakthrough product success without knowing about other factors, this multiple-case study research design has failed to establish the internal validity. Therefore, during interviews, we discussed concerns with key informants and then carefully assessed how and why breakthrough product success resulted from the breakthrough product project team performance measurement system. This was done using logic figures to clarify the cause-effect-cause-effect relations of the key informants. Therefore, we believe that inferences drawn from the interviews and the documentary evidence collected are testable.

As this multiple-case study progressed, various themes and patterns (see Figure 6.1) emerged from the interviews and documentary evidence. We prepared figures intended to link the various themes and issues so that patterns could emerge. In this way, inconsistencies or disconnections can often be identified for us to investigate further. As more pieces of evidence were collected, we expanded the figures, adding new connections and reinterpreting the evidence collected earlier. Also, in the seminars, we showed and discussed the logic figures with key informants to ensure that we had considered relevant factors which may have caused new product success. That is, we attempted to get a limited but comprehensive report about incentive-effort-performance-success connections.

The purpose of this study is to determine whether an open and fair project team performance measurement system eventually led to new product success. Based on the predicted theoretical framework (see Figure 4.8), we attempted to find out whether the incentive-effort-performance-success relationship does exist in the four cases. In addition, based on the interviews and documentary evidence collected, we argued that there is a connection between project team performance measurement system and new product success. That is, the predictive theoretical framework does work in the four cases.

However, we also found out that something was missing in the predictive theoretical framework. Based on a pattern-matching logic, we explained why the relationship exists and what the key incentive is. Therefore, we logically concluded that there is a causal relationship between the open and fair project team performance measurement system and success of project team's output, i.e. new product.

Once the internal validity has been assessed, the third test was to consider the external validity. This case study relies on analytical generalisation. That is, we strive to generalise findings to some broader theory. The theory of the positive effects on an open and fair project team performance measurement system that led to Case A is the same theory that helped to identify Case B making the results generalisable. On the other hand, the theory of the negative effects of an unopened and unfair project team performance measurement system that led to Case C is the same theory that helped to identify Case D making the results generalisable. That is, we used replication logic in this multiple-case study.

Once the external validity of the research study was assessed, the final test was to consider the reliability. In this multiple-case study, we used case study protocol and developed a case study database. We provided detailed guidelines for designing and conducting this case study as well as analysing the interviews context and documentary evidence so the study could be repeated. In designing research study, the objective was to maximise the validity and reliability of the study so that the quality of the research design would be higher. By employing various tactics (e.g. using multiple sources of evidence, using logic models, etc.) to tackle construct validity, internal validity, external validity, and reliability, the researcher believes the quality of this case study is testable.

Additionally, credibility, transferability, dependability, and confirmability criteria were also used to evaluate the quality of this case study analysis. First of all, this case study was conducted in a manner that the four breakthrough product project team performance measurement systems were properly identified and described. We were involved in this study for four years. The five primary benefits of long-term research were persistent study of the project team performance measurement systems, depth of understanding, triangulation, multiple sources of data collection methods, and continuous seminars attended by interviewees and practitioners. The credibility criterion was considered and satisfied.

Secondly, the applicability of the empirical findings to other settings which are sufficiently similar to permit analytic generalisation was also considered and satisfied. This concern is related to the transferability of this holistic case study's findings. Comparing previous multiple theories with the empirical results of this multiple-case study, Cases A, B, C, and D were shown to support both self-categorisation and social identity theories. In addition, this research is generalisable to theoretical propositions. Therefore, the replication and the transferability criterion were considered and satisfied.

Third, this case study's processes were systematic, rigorous, and well documented. The research methodology used in this study, the data collection methods, and the techniques and procedures were used to analyse the data and were explicitly described in Chapter 5. Therefore, the dependability criterion was considered and satisfied.

Finally, the confirmability criterion was considered and fulfilled, because the research processes of this case study were fully described and it is possible to assess whether the findings flow from the data.

8.2 The role of management accounting and management accountants

Our empirical findings confirm the early discussion, in Chapter 1, regarding the existence of a gap between management accounting theory and practice. For example, all interviewees in the four companies perceived that the balanced scorecard strategic management concepts are too abstract and obscure in their meanings. Although Kaplan and Norton (1992, 1993, 1996) claim that when entirely deployed, the balanced scorecard transforms an organisation's vision and strategic planning from an academic exercise into action, practitioners still do not comprehend how to translate vision and strategy into action. All interviewees in the four sample companies agreed that the KPI concepts and processes are fluid and easy to understand and apply.

In Taiwan's high-technology industry, at the present time, most of companies adopt the KPI process rather than the balanced scorecard. Currently, most commercial, governmental, and non-profit organisations have also adopted the KPI process, because the KPI process is particularly simple. Managers prefer a simple and clear management system so that it is understood and accepted by subordinates. Some companies, for example, Companies A and B addressed this problem by holding training courses and promoting continuing education.

According to Maskell and Baggaley (2001), the traditional role of the management accountant is to collect and present financial data, and the traditional role of management accounting systems is focused on transaction-heavy inspection and reconciliation engines. Based on their work experience, Maskell and Baggaley also argue that the role of management accountants should move to team-member and change agent, and the role of management accounting systems should move to lean and vital providers of business insight. Certainly, in today's business environment, change is needed in the methods, approach, and function of management accountants if organisations are to gain competitive advantages in their fields. However, renovations such as new structures, responsibilities, work processes, etc. are not easily successfully implemented or generally accepted by employees of organisations.

In Companies A and B, senior managers such as CEO and PMs recognised that *continuing education* such as training courses held by human resource departments is an important factor in the spread of new management accounting concepts, such as pay by performance, and techniques, such as KPI. In order to develop a good understanding of the knowledge required and techniques available to facilitate managers in measuring and managing team performance within their team, the HR managers set course objectives and require all employees to attend the course (see Figure 8.1). Companies A and B argued that if employees understand and accept the new management accounting technique (i.e. the KPI process), they tend not to resist the new technique. Rather, employees attempt to achieve their tasks.

According to the empirical findings, design and implementation of the KPI performance measurement system was merely the first step for Companies A and B. PMs of Teams A and B understood that performance (including individuals and the entire team) is measured so that the individual and team efforts as well as allocation of corporate resources can be more sensibly managed. Also, managers of Companies A and B realised that the fair and non-discriminatory performance measurement system plays an important role in shaping the belief in each other, the teamwork and pay-for-performance culture, the transferring knowledge and sharing experience (both success and failure), and management commitment.

Although different project teams have different team purposes, one way of motivating and encouraging team-members towards a common team purpose could be similar, (i.e. to measure their performance) in achieving the team purpose. Management and the PM of the team should understand what the team's purpose is. Also, management and the PM of the team should have the knowledge and ability to appropriately stimulate the talents of their people and then assign suitable tasks to them (i.e. individual KPI objectives) in order to achieve the common team purpose.

Management accounting should include the preparation of financial statements and wide-ranging financial information, as well as financial management of the organisation within the management accounting function (Scapens, 1991). Such definition of management accounting is confirmed by our findings. In the four project teams, each member of the team is expected to contribute and play an essential role in shaping the strategies that would help the team to achieve its purpose and guide him or her to future profitability.

In fact, we found out that the interviewees were delighted about their companies' pay and reward structures. The main concerns were: 'How will management allocate *the team reward* to *each member of the team*? What will be the basis for rewarding? and Who will be the one to do this job?' It is normally expected that members of the team are concerned about compensation and reward allocation, because the reward for the team is based on team outcomes achieved, not individual tasks completed. That is, if an individual has completed his or her jobs, undoubtedly, he or she can obtain his or her 'base pay' which is low. If an individual can complete the job effectively, he or she can obtain a 'pay-for-performance' bonus. If an individual wants to obtain his or her shares of *the team reward*, the team outcomes must be achieved.

Despite this, most interviewees (team-members) of Teams C and D felt that 'I have done my share of the work (i.e. my individual objectives). I have no official rights to ask or command other members of the team to do what they should do so that we can achieve the outcomes. I want to achieve the team purpose and then get the reward for the team, but obviously not everyone in the team thinks the same way.' Professional team-members hope that project team performance measurement systems can catch free-riders or under-performance employees and consequently eradicate them. Also, some interviewees of Teams C and D felt that 'it is unfair that I got very little in reward for my hard work. I mean, the money [the team reward] was shared between team-members, but I was the one who saved my team-members. "Unfairness" makes me feel upset and encourages me to be a free-rider too.'

The interviewees of Teams A and B perceived that the quality and performance of their team-members were good and the allocation of the team reward and individual pay-for-performance was objective, reasonable, and acceptable. In fact, management of Companies A and B always encouraged internal communication by sharing both pleasant and disappointing stories. For example, Companies A and B set a 'sharing box' in the company's library so that employees could express their feelings anytime. Apparently, executives' sincere attitude and appropriate tone soothed employees who were wroth or indignant. As the CEO of Company A argued, 'human beings are actually animals with inevitable defects such as taking things for granted, emotions, etc. However, under normal situations, if perceived sincerity is maximised, people are more likely to cooperate with you.'

In addition, different project teams have different project team performance measurement systems, but the way and the objective of measuring performance for each team-member and each team could be similar – as objective as possible. For example, the individual performance of the non-management level in Company A was discussed using criteria such as achieved individual objectives, professional ability, as well as self-actualising ability. All interviewees of Team A perceived

Course Objectives	Suitable Participants
On completion of the individual/team/departmental Key Performance Indicators (KPI's) course individuals should be able to:	➢ Chief Executive Officers
➢ understand how individual/team/departmental objective(s), performance target, and weighting (%) should be linked to personal career planning or team purpose or overall organisation strategy	➢ Chief Financial Officers and Controllers
➢ understand that performance indicators are used as a measure of the achievement of objectives and targets	➢ Financial Analysts and Management and Cost Controllers
➢ understand that during *the KPI delegating authority process*, the majority of the positions vanish and new jobs are created	➢ Departmental Managers
➢ understand that *the KPI delegating authority and rewarding processes* focus on results and key outputs, teamwork (within and between departments), and staff (including management level and non-management level) empowerment/authorisation, and developing individual/team/departmental job descriptions	➢ Supporting Functional Managers and Staff
➢ understand that the outcomes from use of the results of KPI performance measurement can lead to changes in employee coherence and attitude, improvements information and service delivery, and improvements in managerial decision-making	➢ Project Managers
➢ understand that 'no pain, no gain' and 'your pay depends on your performance'	➢ Employees of the Company

Figure 8.1   KPI Training Course Objectives and Participants

that the three widespread perspectives were objective, reasonable, and acceptable. Their primary concern was: 'the results of performance measurement will be used as the basis for rewarding. Will management implement these criteria and performance indicators objectively?'

In fact, Teams B, C, and D used similar criteria to measure their team-members' performance. Coincidentally, most interviewees of Teams B, C, and D showed similar concerns. These interviewees were anxious as their salaries were determined by their performance results. Therefore, if the individual KPI performance measurement results could not be perceived as objective and acceptable, other performance measurement processes or techniques then lose credibility and are ignored or distorted by members of the team or even employees of the company. On the other hand, as long as members of the team perceived that management and the department of human resources tried their best to measure performance as objectively as possible, they were more likely to accept the subjectivity that unavoidably remains or exists in any organisation.

Companies A and B have similar KPI and information distribution processes. First of all, direct managers discuss the individual objectives with their people and then set for each of them reasonable and achievable individual objectives. After discussing and reviewing the agreed individual objectives, performance targets, and weighting, both managers and their subordinates must sign their names and make copies before giving them to the department of human resources. After three months (Company A) or six months (Company B), the results of individual KPI performance measurement was measured by both subordinates (i.e. self-assessment) and their managers. The results of the performance measurement were then sent to departments (each department as a unit) first and subsequently delivered to the department of human resources.

Horngren (1975) distinguishes between the role of cost accountant and management accountant. In practice, however, the role of cost accountant and management accountant is not unambiguous. During the interviewing process, we found that there were no such job positions called 'cost accountant' and/or 'management accountant' in the four sample companies. 'I think the finance experts in our company have played the role of cost accountants ... they provide countless accurate and estimated numbers (e.g. production costs and budgetary information).' The CEO of Company A explained.

Through observing the KPI and information provision processes, we realised that each employee plays an important 'management accountant role.' According to the management accounting literature (e.g. Maskell and Baggaley, 2001; Horngren, 1975; Ryan *et al.*, 2002; Scapens, 1991), the main role of management accounting and accountants is to provide relevant information to serve the needs of the internal users (e.g. managers) of modern businesses. For example, in the department of human resources, the results of individual performance measurement can be used to evaluate and then improve the human resource policies and practices, such as hiring procedures and training approval. To department heads, the results of individual performance measurement (the same information) can also be used to remove low-performing employees. That is, it does not matter who provided the information. As long as such information can help recipients (i.e. users) to make decisions, the provider plays the role of a management accountant – meeting management's need for information, including financial and non-financial.

In conclusion, according to our empirical findings, the role of management accountants (i.e. the PM, the department heads, the secretaries of department heads, and the HR staff) in project team performance measurement systems is to provide comprehensive information – fair, objective, simple, and focused information to effectively measure individuals and team performance. The roles of accounting information (including financial and non-financial information) and management accountants could change from time to time, because it hinges principally on the goals of the organisation and the needs of internal users of the business. However, whether it is relevant or useful accounting information depends on whether it helps managers to make better decisions, i.e. it meets the needs of decision-makers.

8.3   Agents versus stewards

Agency theory is adopted by managers who believe employees must be carefully monitored and controlled in order to obtain production. For example, in a company, if executives believe that the nature of employees is slothful and control is necessary, and if employees are *really* slothful, then the performance of individuals and the outcome of teamwork would be improved. We concur with this argument but wonder *how* executives can control or motivate slothful employees to work hard, improve their behaviour, and in turn increase team effort. In fact, adopting agency theory in a company does not turn slothful or apathetic employees into diligent and passionate members of the team. That is, applying agency theory to slothful and apathetic employees will not improve their performance. Utilising agency theory in this study helps to explore what the key incentives behind controlling systems to motivate employees.

Similar to agency theory, stewardship theory is also seen as a belief behind the organisation. If employees are self-actualising and do not want to be controlled, then when the company adopts stewardship theory, the performance of employees will improve. Towards a team, a company can only adopt either agency theory or stewardship theory. However, an NPD project team consists of members from diverse functions within a company. Therefore, for members of a team, it is possible that not all members are slothful and not all are self-actualising. If in a ten-member project team, five members are slothful, but another five are self-actualising and the company adopts agency theory for the team, then the outcome of the team will be mixed.

In an NPD project team, assuming all members are slothful, and the company believes human nature is essentially bad, the company utilises controlling systems to control members of the team. According to the principle of agency theory, the outcome of the project team should be successful. Assume in another NPD project team, all members are self-actualising and the company believes human nature is essentially good. According to the principle of stewardship theory, the output of the team should also be successful. That is, in theory, as long as the company properly exploits agency or stewardship theories, the efforts of the team will improve and in turn the outcome of teamwork will be successful. However, in practice, the above argument is not always realised.

In addition, although the objective of agency theory is to explain the behaviour of individuals as economic agents, the definition of the term 'agent' in management accounting research is not clear-cut. In Giddens' (1979; 1984) structuration theory, agency refers to an individual's ability to make a difference in the world, i.e. to act as a free human agent. However, the use of the term 'agent' in mainstream accounting research may be opposite to Giddens' assumptions. Ryan *et al.* (2002: 44) argue that 'the agent in agency theory is ... driven by axioms of economically "rational behaviour" to maximize expected utility ... [that is,] the "agent's" behaviour is predictable and determined by the laws of rational choice. In social theory, however, agency refers to the ability of the individual to act autonomously.'

Indeed, in practice, the meaning of the term 'agent' is 'an individual who is authorised to act for another through employment, by contract or clear authority or empowerment.' Under this practical definition, an 'agent' in practice could be an 'agent' in agency theory, which assumes that man is intrinsically self-serving, a 'steward' in stewardship theory, which assumes man is intrinsically self-actualising, or perhaps simply an emotional person. Everyone looks for a workplace where he or she perceives that he or she can accept or handle it (e.g. company's policies and procedures, management style, colleagues, etc.).

'No one was born to be a slothful person or a free-rider,' both the CEO of Company A and the AVP of Company B argued. 'He or she was spoiled by the rotten management control system.' The manage-ment control system in the context of this study is defined as the formal, information-based routines and procedures used by management to maintain and/or improve standards in organisational activities (Simons, 1987). That is to say, the management control system includes information relating to the assignment of decision rights, the pay and reward systems, the project team performance measurement systems, and so on. Assume an employee perceives that there is no clear authority and it does not matter how much work I do, we all get the same pay. Then, even if the employee was a self-actualising man, he or she would eventually change his or her attitude and concepts or prepare to leave the company. Free-riders or slothful people, however, would be happy to stay in the company.

In addition, a business does not want to employ a self-actualising or honest but inefficient or ineffective employee, because his or her performance is inadequate (i.e. does not meet requirements). Conversely, if the employee is an individualistic, opportunistic, self-serving, and/or selfish man, it does not mean that he or she would not work hard or would work inefficiently or ineffectively. In practice, the objective of job interviews is to find out whether the candidate's personalities and professional skills are suitable to the job position he or she applied for, rather than looking for a good man. What a company wants is a person who can contribute to the company.

In practice, similar job positions might require candidates who have different personalities but compatible professional skills. For example, in 2005, Company B had two R&D engineer vacancies, but management was looking for one engineer with good experience in designing prototypes, and another who is a prudent planner in putting the prototypes into action. Everyone has his or her talents or personal comparative advantages. If a good and experienced manager can find out and utilise them, the employee will appreciate it because he can do what he is good at. Additionally, shareholders would be very much delighted because the company benefits from the available talents. The result is a win-win situation.

Emmanuel *et al.* (1990) state that '… the interests of different groups are conflicting. Shareholders are interested in the return on their investment, employees in their wages, customers and suppliers in obtaining an advantageous price, and the local community in having a healthy local economy.' We concur with the first part of this quote 'the interests of different groups are conflicting.' However, we argue that different groups can happily coexist (or compromise) and align with each other on the condition that every group performs its tasks efficiently, i.e. plays its unique role well.

Shareholders are concerned about the return on their investment. Expectedly, shareholders desire to avoid wasting corporate resources and to cut unnecessary costs or expenses. In fact, diligent employees feel the same way. Conscientious employees are much happier to accept the 'do three people's work, get two people's pay' concept than 'get one-person's pay, do two people's jobs' (to cover free-riders or poor performers' work). To shareholders, the problem of moral hazard and adverse selection can be minimised if the company's hiring policies and procedures, pay and reward structures, and performance measurement systems work, i.e. hiring appropriate employees (or the right people) and/or transferring or sweeping low-performing employees (or wrong people) away. The hiring procedures are performed by the senior management. That is, it is management's responsibility to develop an easy teamwork environment for the employees of the company.

To hard-working employees, if management has provided an easy teamwork environment, the only thing the employees need to do is to expend expected efforts in the performance of their tasks. But these employees are still concerned with their salary. What they are concerned about is that 'I am required to expend maximum effort in the performance of individual KPI objectives, but will I receive a reward which fairly and objectively reflects the efforts I performed?' In this situation, if perceived 'openness and objectivity' is maximised, professional employees do not worry about their pay. What professional employees need to do is learn 'how to maximise effectiveness and reasonable work efficiency.[1]' At this time, the interests of shareholders and professional employees are aligned.

Smart customers are interested in obtaining an advantageous price, rather than the lowest price. That is, after comparing the quality and price of different brands of products, as well as the difference in after sales services, a smart customer will choose a product he or she perceives that is worthy to buy. If employees of a company co-work efficiently, the costs and expenses of the products should be at a minimum, but the quality of the products should be higher than other brands. So, the company can offer a reasonable sales price to customers. Currently, the interests of companies and customers have no conflicts. In brief, as long as every group can rationally play its role efficiently, the interests of different groups can be aligned.

It is not difficult to find out that previous agency theory and stewardship theory research seems to be based on one-best-way thinking, i.e. either stewardship theory is correct or agency theory is correct (Davis *et al.*, 1997). However, 'agency theory research is concerned with explaining observed accounting practices.' (Ryan *et al.*, 2002: 76). In addition, positivist agency theory researchers can help the practitioners to understand how the world works (Jensen, 1983). Management accounting researchers can help to explain the reasons for observed management accounting practices. Therefore, the purpose

---

[1]In this study, maximum effectiveness means doing the right things to achieve key objectives. Reasonable work efficiency means doing things right to avoid wasting corporate resources.

of this holistic multiple case study is to explore the specific context of the four cases, and to expand the understanding of the practical context and explain the reasons for observed accounting practices.

In the real-world, everyone works for his or her own interests. Selfishness is just one kind of human nature. Saying a person is selfish does not mean that the person will not work hard for the company. The interests are conflicting due to different groups, but it does not mean that there is no win-win situation for different groups. In practice, at present, most high-technology companies in Taiwan adopt KPI processes to delegate authority, set pay and reward structures, and to evaluate the performance of individuals, teams, and departments (or divisions). Indeed, organisations in Taiwan tend not to use the conventional wisdom of management accounting promoted in the academic literature, because management realises that every employee has his or her talents and needs.

After self-assessment, considerations, and discussions with his or her superior, a mature employee should have enough knowledge to decide how much work he or she can handle within a specific period of time. If an employee asks for more individual KPI objectives, he or she has a chance to get more money on the condition that he or she can meet or exceed or substantially exceed requirements. The employee must make sure that he or she can complete those individual KPI objectives in an efficient and effective way; otherwise he or she may get a negative result. The project team performance measurement system evaluates individual job performance and achievement against individual KPI objectives over a definite period of time (e.g. three months in Company A and six months in Company B).

In addition, in theory, an individual is evaluated only in terms of his or her controllable performance, i.e. an individual needs to take responsibility only when he or she has official rights to make decisions (Scapens, 1991). However, such 'decision-making behaviour and responsibility' in practice does not always represent reality.

As discussed during interviews and as documents revealed, the procedures regarding the approval of breakthrough product projects as well as preparation and structure of the breakthrough product project teams in the four cases are prudent and similar. In addition, the delegation of decision rights to the PM and members of the team, and the design of reward and pay structures of individuals and team are acceptable to the PM and members of the four teams. Therefore, the project team performance measurement system is seen as dissimilar in each of the four cases.

During the third seminar conducted in the four case study sites, the interviewees and managers of Companies C and D admitted that they currently use KPI processes for individuals (both non-management and management levels), project teams, departments (or divisions), and the organisation itself. Since the beginning of 2005, Companies C and D started to implement the KPI processes. After implementing the KPI processes, according to the PM of Team C, 'we found that our team purpose is more focused. The action and behaviour of members of the team is more efficient. The performance of the team-members and the team is more accountable and competitive.' At the same time, the PM of Team D argued that 'when employees trust management, employees are inclined to conquer the fear of new management techniques.'

In fact, after implementing KPI processes, Companies C and D gained many benefits. The companies emphasised that an open and fair project team performance measurement system improves communication between department heads, the PM, and members of the team, as well as helps to identify and plan training needs for individuals and the team. The KPI process and performance measurement identify potential for the future, assist with employees' career planning, and provide effort into payment. An open and fair project team performance measurement system is seen as a competitive advantage in a company. It motivates members of the team to achieve the team purpose and makes members of the team believe that everyone has his or her talents and the goals of the team cannot be achieved unless everyone works together.

8.4 The gap between theory and practice in management accounting

According to Ashton *et al.* (1995), during the late 1950s to the mid-1970s, academics believed that scholars could help to solve the problems that practitioners face. During the early 1980s, there was a significant gap between the theoretical approaches in management accounting textbooks and the methods used by practitioners. During the 1990s, research by academics and practitioners drew significant attention in scholarly literature, but relatively less attention in the academic press. The challenges of globalisation and international competition, the rapid development of technologies, mergers, and the speed of process and product innovations transform management techniques and accounting systems. Ashton *et al.* (1995) observe that academic concern over the perceived gap between theoretical approaches and realistic methods in practice has led to major changes in economic-based management accounting research and to the improvement of other theoretical approaches.

As argued by Ashton *et al.* (1995), the design of accounting systems needs to be connected to the characteristics and environmental context of the organisation and to the motivation and performance evaluation within it. They recommend that a rational model of organisational reality should include environmental factors, organisational processes and structures, the role of human beings, and a predictable system of variables and rules governing their interaction. However, there are some limitations to theoretical assumptions. For example, agency theory helps explore conflicts over control and the contribution of motivation and information, but 'the model of motivation adopted is still that of the "rational economic man" – motivated by self-interest and trading-off his greed against his dislike of work.' (Ashton *et al.*, 1995: 11). Ashton *et al.* (1995) argue that this is nevertheless a naïve and limiting view of motivation.

Scholarly writing needs to stick firmly to the point, such as using only one topic, one theory, and one method. It is possible that scholars attempt to avoid too much detail but neglect some important factors or concerns. The following subsections, using key findings of the four sample cases, gradually give in-depth team descriptions regarding what key success factors mean to practitioners and how to align interests of employees and shareholders by delegating authority and designing open and fair pay structure and performance measurement systems. In addition, by interviewing senior managers in the four sample companies and four project teams, we found some interesting arguments regarding why practitioners agree with academics, but do not practice accordingly.

According to the findings of the four cases, open and fair performance measurement systems of project teams motivated the employees of Teams A and B, which in turn increased new product success. Explicitly, an open and fair performance measurement system in this study is the 'key success factor' for new product success or failure. The term 'key success factor' is a key term for the four sample companies, and its use is encouraged by senior management to describe a competitive advantage that Companies A and B have, but Companies C and D do not. That is, a key success factor for Teams A and B is an incentive which motivates the employees of the team, increases team effort, raises team performance and effectiveness, and eventually promotes a successful new product.

Collins (2001) argues that good-to-great companies understand that the decisive throttle on growth is not markets, or technology, or competition, or products: 'It is one thing above all others: the ability to get and keep enough of the right people.' (Collins, 2001: 54). An open and fair performance measurement system creates a good linkage effect. However, an unofficial or concealed project team performance measurement system produces a contagious effect for the team and even the company. A 'key success factor' is an invisible hand which promotes team effectiveness and performance, which in turn produces a successful team output and attracts professional employees to contribute their talents to the company. The essential message is that professional employees and fair accounting systems interact and influence each other.

The responsibility of senior management is to develop an appropriate corporate culture, to create an easy working environment, to build an open and fair organisational architecture, and to provide a useful means of communication, because only the executive has authority to make managerial decisions. From the authority and responsibility viewpoints, many new product success or failure factors are actually the executive's responsibility. When senior management delegates authority to employees of the team, the assigning task of the senior management has been done, and the task of the team's employees has started. Therefore, the decision rights assignment needs to be clear and successfully put into effect, i.e. a proper decision allocation system should delegate authority.

Empowering means providing employees at all levels within the company with the management accounting information they need so that they can make decisions themselves. In addition, empowerment or authorisation-with-responsibility will make decision allocation systems work effectively. For example, when a company's president makes a merger and acquisition decision, although the CEO does not agree, the CEO will still support and respect the president's decision, because the president has been authorised by the board of directors. If the president makes a good decision (i.e. increasing corporate overall performance), the president can gain a pay-for-performance bonus; however, the president needs to take responsibility (e.g. resign) if he makes a wrong decision. Naturally, the employees at all levels will make decisions carefully and consider the company's interests.

In their paper, Lembke and Wilson (1998: 927) establish that 'teamwork is a function of how team members perceive the team and their role in it.' Lembke and Wilson (1998) utilise social identity and self-categorisation theories to explain the cognitive, evaluative, and emotional processes which motivate individuals to think and work as a team and contribute to the team to the maximum of their ability, which would be advantageous for team purposes. In addition, the premise of Towry's (2003: 1070) study is that 'the effectiveness of [horizontal or vertical incentive systems] depends on the degree to which team members have established a strong psychological attachment, or *team identity*.' Towry (2003) goes on to say that individuals may perceive team tasks assigned by the company as 'a part of the job' or perceive themselves as 'a part of the team.'

In the four cases, the structures of the cross-functional project teams showed the delegation of authority to the employees of the team. In addition, the mutual monitoring systems show the level of team identity in the four cases. Delegating authority and taking responsibility helps employees of the team understand their tasks for the team, and eventually their goal is to work well together and achieve the team's purpose. Even if all of the employees of the team are the right people, the company still needs to give clear job descriptions and appropriately empower them so that they understand their tasks. If all of the employees of the team are inappropriate, the company certainly needs to delegate authority so that they can take responsibility for their actions.

Davis *et al.* (1997: 26–27) find that 'the mixed support for agency and stewardship theories suggests a need to reconcile these differences.' Davis *et al.* (1997) explain that the principal-agent interest divergence or the principal-steward interest convergence may not hold for all members of the team. In this multiple-case study, one of stewardship theory cases produce successful a new product and one of agency theory companies are profitable public companies. Therefore, we do not argue about either agency theory or stewardship theory as the one-best corporate governance system, because both agency and stewardship theories are based on different assumptions on human nature, and adopting agency theory or stewardship theory depends on executives' beliefs, corporate culture, and management philosophy. The essential intention is to find an incentive that encourages members of the team to enhance their ability to contribute to the team.

Kohn (1993: 54) says that 'incentives do not alter the attitudes that underlie our behaviours.' Accordingly, the incentive is the cause of the problem which exists in the company and may rupture the relationship of supervisors and subordinates and the development of teamwork. In the four cases, Companies A, B, C, and D all offered attractive and similar incentive plans to their project teams, but Cases A and B produced successful new products. Findings in Cases C and D suggest that incentive plans cannot work, because Companies C and D failed to offer open and fair performance measurement systems. The essential message from the findings of this multiple-case study is that an attractive incentive plan cannot work without both a proper decision allocation system and an open and fair performance measurement system.

Many organisations in Taiwan propose 'pay revolution' due to the new pension system which started on July 1, 2005. Under the old pension system, which was based on the Labour Standards Law, contributions to employee retirement funds must be paid into a common fund managed by the Taiwanese government, but an employee will lose the benefits if he switches employers or the company he works for goes into bankruptcy. The new pension system, which is based on the Labourers' Pension Law, requires employers to deposit a minimum of 6% of an employee's monthly salary (i.e. base pay) into the employee's individual retirement fund. Obviously, every organisation regards the legal requirement for monthly deposits under the new pension system as a heavy financial burden.

The monthly deposit to an individual's retirement fund is based on an employee's salary, so employers are reorganising their pay structures (see Table 8.1). The base pay is reduced in order to decrease company contributions to individual retirement funds and the heavy financial burden to a company. The new pay structure has raised concerns among both professional and non-professional employees. Non-professional employees fear that they will need to work harder to get enough money or a higher salary. However, professional employees view the new pay structure as a fair opportunity and a sign that the company cares about nothing but ability.

As depicted in Table 8.1, employees at three levels present the decision allocation system within the company. Senior and middle managers and employees have different tasks and responsibilities to the company, so they desire a different level of base pay and bonus. The visible base pay is very low, so employees at all levels certainly will work hard to gain the pay-for-performance bonus. The floated weight percentage of incentives demonstrates that as long as employees have the ability, the company does not care about age, gender, background,

Table 8.1 Pay Revolution

	Pay Structure	
	Base Pay	Pay-for-Performance
Senior Management Level	20%	80%
Middle Management Level	40%	60%
Non-Management Level	60%	40%

or the work experience of employees. The new pay structure clearly combines assigning decision rights to the employees of the team and attractive incentive plans. In addition, the new pay structure is designed to align with shareholder's interests. The salary of a diligent professional is unlimited if he/she achieves the goals which align with the shareholders.

Under the new pay structure, the concern of the employees is not the incentive plans any more. Conversely, what employees suspect is the quality of the performance measurement system. The salary, which includes base pay and pay-for-performance bonus, is determined by the results of the performance measurement. So, employees are sensitive and curious about how the performance is evaluated and by whom. If an attractive pay structure is a commitment by the management to the employees, an open and non-discriminatory performance measurement system should be a sign that shows the management's determination to effectively implement the new pay structure. Professionals will enhance their abilities and contribute their maximum potentials to the company that utilises the 'pay-for-performance' policy.

In practice, incentive plans are always attractive and similar in Taiwanese high-technology companies. When attractive incentive plans do not attract employees any more, good high-technology companies investigate why incentives cannot increase effort and performance. Average high-technology companies determine that incentives are useless. In Cases C and D, due to the unfair performance measurement systems of project teams and the attitudes of the management, members of the teams do not even believe in their companies any longer. If the company can make individual employees of the teams believe that the company will fairly pay team-members by their performance, the effort, effectiveness, and performance of the teams will increase and in turn achieve the team purpose.

Bonner and Sprinkle (2002: 303) 'review[ed] theories and evidence regarding the effects of (performance-contingent) monetary incentives on individual effort and task performance.' Bonner and Sprinkle observed that empirical evidence indicates monetary incentives have widely varying effects on effort, but do not improve performance. In addition, researchers (e.g. Kohn, 1993) examined the effects of incentives on individual performance, but found mixed results regarding the effectiveness of incentives. Researchers (e.g. Bonner and Sprinkle, 2002) emphasise the need to examine the effects of monetary incentives on effort and performance, or the relationships between monetary incentives, effort, and performance. However, few studies inquire '*how* monetary incentives lead to increases in effort' (Bonner and Sprinkle, 2002: 305), or *how* the organisational architecture can be designed to motivate and in turn increase the effort and performance of employees.

The floated pay-for-performance structure implies that salary depends on performance of the employees. That is, under an attractive floated pay structure and open and fair performance measurement systems, higher salary represents higher-quality performance and recognition by the management. Diligent professional employees get a reasonable salary; conversely, slothful or underperforming employees get base pay only. Using overall year-end performance evaluation or a down-sizing plan or shaping policy, employees who are under-performing will be dismissed by the company or quit by themselves. That is the reason why Companies A, B, C, and D authorise employees to decide whether to take the tasks and join the new product project teams. In this case, the company logically aligns employees and shareholders' interests and in turn distinguishes the right people from the wrong people.

During 40 hours of interviews, the 33 informants mostly focused on issues regarding NPD performance measurement systems of project teams, but they also raised five interesting matters. To begin with, Taiwan's government regards capitalism as the only social system consistent with man's rational nature and a basis on the principle of private property and individual rights. A government's job is to protect people's rights rather than to compensate slothful people through social benefits. According to the actions and attitude of the government, the Taiwanese believe that they have to work hard so that after retirement they can look after themselves and their heirs. In practice, a diligent employee will not argue about salary. According to the informants, a diligent employee wants longer working hours and a non-discriminatory evaluation.

The second finding was that a company is under pressure when stakeholders want their relatives to work in the company. The senior managers in the four cases usually accept and hire stakeholders' relatives due to culture-related pressure, but executives also emphasise that the company offers a 'performing area' rather than a 'permanent employment' to their relatives. Underperforming and/or non-professional employees eventually will leave the company as long as management is determined on pay-for-performance policy and open and fair performance evaluation. In addition, Companies A and B believe that slothful employees or free-riders are spoiled by incapable management and an ineffective organisational architecture.

Third, many high-technology companies in Taiwan are meeting the challenge of economic recession by controlling costs through reducing labour costs and shrinking administrative expenses. Some famous public high-technology companies set unreasonable measures for controlling costs. For example, employees at the basic level should go to the toilet no more than three times per day and employees of the marketing department must spend a specific amount of time walking during the course of the day, and so on. However, it is very difficult for employers to observe the actions and performance of the employees all the time. Employees colluded and evaded employers, because the rules are irrational and unachievable. Under this irrational mechanism, employees will not contribute the maximum of their ability to the company, and the company cannot succeed at reducing costs.

Fourth, academic research is divorced from practice under some circumstances. The CEO of Company A recalled that around 1977, researchers proposed that one way to enhance Taiwanese high-technology industry's competitive advantage was to develop semiconductor components in Taiwan. However, the CEO of Company A suspected the academic argument. At that moment, Taiwan did not have enough capital to develop a semiconductor industry, enough ability to control the market, and no mature skills to develop, design and process the technology. That is, although practitioners knew the importance of semiconductor components for Taiwan, the high-technology industry in Taiwan did not have the ability to afford the investment risk regarding critical components.

Finally, in Taiwan, not too many companies currently use the balanced scorecard system. Since the 1990s, the balanced scorecard system has been discussed in many academies of business and has been successfully used in many companies, because both scholars and practitioners believe that the balanced scorecard system has provided a more thorough way to measure performance by quantifying what had been considered intangible assets, such as human capital, information, and culture. Undeniably, since the 1990s, the balanced scorecard system has been adopted by many companies in Taiwan for different reasons. However, later on, most Taiwanese companies abandoned the balanced scorecard system. During interviews, the key informants also claimed that in Taiwan, the balanced scorecard system is not very popular or helpful. 'What I mean is that the balanced scorecard system did not bring the effect and outcome which we expected to us,' the AVP of Company B explained.

The key informants in the four companies perceived that balanced scorecard model is too abstract. The idea is sound, but it is difficult to implement. For example, every professional employee knows that the goals of each business unit should cohere with corporate goals, and the individual objectives should not be opposed to the common purpose of the team. However, in the real-world, an R&D engineer could have more than ten cases on hand, and he or she could sacrifice some cases to save other important or profitable cases.

In addition, the four companies were established by Taiwanese. The senior managers of the four companies want to develop management systems that are suitable to Taiwanese employees and cultural beliefs. Perhaps, not all American management accounting techniques can be successfully transferred or accepted by Taiwanese managers.

From literature, balanced scorecard system as depicted by Kaplan and Norton (1992; 1993) makes effective measurement an integral part of the management process, and enables translating of a company's vision and strategic objectives into sets of performance measures. Kaplan and Norton (1993) claim that balanced scorecard system draws strength from four different perspectives – the financial, customer, internal business processes, and learning and growth, from which to choose measures. Also, Kaplan and Norton (1996) further explain that balanced scorecard system contains three levels of information. The first level pictures the corporate objectives, measures, and goals. The second level translates corporate goals into goals of each business unit. The third level requires both individuals and teams to cohere which of their own objectives would be consistent with the business unit and the corporate objectives. However, in reality, most Taiwanese managers felt that balanced scorecard model is too abstract.

In fact, theory and practice could be not so far apart, on the condition that management accounting researchers have an accurate understanding of the current business environment, the constraints of accounting techniques on the company's activities, and the considerations involved in the election to use or not use simplistic scenarios or complicated mathematical models. That is, in developing new management accounting concepts, techniques, and information, researchers have to identify the information needs and academic knowledge of managers. The researcher explores the relationship of project team performance measurement system and the output of the project team, as well as offering explanations of existing practice. This thesis has focused on issues of direct interest to practitioners and related to their needs, such as how to make their companies more efficient, how to motivate and keep professional employees, and so on.

By tracing and reviewing the development of management accounting, we understand why there are gaps between theory and practice, and what the changing nature regarding the issues in management accounting is. Researchers should pay attention to the complexity of understanding accounting knowledge and practices, and the rapidly changing nature of a series of issues regarding how social factors (e.g. groups, cultures, reward and punishment systems, and the like) affect performance. In conclusion, to close the gap between theory and practice in management accounting, the role of management accounting researchers is to seek to provide 'one step earlier' new accounting concepts, techniques, and information to internal users of organisations.

8.5 Conclusion

After critical reflection and discussions, we infer that an open and fair project team performance measurement system could improve the performance of members of a project team and in turn motivate the members of the team to achieve a common team purpose – producing a successful new product. In addition, it does not matter what kind of person an individual is; if the individual wants to keep the job and get pay-for-performance salary, the individual must complete his or her 'individual objectives' effectively and efficiently. Certainly, the premise is that the company implements an open and fair performance measurement system. If a company distributes the pay among the team-members without considering individual contribution to the team and team output, even professional employees will not contribute extra time for the team. In the end, the company will lose its important assets – professional employees.

In the next chapter, we attempt to connect the empirical work completed, the original research questions, the previous work examined and discussed in the literature chapters, and the new work emerging since this study began. Also, we revisit research questions and give possible answers. In addition, we explain some implications for policy and practice.

9
Conclusions

9.0 Introduction

This chapter summarises the main findings of the study, provides some recommendations, sets out research contributions, shows research limitations, and identifies future research opportunities. The chapter is organised as follows:

- Insights and findings
- Research questions revisited
- Contributions and implications
- Limitations and improvements
- Opportunities for future research
- Conclusion

9.1 Insights and findings

As an old Chinese saying goes, 'it is better to be the head of the chicken than the tail of the ox.' It seems that Taiwanese prefer to be the boss in their own small shops than to be employees in a large company, so most Taiwanese companies always follow a decentralised management model. In addition, the trend of global competition, the development of international products, and the customers' demands for new products have increased the benefits of decentralisation for most international high-technology companies. However, due to diverse assumptions about human nature and concepts of management, executives adopt different levels of control mechanisms. Our findings show that adoption of either agency or stewardship theories leads to diverse management styles, and they do not necessarily contradict each other. This finding is consistent with the literature.

Research (see for example, Davis *et al.*, 1997; and Eisenhardt, 1989) shows that agency theorists believe control is necessary and useful to reduce agency costs. Conversely, stewardship theorists believe that controlling people by any means will not completely succeed. Based on the assumptions of agency theory, companies authorise and assign appropriate employees to suitable project teams. However, due to the management's style of control and the assignment of decision rights, team identity level is weak, and companies certainly need mechanisms to report to the management to help with decision-making. Alternatively, using the assumptions of stewardship theory, companies discuss the requirement of being members of project teams with employees and then empower them so that they can be independent professional employees and learn to take responsibility for their actions. The empirical findings confirmed the earlier research and revealed that both Case B (agency theory) and Case A (stewardship theory) are successful.

The literature shows that social identity and self-categorisation theories help align team-members with the team to achieve a common team goal (see Lembke and Wilson, 1998, for example). The findings show that the four sample companies use their own ways to motivate individuals to join a team, use their skills to performing their team tasks, and then achieve the team purpose. The level of team identity could be influenced by corporate culture, management philosophy, the structure of a team, leadership, and the management style of a PM, and so on. The findings show that team identity is an indispensable process when structuring a project team in the four sample companies. After adopting cognitive and evaluative processes, when the project team has achieved a strong team identity, the most effective way for management to control or evaluate the performance of a team is horizontal in nature and *vice versa*. Literature (see Towry, 2003, for example) and practice are consistent in this aspect.

Literature (see for example, Griffin and Page 1993; 1996) reveals more than 70 factors of new product success/failure. However, in practice, some so-called new product success/failure factors are actually management's basic obligations to employees. For example, in these four cases, both successful and failed cases have achieved the commitment of the senior management involvement, the effectiveness of the structure of the project team, the assignment of a capable project manager and appropriate professional employees, the obligation of corporate resources, communication with NPD processes, and so on. Organisational architecture (e.g. the NPD process, corporate culture, internal and external resources, technology, rewards, incentives, etc.) is management's task and responsibility, as executives have managerial decision rights in NPD practice and on significant policies.

Hayes *et al.* (2005) argue that executives are responsible for the strategic direction of the organisation. They argue that executives play various roles during the process of a project, and their choices shape the nature of their interaction with the project team. To begin with, one management task is mentoring, because before many senior managers got to be senior, they were experienced and successful at running projects. In the second place, during project reviews, executives collaborate in problem-solving between the project teams and other NPD participants. Thirdly, given the cost, risks, and impact of NPD projects on overall company performance, executives play a very legitimate role in their governance and decision-making.

Not all new product projects require senior management involvement, review, and control. There could be many new product projects within a high-technology company, but the use of project teams depends on the level of product innovation the company pursues. That is, if a company does not have a high level of corporate resources, such as a budget, technology, people, etc., there is no need for the company to arrange a breakthrough product project. Responsible executives will evaluate the company's conditions before making any managerial decisions. The senior management takes the final responsibility for the output of a project team. Findings show that a critical new product success/failure factor in the four cases is an incentive that motivates employees of the team, enhances the effectiveness and performance of the team, and in turn promotes the success of the team outcome.

From the structure of a project team, senior management connects external factors (e.g. potential market, technology, and government regulations) and internal considerations (e.g. new product strategy, senior management involvement and determination, corporate resource allocation, and organisational architecture). Each member of a project team could be an indicator of the performance of executives. That is, the performance of executives is evaluated through the structure of a project team. For example, if the quality of the structure of a project team and the effectiveness of senior management involvement are low, executives should take responsibility. Delegating authority and taking responsibility should be equivalent so that the members of the team will perform their tasks deliberately and make relevant decisions appropriately.

Key findings show that an open and non-discriminatory performance measurement system includes the design of measures, the operation of the performance measurement, the use of performance measurement results, and their impact. The senior managers in Cases A and B argued that as the old saying goes, 'people do not do what you expect; they do what you inspect.' Therefore, capable senior managers should review the purpose of the performance measurement results and assess their impact on the actions of the team employees and functions so that unproductive performance measures can be modified in time. The findings show that a great company is able to foresee the linkage or spill-over effects of a performance measure and also manage unexpected effects. In addition, the design of performance measures is always reasonable and acceptable to the employees. However, the essential message is that even perfectly designed performance measures could be useless without effective implementation.

9.2 Research questions revisited

Within-case analysis provides in-depth NPD project team descriptions of each case study. In addition, cross-case analysis compares success-versus-failure groups and finds the differences between the two groups. In this section, the question-and-answer format provides direct answers to the original set of research questions and helps to understand the findings of this study.

> Q1: In computer companies' settings, how are project teams formed and how do they work, including preparation before forming the teams, and to what extent is authority delegated to the teams?

The structure of the breakthrough product cross-functional project team is more-or-less similar within the four cases. As depicted in Figure 9.1, a team is formed (i.e. a project is approved) after considering the possibility of an idea, the appropriateness of corporate resources (e.g. the project budget and the talents of employees), the size of the potential market, the teamwork environment, and the innovative climate and culture. All of the interviewees of the four cases agree that different companies have diverse degrees of product or process innovation, so evaluating internal corporate and external environmental conditions are prerequisites in their companies. When the cross-functional project team is structured and the breakthrough product project is set, senior managers evaluate this NPD project at the end of each NPD process in order to determine whether it is worthwhile to continue investing.

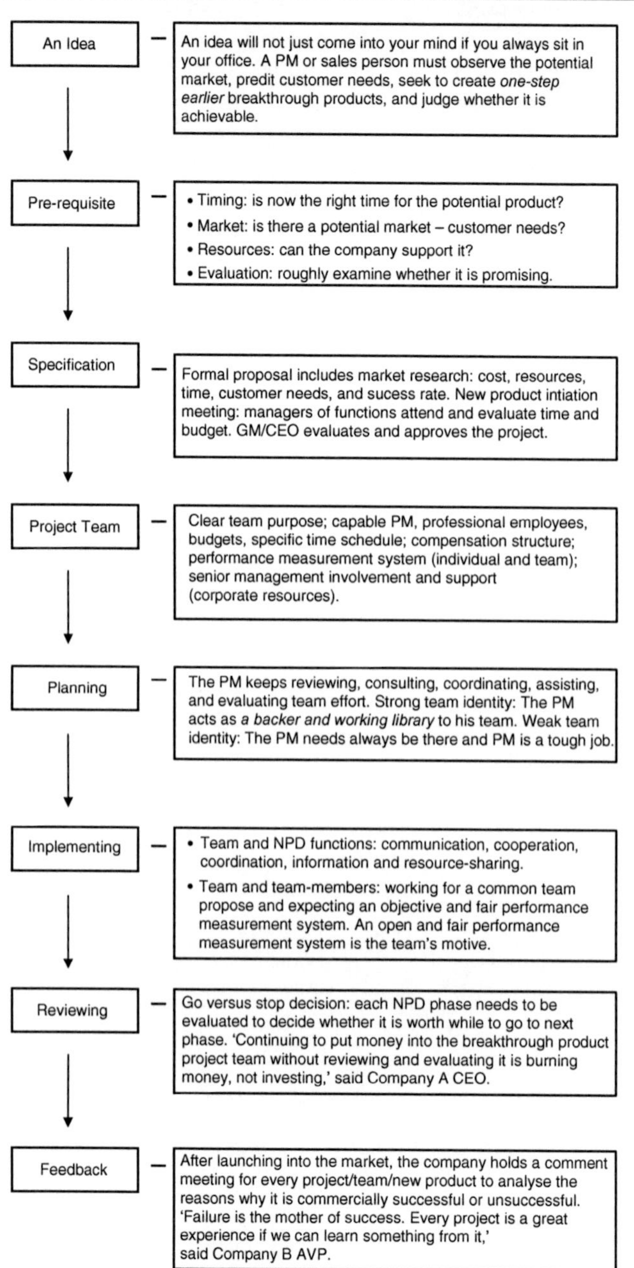

Figure 9.1　Project Thinking

When a new product project is started, a project team is structured to implement it. Practically, before a breakthrough product project is set, the company must evaluate both internal and external variables to see whether it is a good time to proceed with such a big project. Thus, those so-called 'key success factors' for winning NPD business in the literature are essentially prerequisites for forming a cross-functional project team. Regarding the four sample companies, NPD is a senior management level's responsibility, as executives can make managerial decisions, such as approving or terminating NPD projects. Therefore, executives who were interviewed from the four sample companies perceived that key success factors refer to critical causes which motivate team employees to achieve the team purpose and the corporate goal. Figure 9.2 shows the differences between the literature examined and the practices being investigated.

Companies A, B, C, and D all delegate authority to the employees of their cross-functional project teams, but the degree of delegation is different due to diverse assumptions about human nature and management philosophy. The stewardship theory companies (Cases A and

Literature (see Figure2.1; Figure 2.2; Cooper and Kleinschmidt, 1995) Key Success Factors	Practice Findings of Four Cases
I. Strategic Factors: Availability of resources New product strategy R&D spending for NPD	I. Strategic Factors: Executives take responsibility for strategic decisions. Basic considerations before approving a project and forming a team.
II. NPD Factors: Senior management involvement A high-quality NPD process Speed to market Financial/business analysis	II. NPD Factors: One of the tasks of the senior management is to arrange and check each process of NPD, set realist timetable for the team and functions. Senior management involvement is a basic requirement.
III. Internal Factors: An empowering high-quality project team An innovative climate and culture Communication of team and functions	III. Internal Factors: Creating a direct communication, an easy teamwork, an innovative environment is the senior management's responsibility.
IV. External Factors: Potential market Government regulation	IV. External Factors: Before approving a project, market research is used.

Figure 9.2   The Issue of Key Success Factors: Literature versus Practice

D) fully decentralise, empower, and delegate authority to the employees of project teams so that team-members can learn from and communicate with others who come from diverse fields, make timely decisions and take responsibility for their actions. The agency theory companies (Cases B and C) delegate authority to the employees of project teams so that team-members understand their tasks and also supervises team-members using reporting systems. Management textbooks (see Brickley *et al.*, 2004; Milgrom and Roberts, 1992, for example) concur on this approach.

The PM belongs to an independent business unit and is part of senior management. He/she will take final responsibility of the team. The four sample companies all appoint experienced PMs to manage the breakthrough product project teams. Companies C and D assigned appropriate team-members to the teams after meeting with the functional managers. However, before assigning employees to the team, Companies C and D also encourage the employees to willingly join or to recommend professional employees to work in the team. Companies A and B strongly encourage employees to willingly join a team and authorise the PM, functional managers, and employees to clarify job descriptions and qualifications for the project team.

However, due to strong team identity and self-categorisation, the members of Teams A and B communicate with each other and solve task conflicts within their teams. In other words, Teams A and B use horizontal incentive systems instead of reporting to top management. Therefore, members of Teams A and B established strong rapport with each other. Conversely, senior managers of Companies C and D preferred to control their employees by reporting procedures. Thus, members of Teams C and D monitor each other's actions. If team-members in Teams C and D are not satisfied with each other's behaviour, they report directly to their superiors. Eventually, members of Teams C and D treat teamwork as a part of their jobs. Previous literature consistent with such practices for both team management (see for example, Cohen and Bailey, 1997; and Towry, 2003) and team identity (see for example, Lembke and Wilson, 1998; and Rowe, 2004).

In the four cases, the PM's task was to communicate, integrate, and assist the members of the project team. The project team needs cooperation and communication with NPD functions, so the PM is responsible to answer task-related questions and provide assistance when members of the team ask for guidance. That is, the task of the PM is determined by requirements of the team-members and NPD functions. The team leader's duty is not consistent with the Harvard auto study (see Clark *et al.*, 1987; Clark and Fujimoto, 1991; and Hayes *et al.*, 1988). In the four cases, each team-member has individual objectives (KPI) and professional skills in his or her field. However, not all of the team-members are collectivists or opportunists. That is, agency or stewardship theories do not hold for all of the employees in the four cases. Both the psychological and sociological literature (Davis *et al.*, 1997; Donaldson and Davis, 1991; Doucouliagos, 1994) concur on this point.

> Q2: In what areas is performance measured for project teams, and how are internal project team performance measurement systems operated and compared to the theoretical recommendations of the literature?

In each of the four cases, the project team consists of a PM and 10–15 cross-functional team-members. Since the four breakthrough product projects take roughly one year to accomplish and launch the products, members of the teams cannot wait to be paid until the job is completed. In fact, the four sample companies paid the employees of the teams monthly according to their performance. Therefore, it is necessary to examine how the company evaluates the PM and team individuals.

For the individual (non-management level) members of teams, the four sample companies arranged individual KPI for their team employees. Basically, every three months or six months, the individual and his or her direct supervisor have a discussion, and then fixed individual objectives and performance measurements are weighed together. After the three-month or six-month review, the individual's direct supervisor evaluates the individual's performance, and then decides whether he or she meets an acceptable level of performance. If the individual has underperformed (i.e. failed to achieve his or her objectives), the individual has to fill out an improvement form (with the reviewing manager and direct supervisor) and has three months (Case A) or six months (Case B) to improve his or her performance, or the individual must quit or be dismissed. Finally, at the end of every year, functional managers evaluate their people based on job knowledge, quality, productivity, dependability, teamwork, customer satisfaction, initiative, planning and organisation, flexibility, and judgement in order to decide the year-end bonus or promotion.

A PM (management level) has three-monthly (Case A) or six-monthly (Case B) personal KPI evaluations and a year-end evaluation as well. In addition, the measurement factors place emphasis mainly on management ability, negotiation ability, efficiency, reputation, and job knowledge. The project team comes to an end when its output – the breakthrough product – is launched on the market. However, the responsibility of the PM continues until the product is withdrawn.

Regarding the breakthrough product project team, the types and areas of outcomes measured are more-or-less similar within the four sample companies (see Figure 9.3). In the four companies, executives measured not only financial performance (e.g. met profit goals, ROI, IRR, etc.) but also non-financial performance (e.g. the international organisation for standardisation (ISO) standards, awards from prestigious information technology media around the world, comments in professional computer magazines, or sales ranking in computer shops).

'Using the same indicators to measure the products does not mean allocating the same bonus to the teams,' the AVP of Company B emphasised. 'For example, we all know market share measure is important, but how much market share is good to receive how much bonus? It depends on each company's focus and strategy.' Executives used the results of the performance measurement (see Figure 9.3) to make promotion decisions, re-allocate corporate resources, and so on. 'Getting the results of the performance measurement is a task; exploiting the results of the performance measurement is an art,' the CEO of Company A described. 'Designing measures is not difficult at all, but the point is how to use them.'

> Q3: Are the uses or purposes of project team performance measurement results and their impact realised in practice?

Companies set performance measurement systems for various purposes and expect some impacts that affect actions of the employees. Figure 9.4 shows reasons why the four sample companies set the performance measurement systems and the expectations the four sample companies attempted to reach. Companies A and B set the performance measurement systems for the breakthrough product project teams for the purpose of individual evaluation, resource allocation, managerial decision-making, communication, continuous improvement, and correction. Companies A and B also achieved these purposes with good results. Conversely, Companies C and D primarily intended to control the actions of the employees and help determine individual incentives, allocation of corporate resources, managerial decisions, communication, continuous improvement, and timely correction. However,

Literature (see Figure 3.2; Figure 3.3)	Practice			
	A	B	C	D
I. Objective Performance				
a. Financial Indicators:				
• Product revenue or savings in production costs	√	√	√	√
• Profitability of product (meet profit goals or ROI or IRR)	√	√	√	√
• Market share of product	√	N	N	√
• Relative revenues within company	N	N	√	N
b. Innovation Indicators:				
• Patent	√	√	√	√
		ISO		
		Awards		
II. Perceptions Performance				
• Team and management rated overall technical performance of project	√	√	√	√
• Team and management rated performance for overall team performance	√	√	√	√
• Team and management rated performance for quality of teamwork	√	√	N	N
• Failure (cancellation and success (profitability) as rated by management	√	N	N	√
III. Strategic Performance				
a. Customer Satisfaction Indicators:				
• Appearance and functionality	√	√	√	√
• Quality of service	√	√	N	N
		Magazines		
		Sales Ranking		
b. Operational Indicators:				
• Speed	N	N	√	√
• Flexibility	√	√	√	√
• Productivity	√	√	√	√
• Schedule, budgets, innovation, efficiency	√	√	√	√

* N represents not available in the company

Figure 9.3   The Areas Measured in Team Outcomes: Literature vs. Practice

Literature (see Figure 3.4 and Figure 3.5)	Practice			
Purposes versus the Impact of Performance Measurement Results	A	B	C	D
I. Uses and Purposes				
a. Individual Evaluation:				
• Deciding on individual incentives	√	√	X	X
• Replacing/Dismissing/Transferring	√	√	X	X
b. Resource Allocation:				
• Arranging resources for project team	√	√	√	√
c. Managerial Decision-Making:				
• Cancelling of project	N	N	X	X
• Reorientation of project	√	√	X	X
• Timing for launching	√	√	N	N
d. Communication:				
• Communicating objectives, agreements, and rules	√	√	X	X
e. Continuous Improvement:				
• Learning from team-members	√	N	X	X
f. Correction:				
• Defining corrective actions	√	√	X	X
II. Impacts				
a. Individual Evaluation:				
• Increasing effectiveness of the team				
• Increasing employee motivation in the team	√	√	X	X
b. Resource Allocation:	√	√	X	X
• Increasing appropriateness and efficiency of resources				
c. Managerial Decision-Making:	√	√	X	X
• Well-balanced arbitration and decision-making				
d. Communication:	√	√	X	X
• Enhancing communication of the team and management				
• Modernising information access	√	√	X	X
• Improving development of common understanding among the players involved in NPD activity	√	√	X	X
e. Continuous Improvement:	√	√	X	X
• Improving the defined team outcomes				
• Enabling performance benchmarking with other projects/companies	√	√	X	X
f. Correction:	√	√	X	X
• Correcting relevant mistakes on time	√	√	X	X

* √ means companies set and achieve their purposes and get the desired impact. X means companies set, but fail to achive their purposes or get the desired impact. N means the purpose is not set.

Figure 9.4 The Issue of Uses and the Impact of Measurement Results: Literature versus Practice

Companies C and D both failed to achieve the aims of fair individual evaluation, appropriate resource allocation, proper decision-making, communication, continuous improvement, or timely correction.

Obviously, Companies A and B utilised the performance measurement systems as the incentive to motivate team-members. An open and fair performance measurement system of an NPD project team sends a good message to employees. Conversely, although Companies C and D set similar measures, purposes, and impacts of performance measurement systems to Companies A and B, Companies C and D failed in *implementation*. For example, Companies C and D did not return results to the individuals. Both NPD project team (Brown and Eisenhardt, 1995; Cohen and Bailey, 1997) and performance measurement literature (Busby, 1999; Godener and Söderquist, 2004; Hertenstein and Platt, 2000; Kaplan and Norton, 1993; Kerssens-van Drongelen and Bilderbeek, 1999; Kerssens-van Drongelen and Cook, 1997) concur on these purposes and impacts.

Q4: What are the key impacts of the NPD performance measurement results on the behaviour of the members of the project teams and functional departments?

Individuals, such as an R&D engineer, could run ten or more new product projects together, and the number of projects depends on the degree of product innovation. Each project team deals with one project, but there is no fixed timetable for every case. In reality, after launching the breakthrough product on the market, the project team comes to an end. Since project team-members come from diverse functions, team-members will return to their own departments and concentrate on other new product projects. The leader and members who work on the same team this time may not work together again for other projects. Conversely, the functional managers are familiar with their people's talents, professional areas, and the time schedule. Therefore, all interviewees agreed that PMs will be more suitable to evaluate the team-members. However, the four sample companies all delegated managers of NPD functional departments to evaluate the performance of their people on the project teams.

Responsible functional managers will not evaluate their people by their intentions, because they understand that what professional employees want is an open and fair performance measurement system. When a functional manager frequently takes the time to ask about his people's progress and offers the utilisation of seminar rooms, departmental libraries, and corporate resources, employees in the functional department feel senior management's involvement, commitment, and determination. The functional manager's attitude convinces people that the company welcomes diligent employees and is eager to develop an easy work environment for them.

The functional managers in Companies A and B discussed task assignment, time management, and the degree of process and product innovations with PMs and employees of the teams and ensured that employees have enough time to run appropriate projects. The functional managers first considered the employees' skills before allocating tasks and evaluating their overall performance, because functional managers believe that a tight schedule causes employees to sacrifice some projects while focusing on other projects in order to gain higher performance. Therefore, Companies A and B consider and discuss the schedule of each employee before assigning any tasks. The performance measurement results motivate members of the project team to contribute their potential and also convince the employees that the company is worth remaining loyal to.

Although the functional managers in Companies C and D assigned professional employees to the project teams, the managers did discuss with their people whether they are willing and have enough time to do this breakthrough product project. The employees could refuse the assignment if they felt they did not have enough time. However, if the employees accepted the tasks, employees needed to practice their tasks and meet the deadlines of each process. From the interviews, professional employees do not mind working long or hard as long as they feel that it is worthwhile. However, Companies C and D treated performance measurement as a routine procedure and kept the results of performance measurement, so professional employees felt that their efforts had no response and no return and distrusted the commitment of the senior management. They eventually left the company.

9.3 Contributions and implications

In this study we followed most of the methodological procedures and basic techniques introduced by Ryan *et al.* (2002) and Yin (2003), such as using a case study protocol, adopting an interview protocol, maintaining a chain of evidence, using replication logic, establishing a case study database, and so on. In this multiple-case study, each individual case is significant and reveals new insights and evidence from different perspectives has increased the quality of the case studies.

In this section, we identify the contributions being made to theory and practice. We can identify three contributions to previous agency theory and stewardship theory research. First, we provide a much more detailed comparison and description of agency theory and stewardship theory: its language, definitions of terms, boundaries, units of analysis, and psychological and situational mechanisms. Second, we do not assume that stewardship theory is wrong or inferior to agency theory, or vice versa, as previous researchers have stated. We attempt to show the differences between agency theory and stewardship theory by describing the definitions, underlying assumptions, and theoretical limits. A framework for agency and stewardship theories is provided (see Figure 4.2).

Finally, based on the findings of the four empirical cases, we discover that in practice, adopting agency theory or stewardship theory is not the main concern or objective to management. All of the practitioners (i.e. interviewees) of the four companies had never heard about agency theory or stewardship theory before the interviews. Further, the empirical findings in the four cases show that managers choose to behave either as stewards or agents and employees choose to behave either as professional employees or free-riders, contingent on the project team performance measurement systems. That is, if the project team performance measurement system can work transparently and objectively, the managers will choose to believe that the shareholder-manager interests are aligned and professional employees will be happy to work efficiently for the company.

Furthermore we expand the current literature. First, we connect the breakthrough product project team performance measurement system and the breakthrough product success. In management accounting research, it is not difficult to get numerous research regarding performance measurement, new product design and development, and agency theory. In addition, in management accounting literature, it is easy to review the new product design and development literature, performance measurement literature, corporate governance literature, etc. However, there is little related literature which connects the project team performance measurement system and new product success altogether. We consider our research as an avenue for a new area of management accounting research.

Second, we provide a much more detailed study of breakthrough products. Previous new product design and development research and literature have mostly focused on continuous products, rather than breakthrough products. However, breakthrough products are contributors to the company's survival. The few studies on the breakthrough innovation are disproportionate to the significance of breakthrough products. Thus, researchers cannot ensure whether present studies about factors of new product success or failure improve breakthrough product and process innovations. Therefore, we attempt to contribute to new management concepts and devices to help practitioners to increase the possibility of successful breakthrough innovation.

Third, Taiwan's high-technology sector is studied. Most studies analyse successful Japanese, American, and European auto or pharmaceutical industries, but it is probable that their results might not extend to other countries and other industries. Using NPD literature, we examine the high-technology sector in Taiwan. Finally, we construct a theoretical framework, based on the findings and results of management accounting research and literature. This theoretical framework could be tested by other researchers in a quantitative and/or qualitative way.

After examining this multiple-case empirical study, we propose the following propositions. These propositions reflect our critical inferences of what is probable and supposed by this research. These propositions[1] help in identifying the relevant information about the unit of analysis – project teams, and cover all related factors specifically within feasible limits.

Proposition 1

Corporate resources and NPD commitment should be the initial prerequisites before structuring a new product project team, not the critical factors or drivers of new product success or failure.

In the four cases, no matter whether the teams were commercially successful or failed project teams, before executing NPD projects and structuring project teams, key findings show that all companies considered internal (e.g. corporate resources) and external (e.g. markets) factors to see whether they have enough ability to execute breakthrough product projects and the success probability. NPD commitment includes

---

[1]The propositions are based on the empirical findings of the four Taiwanese cases. The propositions may not apply in all situations. In this study, we do not intend to generalise from the four Taiwanese cases and say that all companies in the world will match all of these propositions. The purpose is to propose some common findings in the four cases and then in the future, researchers can further investigate them.

the senior management's full involvement, new product strategy, and the structure of project teams. 'In my personal opinion, "senior management involvement," for example, is just a signal by the employees to the company,' the AVP of Company B emphasised. 'Without senior management involvement (senior managers' attitude), the success probability goes down.' That is, initial preparation and the executives' attitudes indicate commitment to the employees.

Proposition 2

Social identity and self-categorisation, which guide the members of the team to a common team purpose, are more likely to achieve team cohesion, to encourage employees to perceive themselves as a team, to integrate team-specific communication, and to help to clarify the decision allocation, the incentive, and the performance measurement systems.

In the four cases, key findings show that self-categorisation and social identity are like a 'natural process' and the difference between the four cases is the level of team identity. The level of team identity is decided by the way the companies structure them. 'If team-members get along with each other very well, the team has a strong identity, and executives do not need to control the team,' the CEO of Company A explained. 'It is something about your company's culture.' The findings show that the teams with strong team identity do not need to be controlled; conversely, executives of Companies C and D chose vertical incentive systems to monitor the teams without strong team identity.

Proposition 3

Agency and stewardship theories express diverse management styles, different degree of authorisation or empowerment, and different control mechanisms, rather than the one-best-way to corporate governance.

'In our Company, we do not like to control employees. Employees do not like to be controlled either,' the CEO of Company A said. 'However, not every NPD project is successful in the company.' Conversely, the CEO of Company C and the VP of Company D both emphasised that Companies C and D 'were' successful innovative technology companies in Taiwan and they never changed the way they governed themselves. Neither agency theory nor stewardship theory provides the one-best-way for corporate governance. 'Adopting agency theory or stewardship theory depends on the leader's management philosophy,' the AVP of Company D explained. 'I believe no literature will tell you agency theory will make your company succeed, or stewardship theory will make your company fail.'

Proposition 4

When delegating authority to members of the team and setting the rewards, the members should show professional care for their tasks without complaints about pay structure, but expect an open and fair performance measurement system.

Key findings show that pay structure is decided by the management, but professional employees will not waste time complaining about it. The premise is that professional employees believe the company will measure their performance fairly and objectively. '"Fairness" is a valuable asset in our company and is a competitive advantage in Taiwan's high-technology sector,' the CEO of Company A proudly claimed. 'Before asking employees to contribute their talents to the company, the company should create a fair and easy working environment for them in advance.' The CEO of Company C and the VP of Company D agree with the CEO of Company A and are currently re-forming their performance measurement systems to address the problem of losing professional employees.

Proposition 5

A proper decision allocation system should appropriately delegate authority to members of the team in order to achieve the common team purpose.

Key findings show that executives delegate authority to professional employees due to their qualifications, not job positions. Delegating authority is helpful to team-members to achieve the common team purpose. 'Detailed job descriptions are annoying, but at least they offer a way you should follow,' the CEO of Company C explained. 'Besides, if anything goes wrong, we know who should take responsibility for it.' The AVP of Company B also recommended that 'individual KPI should be known by all members of the team,' because he believes that 'openness' would be very helpful to align the interests of members of the team and to help team-members in achieving the common team goal.

Proposition 6

An efficient and effective performance measurement system should be able to evaluate employees' performance fairly, play an important role in reviewing and inspecting the system of assigning decision rights, and assist the incentive system.

In the four cases, the key findings show that one of the purposes of a performance measurement system is to keep professional employees in and/or sweep low-performing employees out. Also, executives award pay-for-performance bonuses according to the results of the performance measurement. Therefore, it is important to evaluate employees' performance properly and fairly, because it is a way to show the management's selection on the 'professional employees only' policy. Key findings also show that a complete performance measurement system includes the design and the operation of performance measures as well as the uses and impacts of the results of performance measurement. 'I personally worked in other high-technology companies in Taiwan when I was young and inexperienced,' the CEO of Company C admitted. 'It is very easy to know what performance measures other companies use, but it seems we missed an important part.'

Proposition 7

An open and fair performance measurement system could become the catalyst which influences new product success or failure, given appropriate delegated authority, explicit responsibility, clear punishment rules, and an attractive pay structure.

As shown in Figure 9.3, executives in the four companies all used the same performance measures for their project teams. No matter whether they had commercially successful or commercially failed project teams, they were required to achieve 'speed' and 'flexibility' standards. 'It is not difficult to meet the deadline. If I asked the PM to submit the product tomorrow, they would submit it tomorrow,' the VP of Company D explained. 'Why do we set these measures [see Figure 9.3] for our team? We will not indefinitely invest. It is something about "budgeting," i.e. money.' An open and fair performance measurement system is seen as the management's ultimate goal, motivating employees to spend their whole life working in the company. Also, an open and fair performance measurement system is the incentive to align employees' interests and shareholders' interests. That is, an open and fair performance measurement system can create a 'win-win' situation for both employees and shareholders.

9.4 Limitations and improvements

In this multiple-case (holistic) study research, considerable care and attention has been given to the collection and evaluation of interview and documentary evidence, which is used in developing and generalising theory. That is, this case study research has its own severity and is capable of generalisation. However, we acknowledge that there are still some limitations that have to be taken into consideration in interpreting our findings. In this section, we attempt to identify these limitations.

First, there is the limitation of resources. This case study research occurs in a particular country; Taiwan. After considering restricted resources such as limited research budgets, time, and access to case study sites with ease, etc., we allocated all resources to Taiwan's high-technology sector. If we had full financial support and access to any countries' case study sites with ease, we would have liked to study at least two countries that are believed to have similar and/or different cultures, and do comparisons regarding the same industry in different countries. It is possible that high-technology companies in different countries have diverse perceptions about team effectiveness, motivation, new product success, and/or new product failure due to different social values and leadership.

The second limitation stems from the nature of business confidentiality. Companies A, B, C, and D all strongly recommended that the latest breakthrough product project team is more suitable for research purposes. In addition, the senior managers of Companies C and D suggested that the latest project team in their companies is the consequence of ineffective corporate governance. Under particular circumstances, we respected and accepted the practitioners' professional opinions and suggestions. Therefore, we did not have a choice of the project to be studied in each company but we followed the suggestion of the companies. However, it turned out to be the most recent project that we studied in each company.

The third limitation of this research is caused by necessary generalisation. The four cases are anecdotal and may not be generalisable to other situations. In fact, if the four sample companies agree, we could design multiple embedded cases and conduct a survey at each case study site. The data would become more quantitative, focusing on the perceptions of team employees and senior management. The data could be used, along with documentary evidence, to interpret the success or failure and operations in the given cases.

The final limitation of this case study research is that the four cases are static and historical. Although the four cases are the latest breakthrough products in the four participating companies, they are nevertheless team logs and archival data at the present. We could not observe the motions of senior managers and the actions of members of the teams. In this case study, one of the authors worked as a visitor who visited the case study sites and interviewed subjects of the research. Therefore, the researcher needs to infer from the interviews and documentary evidence. If the researcher was to do the same multiple-case study all over again, and if the sample companies allowed, the researcher would like to do a few things differently. For example, the researcher could become a *participant* so that the researcher could obtain insights into the everyday workings of each company.

9.5 Opportunities for future research

We have attempted to draw a broad outline of the operation and effect of project team performance measurement systems that are presently somewhat neglected in contemporary management accounting literature, and that provide the underpinnings of self-categorisation theory and social identity theory. In addition, in this case study research, we have showed that both agency theory and stewardship theory could be correct, because both Cases A (stewardship relationships) and B (agency relationships) are successful. Certainly, more fine-grained analyses are required, which would incorporate larger samples (more breakthrough product project teams), the examination of new variables (factors), and empirical testing. In the future, researchers could inquire into the design, operation, and effect of KPI project team performance measurement systems in different companies, and examine their relative importance, their interactions, and the variables that affect them.

In this study, we attempted to highlight the significance and consequence of locating the four breakthrough product project teams within the context of the broader organisational, economic, and social systems of which the four project teams are part. A breakthrough product project team in a particular Taiwanese high-technology company will have evolved with the development of the business. Therefore, acting on Jensen's (1983) recommendations, in this study, we expanded the four project teams to studying interrelations with other and associated systems, such as the project team performance measurement system, reward and punishment system, and the assignment of decision rights.

The holistic model of studying all aspects of a breakthrough product project team is obviously unachievable, and we must be satisfied with appropriations. Therefore, we placed some limits on the subject matter. We placed boundaries on the area of breakthrough product project team, and made those boundaries explicit. This permits an in-depth holistic case study research of the area, and allows other researchers to expand the work into other areas. The purpose of the case study research was to get theoretical generalisations. In addition, the process of theoretical generalisation in this case study can expand the understandings of the field of study into larger social systems, as more case studies are undertaken. In the future, surveys can contribute by examining more cases.

In this study, we constructed an empirical framework (see Figure 7.5), based on the findings of empirical work, for overseeing the effects of performance-contingent incentives, the uses and impacts of the results of the project team performance measurement system on team efforts, effectiveness, and new product success. This empirical framework can be a model in further quantitative research. In addition, the role of management accounting and management accountants is to meet the needs of users internal to the business. Therefore, in the future, management accounting should not be restricted or limited to mathematical models only, but it should be studied and investigated as a social construct (Broadbent, 1999).

Findings of this empirical work may be relevant for at least four different audiences who have substantive interests in organisational, management, and accounting areas. This includes disciplinarians (e.g. management, organisation studies, etc.), methodologists and theorists (e.g. case study researchers, interviewers, etc.), practitioners (e.g. managers, entrepreneurs, etc.), and politicians (e.g. societal or fiscal policy-makers, etc.) are all possible audiences and/or future researchers.

For disciplinarians, the findings of this case study suggest that management should find out the cause of a problem before giving remedies. Also, control is not the only management mechanism in today's business environment. After the research was completed, some new questions arose: Can the management's concepts and leadership influence and determine the success or failure of a project team? Does the relationship of an open and fair performance measurement system and the outcomes of a work team, parallel team, or management team exist? Does the relationship between an open and fair performance measurement system, and the success or failure of the output of the project team exist in different industries? Is an open and fair performance measurement system important to small business in Taiwan as well as high-technology companies? Future research addressing these new questions would improve our understanding by gaining a comprehensive picture regarding an open and fair performance measurement system.

For methodologists, this holistic multiple-case study provides readers with a series of systematic methodological procedures to be followed in future research. The most relevant evidence from interviews and documents for each case study has been investigated in-depth. Also, the four processed cases and the cross-case conclusions have not been prejudiced by undue attention to any one of the cases. In the future, methodology researchers can work as investigators or auditors of this case study research. We argue that the test of reliability is satisfied. So, a later investigator should be able to follow the same procedures as described in this study and conduct the same case study all over again. The next investigator should reach similar findings and conclusions. That is, in the future, another investigator can act as an auditor and perform a reliability check.

Theorists, in the future, can focus on the alignment of multiple theories from different perspectives, such as sociological, philosophical, political, and economical constructs. Our theory is that an open and fair project team performance measurement system could be an incentive to members of a team and eventually will motivate members of the team to achieve a common team purpose – a successful new product. We perceive that a capable theorist should be able to utilise theories to help practitioners, and not be divorced from their practices. Due to the findings of this empirical work, a research project in the future could survey more case studies in order to examine whether a relationship between an open and fair performance measurement system and new product success or failure exists.

Practitioners would be interested to know the findings in this case study. The managers in the four cases realised that they play an important role in performance measurement systems. A capable manager should understand that the actions and performance of employees are influenced by the way their superior managers evaluate them. In addition, senior managers have given more attention to cautiously recruiting and objectively evaluating employees so that the company can appropriately distribute the salary budget to professional employees. Also, new high-technology companies which attempt to start their own brand products can gain knowledge from this study. High-technology companies in Taiwan can take advantage of the findings in this empirical study by considering whether they have established and aligned proper decision allocation systems, attractive pay structures, appropriate reward and punishment systems, and open and fair performance measurement systems for their project teams.

For politicians, before creating any fiscal policy, they must consider the positive and negative effects after announcing and implementing government policy. A capable politician is supposed to be able to judge the circumstances of society, predict the actions of entrepreneurs and citizens, and deal with the consequences of policy implementation. It is not difficult to anticipate that a man will attempt his best to defend his rights. For example, if an entrepreneur's profits are damaged by government policy, the entrepreneur will transfer his losses to his employees or customers. If the cost can be completely transferred to an innocent third party, politicians will be blamed by the people. This policy is harmful to society, and people will feel upset with the government. The government someday will lose credibility.

For example, Taiwan's government established a reformed pension system which provides Taiwan's aging society with a monetary safety net, improves government finances, and helps the financial industry. Although the new pension system began on July 1, 2005, some good organisations reformed their pay structures and compensation plans several years ago. The implementation of the reformed pension system has enhanced the effectiveness of the labour force and employment in organisations. Obviously, the outcomes of this new pension regulation are supportive of some entrepreneurs and professional employees. Therefore, researchers can contribute by examining and predicting the effects of new government regulations.

9.6   Conclusion

We use self-categorisation and social identity theories to understand the coherence of teamwork that can arise between members of the project team. However, organisational relationships may be more com-plex than those analysed through self-categorisation and social identity theories. This study adds to the understanding of project team performance measurement systems by comparing the four selected cases.

We extend previous performance measurement and new product success/failure research by exploring and explaining the relationship between the project team performance measurement system and new product success. Our theory is that an open and fair KPI project team performance measurement system will eventually motivate or even force members of the team to achieve a common team purpose. This study also adds to previous agency and stewardship research by finding that adopting agency theory or stewardship theory is based on the management philosophy and beliefs, rather than one-best-way thinking in corporate governance.

Finally, we suggested some avenues for future management and accounting research. We suggested a need for more fine-grained analysis of samples (i.e. breakthrough product project teams) and the examination of new variables. In brief, a variety of theoretical and empirical research projects are essential to help fully understand the relationship between different project team performance measurement systems and the outputs of those project teams.

Bibliography

Aaker, D.A. (2005) *Strategic Market Management*, 7th ed., Hoboken, NJ: John Wiley.

Abdel-khalik, A.R. and Ajinkya, B.B. (1979) *Empirical Research in Accounting: A Methodological Viewpoint*, American Accounting Association, Accounting Education Series, Vol.4.

Adler, P.S., Mandelbaum, A., Nguyen, V. and Schwerer, E. (1995) 'From Project to Process Management: An Empirically-based Framework for Analyzing Product Development Time', *Management Science*, 41(3): 458–484.

Ali, A. (1994) 'Pioneering versus Incremental Innovation: Review and Research Propositions', *Journal of Product Innovation Management*, 11: 46–61.

Allen, T.J. (1971) 'Communications, Technology Transfer, and the Role of Technical Gatekeeper', *R&D Management*, 1: 14–21.

Allen, T.J. (1977) *Managing the Flow of Technology*, Cambridge, MA: MIT Press.

Altheide, D.L. (1996) *Qualitative Media Analysis*, Thousand Oaks, California: Sage.

Amabile, T.M. (1993) 'Rethinking Rewards', *Harvard Business Review*, November–December: 42–43.

Ancona, D.G. and Caldwell, D.F. (1992) 'Demography and Design: Predictors of New Product Team Performance', *Organization Science*, 3(3): 321–341.

Anderson, S.W., Hesford, J.W. and Young, S.M. (2002) 'Factors Influencing the Performance of Activity Based Costing Teams: A Field Study of ABC Model Development Time in the Automobile Industry', *Accounting, Organizations and Society*, 37: 195–211.

Appelbaum, E. (1993) 'Rethinking Rewards', *Harvard Business Review*, November–December: 38–39.

Ashton, D., Hopper, T. and Scapens, R.W. (1995) 'The changing nature of issues in management accounting' in D. Ashton, T. Hopper and R.W. Scapens (eds) *Issues in Management Accounting*, 2nd ed., London: Prentice Hall, 1–20.

Baiman, S. (1982) 'Agency Theory in Management Accounting: A Survey', *Journal of Accounting Literature*, 1: 154–213.

Baker, G., Jensen, M. and Murphy, K.J. (1988) 'Compensation and Incentives: Practice versus Theory', *Journal of Finance*, 43: 593–616.

Balachandra, R. and Friar, J.H. (1997) 'Factors for Success in R&D Projects and New Product Innovation: A Contextual Framework', *IEEE Transactions on Engineering Management*, 44(3): 276–287.

Bart, C.K. (1991) 'Controlling New Products: A Presidential Perspective', *Journal of Product Innovation Management*, 8: 4–17.

Bart, C.K. (1999) 'Controlling New Products: A Contingency Approach', *International Journal of Technology Management*, 18(5/6/7/8): 395–413.

Beer, M. (1993) 'Rethinking Rewards', *Harvard Business Review*, November–December: 39–42.

Blumer, H. (1978) 'Methodological Principles of Empirical Science' in N.K. Denzin (ed) *Sociological Methods: A Sourcebook*, McGraw-Hill.

Bonner, S.E. (1999) 'Commentary: Judgment and Decision-Making Research in Accounting', *Accounting Horizons*, 13(4): 385–398.

Bonner, S.E. and Sprinkle, G.B. (2002) 'The Effects of Monetary Incentives on Effort and Task Performance: Theories, Evidence, and a Framework for Research', *Accounting, Organizations and Society*, 27: 303–345.

Booz-Allen, S. and Hamilton, S. (1982) *New Product Management for the 1980's*, New York: Booz, Allen and Hamilton Inc.

Bourgeois, L.J. III and Eisenhardt, K.M. (1988) 'Strategic Decision Processes in High Velocity Environments: Four Cases in the Microcomputer Industry', *Management Science*, 34(7): 816–835.

Bourne, M., Mills, J., Wilcox, M., Neely, A. and Platts, K. (2000) 'Designing, Implementing and Updating Performance Measurement Systems', *International Journal of Operations & Production Management*, 20(7): 754–771.

Boyatzis, R.E. (1998) *Transforming Qualitative Information: Thematic Analysis and Code Development*, Thousand Oaks, CA: Sage.

Brickley, J.A., Smith, Jr. C.W. and Zimmerman, J.L. (2004) *Managerial Economics and Organizational Architecture*, 3rd ed., Boston, Mass: McGraw-Hill/Irwin.

Broadbent, J. (1999) 'The State of Public Sector Accounting Research – The APIRA Conference and Some Personal Reflections', *Accounting, Auditing & Accountability Journal*, 12(1): 52–57.

Bromwich, M. and Bhimani, A. (1989) *Management Accounting: Evolution not Revolution*, Chartered Institute of Management Accountants (CIMA).

Brown, S.L. and Eisenhardt, K.M. (1995) 'Product Development: Past Research, Present Findings, and Future Directions', *Academy of Management Review*, 20(2): 343–378.

Bryman, A. and Bell, E. (2003) *Business Research Methods*, New York: Oxford University Press.

Busby, J.S. (1999) 'Problems in Error Correction, Learning and Knowledge of Performance in Design Organizations', *IIE Transactions*, 31: 49–59.

Bushe, G.R. and Shani, A.B. (1991) *Parallel Learning Structures: Increasing Innovation in Bureaucracies*, Reading, MA: Addison-Wesley.

Chaturvedi, K.J. and Rajan, Y.S. (2000) 'New Product Development: Challenges of Globalization', *International Journal of Technology Management*, 19 (7/8): 788–805.

Chen, C.C. and Meindl, J.R. (1991) 'The Construction of Leadership Images in the Popular Press: The Case of Donald Burr and People Express', *Administrative Science Quarterly*, 36: 521–551.

Chiu, J.S. and Chang, D.L. (1979) 'Management Accounting in Taiwan', *Management Accounting*, June: 50–55.

Chua, W.F. (1986) 'Radical Developments in Accounting Thought', *The Accounting Review*, LXI(4): 601–632.

Clark, K.B., Chew, W.B. and Fujimoto, T. (1987) Product Development in the World Auto Industry, *Brookings Papers on Economic Activity*, 3: 729–781.

Clark, K.B. and Fujimoto, T. (1990) 'The Power of Product Integrity', *Harvard Business Review*, November–December: 107–118.

Clark, K.B. and Fujimoto, T. (1991) *Product Development Performance: Strategy, Organization and Management in the World Auto Industry*, Boston, MA: Harvard Business School Press.

Coates, J.B., Smith, J.E. and Stacey, R.J. (1983) 'Results of a Preliminary Survey into the Structure of Divisionalised Companies, Divisionalised Performance Appraisal and the Associated Role of Management Accounting' in D. Cooper,

R. Scapens and J. Arnold (eds), *Management Accounting Research and Practice*, Institute of Cost and Management Accountants: 265–282.

Cohen, S.G. and Bailey, D.E. (1997) 'What Makes Teams Work: Group Effectiveness Research from the Shop Floor to the Executive Suite', *Journal of Management*, 23(3): 239–290.

Collins, J. (2001) *Good to Great*, London: Random House Business Books.

Collis, J. and Hussey, R. (2003) *Business Research: A Practical Guide for Undergraduate and Postgraduate Students*, 2nd ed., Palgrave Macmillan: Basingstoke.

Colville, I. (1981) 'Reconstructing 'Behavioural Accounting'', *Accounting, Organizations and Society*, 6(2): 119–132.

Cooper, R.G. (1979a) 'Identifying Industrial New Product Success: Project NewProd', *Industrial Marketing Management*, 8(2): 124–135.

Cooper, R.G. (1979b) 'The Dimensions of Industrial New Product Success and Failure', *Journal of Marketing*, 43(3): 93–103.

Cooper, R.G. (1988a) 'Predevelopment Activities Determine New Product Success', *Industrial Marketing Management*, 17: 237–247.

Cooper, R.G. (1988b) 'The New Product Process: A Decision Guide for Management', *Journal of Marketing Management*, 3(3): 238–255.

Cooper, R.G. (1990) 'Stage-gate Systems: A New Tool for Managing New Products', *Business Horizons*, May-June: 44–56.

Cooper, R.G. (1995) *When Lean Enterprises Collide: Competing Through Confrontation*, Boston, MA: Harvard Business School Press.

Cooper, R.G. (1996) 'Overhauling the New Product Process', *Industrial Marketing Management*, 25: 465–482.

Cooper, R.G. and Kleinschmidt, E.J. (1986) 'An Investigation into the New Product Process: Steps, Deficiencies and Impact', *Journal of Product Innovation Management*, 3(2): 71–85.

Cooper, R.G. and Kleinschmidt, E.J. (1987a) 'New Products: What Separates Winners from Losers?' *Journal of Product Innovation Management*, 4(3): 169–184.

Cooper, R.G. and Kleinschmidt, E.J. (1987b) 'Success Factors in Product Innovation', *Industrial Marketing Management*, 16(3): 215–233.

Cooper, R.G. and Kleinschmidt, E.J. (1988) 'Resource Allocation in the New Product Process', *Industrial Marketing Management*, 17(3): 249–262.

Cooper, R.G. and Kleinschmidt, E.J. (1990) 'New Product Success Factors: A Comparison of "Kills versus Success and Failure"', *R&D Management*, 20(1): 47–63.

Cooper, R.G. and Kleinschmidt, E.J. (1991) 'New Product Processes at Leading Industrial Firms', *Industrial Marketing Management*, 20: 137–147.

Cooper, R.G. and Kleinschmidt, E.J. (1993) 'Major New Products: What Distinguishes the Winners in the Chemical Industry?', *Journal of Product Innovation Management*, 10(2): 90–111.

Cooper, R.G. and Kleinschmidt, E.J. (1995) 'Benchmarking the Firm's Critical Success Factors in New Product Development', *Journal of Product Innovation Management*, 12(5): 374–391.

Cooper, R.G. and Kleinschmidt, E.J. (1996) 'Winning Businesses in Product Development: The Critical Success Factors', *Research • Technology Management*, July-August: 18–29.

Crawford, C.M. and Di Benedetto, C.A. (2003) *New Products Management*, 7th ed., Boston: McGraw-Hill.

Creswell, J.W. (1998) *Qualitative Inquiry and Research Design: Choosing among Five Traditions*, Thousand Oaks, California: Sage.

Cusumano, M.A. and Nobeoka, K. (1992) 'Strategy, Structure and Performance in Product Development – Observations from the Auto Industry', *Research Policy*, 21: 265–293.

Davila, A. (2003) 'Short-term Economic Incentives in New Product Development', *Research Policy*, 32: 1397–1420.

Davila, T. (2000) 'An Empirical Study on the Drivers of Management Control Systems' Design in New Product Development', *Accounting, Organizations and Society*, 25: 383–409.

Davis, D. (1985) 'New Projects: Beware of False Economies', *Harvard Business Review*, March–April: 95–101.

Davis, J.H., Schoorman, F.D. and Donaldson, L. (1997) 'Toward a Stewardship Theory of Management', *Academy of Management Review*, 22(1): 20–47.

Denzin, N.K. (1971) 'Symbolic Interactionism and Ethnomethodology' in J.D. Douglas (ed) *Understanding Everyday Life: toward the Reconstruction of Sociological Knowledge*, London: Routledge and Kegan Paul.

Donaldson, L. (1990) 'The Ethereal Hand: Organizational Economics and Management Theory', *Academy of Management Review*, 15(3): 369–381.

Donaldson, L. and Davis, J.H. (1991) 'Stewardship Theory or Agency Theory: CEO Governance and Shareholder Returns', *Australian Journal of Management*, 16(1): 49–64.

Doucouliagos, C. (1994) 'A Note on the Evolution of Homo Economicus', *Journal of Economics Issues*, 3: 877–883.

Drury, C. (2004) *Management and Cost Accounting*, 6th ed., London: Thomson.

Edgett, S., Shipley, D. and Forbes, G. (1992) 'Japanese and British Companies Compared: Contributing Factors to Success and Failure in NPD', *Journal of Product Innovation Management*, 9: 3–10.

Eisenhardt, K.M. (1989) 'Agency Theory: An Assessment and Review', *Academy of Management Review*, 14(1): 57–74.

Eisenhardt, K.M. and Tabrizi, B.N. (1995) 'Accelerating Adaptive Processes: Product Innovation in the Global Computer Industry', *Administrative Science Quarterly*, 40: 84–110.

Emmanuel, C., Otley, D. and Merchant, K. (1990) *Accounting for Management Control*, 2nd ed, London: Chapman and Hall.

Emmanuelides, P.A. (1993) 'Toward an Integrative Framework of Performance in Product Development Projects', *Journal of Engineering and Technology Management*, 10: 363–392.

Evans, J.H. III, Hannan, R.L., Krishnan, R. and Moser, D.V. (2001) 'Honesty in Managerial Reporting', *The Accounting Review*, 76(4): 537–559.

Fama, E.F. (1980) 'Agency Problems and the Theory of the Firm', *Journal of Political Economy*, 88(2): 288–307.

Fama, E.F. and Jensen, M.C. (1983) 'Separation of Ownership and Control', *Journal of Law and Economics*, XXVI: 301–325.

Ferreira, L.D. and Merchant, K.A. (1992) 'Field Research in Management Accounting and Control: A Review and Evaluation', *Accounting, Auditing & Accountability Journal*, 5(4): 3–34.

Frankl, V.E. (1984) *Man's Search for Meaning*, New York: Touchstone Books, 134.

Friedman, M. (1953) 'The Methodology of Positive Economics' in M. Friedman (ed) *Essays in Positive Economics*, Chicago: University of Chicago Press, 23–47.

Ghosh, D. and Lusch, R.F. (2000) 'Outcome Effect, Controllability and Performance Evaluation of Managers: Some Field Evidence from Multi-outlet Businesses', *Accounting, Organizations and Society*, 25: 411–425.

Giddens, A. (1979) *Central Problems in Social Theory: Action, Structure and Contradiction in Social Analysis*, London: Macmillan.

Giddens, A. (1984) *The Constitution of Society*, Cambridge: Polity Press.

Godener, A. and Söderquist, K.E. (2004) 'Use and Impact of Performance Measurement Results in R&D and NPD: An Exploratory Study', *R&D Management*, 34(2): 191–219.

González, F.J.M. and Palacios, T.M.B. (2002) 'The Effect of New Product Development Techniques on New Product Success in Spanish Firms', *Industrial Marketing Management*, 31: 261–271.

Green, S.G. (1995) 'Top Management Support of R&D Projects: A Strategic Leadership Perspective', *IEEE Transactions on Engineering Management*, 42(3): 223–232.

Gregory, G. and J. Piper (1983) 'A Study of the Raw Material Recorder Decisions in Small Batch Manufacturing Companies' in D. Cooper, R. Scapens and J. Arnold (eds) *Management Accounting Research and Practice* (Institute of Cost and Management Accountants): 318–362.

Griffin, A. (1997) *Drivers of NPD Success: The PDMA Report*, Chicago.

Griffin, A. and Hauser, J.R. (1996) 'Integrating R&D and Marketing: A Review and Analysis of the Literature', *Journal of Product Innovation Management*, 13(3): 191–215.

Griffin, A. and Page, A.L. (1993) 'An Interim Report on Measuring Product Development Success and Failure', *Journal of Product Innovation Management*, 10: 291–308.

Griffin, A. and Page, A.L. (1996) 'PDMA Success Measurement Project: Recommended Measures for Product Development Success and Failure', *Journal of Product Innovation Management*, 13: 478–496.

Grupp, H., Münt, G. and Schmoch, U. (1996) 'Knowledge-Intensive and Resource-Concerned Growth in Germany', *Research Evaluation*, August: 93–104.

Hackman, J.R. (1990) *Groups that Work (and those that Don't): Creating Conditions for Effective Teamwork*, San Francisco: Jossey Bass.

Hägg, I. and Hedlund, G. (1979) '"Case Studies" in Accounting Research', *Accounting, Organizations and Society*, 4(1/2): 135–143.

Hansen, C.J. (1995) 'Writing the Project Team: Authority and Intertextuality in a Corporate Setting', *The Journal of Business Communication*, 32(2): 103–122.

Hatzichronoglou, T. (1997) 'Revision of the High-Technology Sector and Product Classification', *STI Working Paper 1997/2*, OECD, Paris.

Hawkins, S.A. and Hastie, R. (1990) 'Hindsight: Biased Judgments of Past Events After The Outcomes Are Known', *Psychological Bulletin*, 107: 311–327.

Hayes, R.H., Pisano, G.P., Upton, D.M. and Wheelwright, S.C. (2005) *Operations, Strategy, and Technology: Pursuing the Competitive Edge*, Wiley.

Hayes, R.H., Wheelwright, S.C. and Clark, K. (1988) *Dynamic Manufacturing*, New York: The Free Press.

Hertenstein, J.H. and Platt, M.B. (2000) 'Performance Measures and Managment Control in New Product Development', *Accounting Horizons*, 14 (3): 303–323.

Hesterly, W.S., Liebeskind, J. and Zenger, T.R. (1990) 'Organizational Economics: An Impending Revolution in Organization Theory?', *Academy of Management Review*, 15(3): 402–420.

Hickson, D.J., Butler, R.J., Cray, D., Mallory, G.R. and Wilson, D.C. (1986) *Top Decisions: Strategic Decision-Making in Organizations*, San Francisco, CA: Jossey-Bass.

Hill, R.J. (1978) 'On the relevance of methodology' in N.K. Denzin (ed) *Sociological Methods: A Sourcebook*, McGraw-Hill.

Hirsch, P., Michaels, S. and Friedman, R. (1987) '"Dirty Hands" versus "Clean Models"', *Theory and Society*, 16(3): 317–336.

Hogg, M.A. and Abrams, D. (1993) 'Towards a single-process uncertainty reduction model of social motivation in groups' in M.A. Hogg and D. Abrams (eds) *Group Motivation: Social Psychological Perspectives*, New York: Harvester Wheatsheaf.

Hopkins, D.S. (1980) 'New Products Winners and Losers', *The Conference Board Report*, 1–34.

Hopwood, A.G. (1972) 'An Empirical Study of the Role of Accounting Data in Performance Evaluation', *Journal of Accounting Research*, Supplement, 156–182.

Horngren, C.T. (1975) 'Management Accounting: Where are We?' in Management Accounting and Control, University of Wisconsin-Madison.

Horngren, C.T., Bhimani, A., Foster, G. and Datar, S.M. (1999) *Management and Cost Accounting*, London: Prentice-Hall Europe.

Huberman, A.M. and Miles, M.B. (1994) 'Data management and analysis methods' in N.K. Denzin and Y.S. Lincoln (eds) *Handbook of Qualitative Research*, Thousand Oaks, CA: Sage, 428–444.

Hughes, G.D. and Chafin, D.C. (1996) 'Turning New Product Development into a Continuous Learning Process', *Journal of Product Innovation Management*, 13(2): 89–104.

Iansiti, M. (1992) *Science-based Product Development: An Empirical Study of the Mainframe Computer Industry*, Working Paper, Cambridge, MA: Harvard Business School.

Iansiti, M. (1993) 'Real-world R&D: Jumping the Product Generation Gap', *Harvard Business Review*, 71(3): 138–147.

Imai, K., Ikujiro, N. and Takeuchi, H. (1985) 'Managing the new product development process: how Japanese companies learn and unlearn' in R.H. Hayes, K. Clark and C. Lorenz (eds) *The Uneasy Alliance: Managing the Productivity-Technology Dilemma*, Boston, Mass.: Harvard Business School Press, 337–375.

Ittner, C.D. and Larcker, D.F. (1995) 'Total Quality Management and the Choice of Information and Reward Systems', *Journal of Accounting Research*, 33(Supplement): 1–34.

Jenkins, S., Forbes, S. and Durrani, T.S. (1997) 'Managing the Product Development Process – (Part I: An Assessment)', *International Journal of Technology Management*, 13(4): 359–378.

Jenkins, G.D., Gupta, N., Mitra, A. and Shaw, J.D. (1998) 'Are Financial Incentives related to Performance? A Meta-analytic Review of Empirical Research', *Journal of Applied Psychology*, 83(5): 777–787.

Jensen, M.C. (1983) 'Organization Theory and Methodology', *The Accounting Review*, LVIII(2): 319–339.

Jensen, M.C. and Meckling, W.H. (1976) 'Theory of the Firm: Managerial Behavior, Agency Costs, and Ownership Structure', *Journal of Financial Economics*, 3(4): 305–360.

Jensen, M.C. and Meckling, W.H. (1994) 'The Nature of Man', *Journal of Applied Corporate Finance*, 7(2): 4–19.

Jensen, M.C and Meckling, W.H. (1995) 'Specific and General Knowledge, and Organizational Structure', *Journal of Applied Corporate Finance*, 8(2): 4–18.

Johnson, H.T. and Kaplan, R.S. (1987) *Relevance Lost – The Rise and Fall of Management Accounting*, Harvard Business School Press.

Kahn, K.B. (1996) 'Interdepartmental Integration: A Definition with Implications for Product Development Performance', *Journal of Product Innovation Management*, 13(2): 137–151.

Kaplan, R.S. (1983) 'Comments on Wilson and Jensen', *The Accounting Review*, LVIII(2): 340–346.

Kaplan, R.S. and Norton, D.P. (1992) 'The Balanced Scorecard: Measures that Drive Performance', *Harvard Business Review*, January-February: 71–79.

Kaplan, R.S. and Norton, D.P. (1993) 'Putting the Balanced Scorecard to Work', *Harvard Business Review*, September–October: 134–147.

Kaplan, R.S. and Norton, D.P. (1996) 'Using the Balanced Scorecard as a Strategic Management System', *Harvard Business Review*, January-February: 75–85.

Katz, R. (1982) 'The Effects of Group Longevity on Project Communication and Performance', *Administrative Science Quarterly*, 27: 81–104.

Katz, R. and Allen, T.J. (1985) 'Project Performance and the Locus of Influence in the R&D Matrix', *Academy of Management Journal*, 28: 67–87.

Keller, R.T. (1994) 'Technology-information Processing Fit and the Performance of R&D Project Groups: A Test of Contingency Theory', *Academy of Management Journal*, 37(1): 167–179.

Kerssens-van Drongelen, I.C. and Bilderbeek, J. (1999) 'R&D Performance Measurement: More than Choosing a Set of Metrics', *R&D Management*, 29(1): 35–46.

Kerssens-van Drongelen, I.C. and Cook, A. (1997) 'Design Principles for the Development of Measurement Systems for Research and Development Processes', *R&D Management*, 27(4): 345–357.

Kleinschmidt, E.J. and Cooper, R.G. (1991) 'The Impact of Product Innovativeness on Performance', *Journal of Product Innovation Management*, 8: 240–251.

Kohn, A. (1993) 'Why Incentive Plans Cannot Work', *Harvard Business Review*, September–October: 54–63.

Kotler, P. (1997) *Marketing Management Analysis: Planning, Implementation and Control*, 8th ed., New Jersey: Prentice Hall.

Krishnan, V. and Ulrich, K.T. (2001) 'Product Development Decisions: A Review of the Literature', *Management Science*, 47(1): 1–21.

Kuzel, A.J. (1992) 'Sampling in qualitative inquiry' in B.F. Crabtree and W.L. Miller (eds) *Doing Qualitative Research* (Research Methods for Primary Care Series, Vol. 3), Newbury Park, CA: Sage, 31–44.

Kvale, S. (1988) 'The 1000-Page Question', *Phenomenology + Pedagogy*, 6(2): 90–106.

Lebby, A.M. (1993) 'Rethinking Rewards', *Harvard Business Review*, November–December: 42.

Lembke, S. and Wilson, M.G. (1998) 'Putting the "Team" into Teamwork: Alternative Theoretical Contributions for Contemporary Management Practice', *Human Relations*, 51(7): 927–944.

Leonard-Barton, D. (1992) 'Core Capabilities and Core Rigidities: A Paradox in Managing New Product Development', *Strategic Management Journal*, 3: 111–125.

Leonard-Barton, D. and Wilson, E. (1994) 'Commercializing Technology: Imaginative Understanding of User Needs', *Harvard Business School*, Cambridge, MA, Case Study N9-694-102.

Levi, D. and Slem, C. (1995) 'Team Work in Research and Development Organizations: The Characteristics of Successful Teams', *International Journal of Industrial Ergonomics*, 16: 29–42.

Llewelyn, S. (2003) 'Methodological Issues What Counts as "Theory" in Qualitative Management and Accounting Research? Introducing Five Levels of Theorizing', *Accounting, Auditing & Accountability Journal*, 16(4): 662–708.

Loch, C., Stein, L. and Terwiesch, C. (1996) 'Measuring Development Performance in the Electronics Industry', *Journal of Product Innovation Management*, 13(1): 3–20.

Lundqvist, M., Sundgren, N. and Trygg, L. (1996) 'Remodularization of a Product Line: Adding Complexity to Project Management', *Journal of Product Innovation Management*, 13(4): 311–324.

Lynn, G.S., Morone, J.G. and Paulson, A.S. (1996) 'Marketing and Discontinuous Innovation: The Probe and Learn Process', *California Management Review*, 38: 8–37.

Mahajan, V. and Wind, J. (1986) 'New Products Models: Practice, Shortcomings, and Desired Improvements', *Journal of Product Innovation Management*, 9: 128–139.

Maidique, M.A. and Zirger, B.J. (1984) 'A Study of Success and Failure in Product Innovation: The Case of the U.S. Electronics Industry', *IEEE Transactions in Engineering Management*, 4: 192–203.

Maidique, M.A. and Zirger, B.J. (1985) 'The New Product Learning Cycle', *Research Policy*, 14: 299–313.

Mangham, I. (1978) *Interactions and Interventions in Organizations*, New York: Wiley.

March, J.G. and Simon, H.A. (1993) *Organizations*, 2nd ed., New York: Blackwell.

Maskell, B.H. and Baggaley, B.L. (2001) 'Future of Management Accounting in the 21st Century', *Journal of Cost Management*, January/February.

McAdams, J. (1993) 'Rethinking Rewards', *Harvard Business Review*, November–December: 43–44.

McKinnon, J. (1988) 'Reliability and Validity in Field Research: Some Strategies and Tactics', *Accounting, Auditing & Accountability Journal*, 1 (1): 34–54.

Meyers, P.W. and Tucker, F.G. (1989) 'Defining Roles for Logistics during Routine and Radical Technological Innovation', *Journal of the Academy of Marketing Science*, 17: 73–82.

Miles, M.B. and Huberman, A.M. (1994) *Qualitative Data Analysis: An Expanded Sourcebook*, 2nd ed., Thousand Oaks CA: Sage.

Milgrom, P. and Roberts, J. (1992) *Economics, Organization and Management*, Englewood Cliffs, NJ: Prentice Hall.

Millson, M.R. and Wilemon, D. (2002) 'The Impact of Organizational Integration and Product Development Proficiency on Market Success', *Industrial Marketing Management*, 31: 1–23.

Mishler, E.G. (1990) 'Validation in Inquiry-Guided Research: The Role of Exemplars in Narrative Studies', *Harvard Educational Review*, 60: 415–441.

Moenaert, R.K. and Souder, W.E. (1990) 'An Information Transfer Model for Integrating Marketing and R&D Personnel in New Product Development Projects', *Journal of Product Innovation Management*, 7(2): 91–107.

Mohrman, S.A., Cohen, S.G. and Mohrman, Jr. A.M. (1995) *Designing Team-based Organizations: New Forms for Knowledge Work*, San Francisco: Jossey-Bass.

Montoya-Weiss, M.M. and Calantone, R.J. (1994) 'Determinants of New Product Performance: A Review and Meta Analysis', *Journal of Product Innovation Management*, 11(5): 397–417.

Morgan, G. and Smircich, L. (1980) 'The Case for Qualitative Research', *Academy of Management Review*, (5): 491–500.

Morone, J.G. (1993) *Winning in High-Tech Markets: The Role of General Management: How Motorola, Corning, and General Electric Have Built Global Leadership Through Tech*, Cambridge, MA: Harvard Business School Press.

Nadler, D.A. and Ancona, D. (1992) 'Teamwork at the top: creating executive teams that work' in D.A. Nadler, M.S. Gerstein and R.B. Shaw (eds) *Organizational Architecture: Designs for Changing Organizations*, San Francisco: Jossey-Bass, 209–231.

Nixon, B. (1998) 'Research and Development Performance Measurement: A Case Study', *Management Accounting Research*, 9 (3): 329–355.

OECD (Organisation for Economic Co-operation and Development) (2003) *OECD Science, Technology and Industry Scoreboard 2003 – Towards a Knowledge-based Economy*, Paris, pp. 1–73.

Otley, D. and Fakiolas, A. (2000) 'Reliance on Accounting Performance Measures: Dead End or New Beginning?', *Accounting, Organizations and Society*, 25: 497–510.

Pande, P.S., Neuman, R.P. and Cavanagh, R.R. (2000) *The Six Sigma Way: How GE, Motorola, and Other Top Companies Are Honing Their Performance*, McGraw-Hill.

Parker, G.M. (1994) *Cross-functional Teams: Working with Allies, Enemies, and other Strangers*, San Francisco: Jossey Bass.

Pascale, R.T. and Athos, A.G. (1982) *The Art of Japanese Management: Applications for American Executives*, Harmondsworth, Middlesex: Penguin Books.

Patton, M.Q. (1990) *Qualitative Evaluation and Research Methods*, 2nd ed., Newbury Park, CA: Sage.

Pelled, L.H. and Adler, P.S. (1994) 'Antecedents of Intergroup Conflict in Multifunctional Product Development Teams: A Conceptual Model', *IEEE Transactions on Engineering Management*, 41(1): 21–28.

Pettigrew, A. (1997) 'What Is A Processual Analysis?', *Scandinavian Journal of Management*, 13: 337–348.

Perrow, C. (1986) *Complex Organizations: A Critical Essay*, New York: McGraw-Hill.

Peters, T.J. and Waterman, Jr. R.H. (1982) *In Search of Excellence: Lessons from America's Best-Run Companies*, New York: Harper & Row.

Philliber, S.G., Schwab, M.R. and Samsloss, G. (1980) *Social Research: Guides to a Decision-Making Process*, Itasca, IL: Peacock.

Pike, R.H. (1988) 'An Empirical Study of the Adoption of Sophisticated Capital Budgeting Practices and Decision-Making Effectiveness', *Accounting and Business Research*, 18 (72): 341–351.

Poolton, J. and Barclay, I. (1998) 'New Product Development from Past Research to Future Applications', *Industrial Marketing Management*, 27: 197–212.

Prasad, P. (1993) 'Symbolic Processes in the Implementation of Technological Change: A Symbolic Interactionist Study of Work Computerization', *Academy of Management Journal*, 36(6): 1400–1429.

Quinn, J.B. (1985) 'Managing Innovation: Controlled Chaos', *Harvard Business Review*, May–June, 73–84.

Quinn, J.B., Anderson, P. and Finkelstein, S. (1996) 'Managing Professional Intellect: Making the Most of the Best', *Harvard Business Review*, March–April: 71–80.

Robey, D. (1991) *Designing Organizations*, Burr Ridge, IL: Richard D. Irwin.

Rothwell, R. (1972) *Factors for Success in Industrial Innovations from Project SAPPHO – A Comparative Study of Success and Failure in Industrial Innovation*, Brighton, Sussex, England: S.P.R.U.

Rothwell, R., Freeman, C., Horsley, A., Jervis, V.T.P., Robertson, A. and Townsend, J. (1974) 'SAPPHO Updated – Project Sappho Phase II', *Research Policy*, 3(3): 258–291.

Rowe, C. (2004) 'The Effect of Accounting Report Structure and Team Structure on Performance in Cross-Functional Teams', *The Accounting Review*, 79(4): 1153–1180.

Rubenstein, R., Chakrabarty, R., O'Keefe, R., Souder, R. and Young, R. (1976) 'Factors Influencing Innovation Success at the Project Level', *Research Management*, 19(3): 15–20.

Ryan, B., Scapens, R.W. and Theobald, M. (2002) *Research Method and Methodology in Finance and Accounting*, 2nd ed., London: Thomson.

Scapens, R.W. (1990) 'Researching Management Accounting Practice: The Role of Case Study Methods', *British Accounting Review*, 20(3): 260–279.

Scapens, R.W. (1991) *Management Accounting – A Review of Recent Development*, 2nd ed., London: Macmillan.

Shocker, A.D. and Srinivasan, V. (1979) 'Multiattribute Approaches for Product Concept Evaluation and Generation: A Critical Review', *Journal of Marketing Research*, 16: 159–180.

Silverman, D. (2001) *Interpreting Qualitative Data: Methods for Analysing Talks, Text and Interaction*, 2nd ed., London: Sage.

Simons, R. (1987) 'Accounting Control Systems and Business Strategy: An Empirical Analysis', *Accounting, Organizations and Society*, 12(4): 357–374.

Söderquist, K.E. and Nellore, R. (2000) 'Information Systems in Fast Cycle Development: Identifying User Needs in Integrated Automotive Component Development', *R&D Management*, 30(3): 199–211.

Song, X.M., Neeley, S.M. and Zhao, Y. (1996) 'Managing R&D-Marketing Integration in the New Product Development Process', *Industrial Marketing Management*, 25: 545–553.

Stake, R.E. (1994) 'Case studies' in N.K. Denzin and Y.S. Lincoln (eds) *Handbook of Qualitative Research*, Thousand Oaks, CA: Sage, 236–247.

Subramaniam, M., Rosenthal, S. R. and Hatten, K. J. (1998) 'Global New Product Development Processes: Preliminary Findings and Research Propositions', *Journal of Management Studies*, 35(6): 773–796.

Taiwan Stock Exchange Corporation (TSEC) 'Criteria for Review of Securities Listings, Chapter II The Listing of Domestic Securities, Section 1 The Listing of Stock, Article 5'. Online. Available at: http://www.tse.com.tw/en/ (accessed 14 February 2006).

Tajfel, H. (1982) 'Social Psychology of Intergroup Relations', *Annual Review of Psychology*, 33: 1–39.

Tajfel, H. and Turner, J.C. (1986) 'The social identity theory of intergroup behavior' in S. Worchel and W.G. Austin (eds) *Psychology of Intergroup Relations*, 2nd ed., Chicago: Nel-son-Hall.

Takeuchi, H. and Nonaka, I. (1986) 'The New Product Development Game', *Harvard Business Review*, January: 137–146.

Terwiesch, C., Loch, C. and Niederkofler, M. (1998) 'When Product Development Performance Makes a Difference: A Statistical Analysis in the Electronics Industry', *Journal of Product Innovation Management*, 15: 3–15.

Thomke, S. and Hippel, E. (2002) 'Customers as Innovators – A New Way to Create Value', *Harvard Business Review*, April: 74–81.

Time. (1984) 'Capitalism in the Making', April 30: 62.

Tomkins, C. and Groves, R. (1983a) 'The Everyday Accountant and Researching his Reality', *Accounting, Organizations and Society*, 8(4): 361–374.

Tomkins, C. and Groves, R. (1983b) '"The Everyday Accountant and Researching his Reality": Further Thoughts', *Accounting, Organizations and Society*, 8(4): 407–415.

Tomkovich, C. and Miller, C. (2000) 'Perspective-riding the Wind: Managing New Product Development in the Age of Change', *Journal of Product Innovation Management*, 17(6): 413–432.

Tosi, H.L. Brownlee, A.L., Silva, P. and Katz, J.P. (2003) 'An Empirical Exploration of Decision-making Under Agency Controls and Stewardship Structure', *Journal of Management Studies*, 40(8): 2053–2071.

Towry, K.L. (2003) 'Control in a Teamwork Environment – The Impact of Social Ties on the Effectiveness of Mutual Monitoring Contracts', *The Accounting Review*, 78(4): 1069–1095.

Turner, J.C. (1987) *Rediscovering the Social Group: A Self-Categorization Theory*, Oxford: Basil Blackwell.

Tushman, M.L. and Anderson, P. (1986) 'Technological Discontinuities and Organizational Environments', *Administrative Science Quarterly*, 31: 439–465.

Tushman, M.L. and Nadler, D. (1986) 'Organizing for Innovation', *California Management Review*, 28: 74–92.

Ulrich, K.T. and Eppinger, S.D. (2004) *Product Design and Development*, 3rd ed., McGraw-Hill.

Ulwick, A.W. (2002) 'Turn Customer Input into Innovation', *Harvard Business Review*, January: 91–97.

Veryzer, Jr. R.W. (1998) 'Discontinuous Innovation and the New Product Development Process', *Journal of Product Innovation Management*, 15: 304–321.

Wall Street Journal. (1992) 'New-product Troubles have Firms Cutting back', Jan. 13: B1.

Wall Street Journal. (1999) 'Linking Pay to Performance is becoming a Norm in the Workplace', *115*(April 6): 1.

Wellins, R.S., Byham, W.C. and Dixon, G.R. (1994) *Inside Teams: How 20 World-Class Organizations are Winning through Teamwork*, San Francisco, CA: Jossey-Bass.

Wellins, R.S., Byham, W.C. and Wilson, J.M. (1991) *Empowered Teams: Creating Self-directed work Groups that Improve Quality, Productivity, and Participation*, San Francisco, CA: Jossey-Bass.

Werner, B.M. and Souder, W.E. (1997) 'Measuring R&D Performance – State of the Art', *Research°DTechnology Management*, 40(2): 34–42.

Wheelwright, S.C. and Clark, K.B. (1992) *Revolutionizing Product Development*, New York: The Free Press.

Wind, J. and Mahajan, V. (1997) 'Issues and Opportunities in New Product Development: An Introduction to the Special Issue', *Journal of Marketing Research*, XXXIV(February): 1–12.

Wolters, D.S. (1993) 'Rethinking Rewards', *Harvard Business Review*, November–December: 45–49.

Wruck, K.H. and Jensen, M.C. (1994) 'Science, Specific Knowledge, and Total Quality Management', *Journal of Accounting and Economics*, 18: 247–287.
Yin, R.K. (2003) *Case Study Research: Design and Methods*, 3rd ed., Beverly Hills, CA: Sage.
Zirger, B.J. and Maidique, M.A. (1990) 'A Model of New Product Development: An Empirical Test', *Management Science*, 36(7): 867–883.

Appendices

Appendix A   Protocol[1] for conducting a multiple-case study of NPD practices

A. Introduction to the case study and purpose of protocol
    A1. Research questions
    A2. Theoretical framework
    A3. Interview protocol in guiding interviews

B. Data collection and recording procedures
    B1. Name of sites to be visited, name, email, cell phone of contact person
    B2. Data collection plan: the calendar period for the site visits, the amount of time to be used for each visit, and the level of effort to do each case study
    B3. Preparation prior to site visits: identifies specific documents to be reviewed and where documents can be accessed

C. Outline of case study report
    C1. The background of each case
    C2. The key results of each case
    C3. Outcome from the practice

D. Case study questions
    D1. NPD activities
        a. What are the characteristics of your company's new products? Why?
        b. What is the role of NPD in your company? Why?

    D2. Organisations
        a. What is your company's management philosophy? Why?
        b. Whether your company provides a NPD environment?
        c. Whether your company has qualified resources?

    D3. Breakthrough product project team
        a. How does your company assign the project team leader? Why?
        b. How does the project team be formed? Why?
        c. How does your team cooperate and communicate? Why?

    D4. Organisational structures
        a. Do you think the delegation of authority is appropriate? Why?
        b. Are you satisfied with the reward plan? Why?
        c. What measures do you think would best evaluate the project team? Why you think these measures would be most appropriate?
        d. Why existing measures of your company are different from the measures which you think would be more appropriate?

    D5. Other:
        a. Technology: whether advance quickly? Why?
        b. Computer Market: whether support innovation? Why?
        c. Electronic Industry: whether it is a mature industry? Why?
        d. Government Regulation: whether support new product innovation? Why?

---

[1]This is a draft for conducting the multiple-case study. Questions are flexible.

Appendix B Interview protocol

Interview Protocol
Case Study: Breakthrough Project Team & New Product Performance Measures

Time Started:
Date:
Place:
Interviewee/Position:
Time Finished:

[Briefly describe the purpose of this study. Business card. Confidentiality. Eye contact.]

[Why] Questions:
1. NPD activities (Process, Role, Environment …)

2. Organisations (Corporate Culture, New Product Strategy …)

3. Breakthrough product project teams (Formation, Project Manager, Members …)

4. Organisational architecture (Decision Allocation, Reward & Punishment, Performance Measurement …)

5. Technology, market, industry, government regulations (Stable, Mature, Patents …)

[Thank informant for participating in this interview. 'One single conversation with you is more enlightening than a decade's study.' Assure confidentiality of informants and potential future interviews. Email or telephone contact? Write a thank you email]

Appendix C   The process of analytic induction for this study

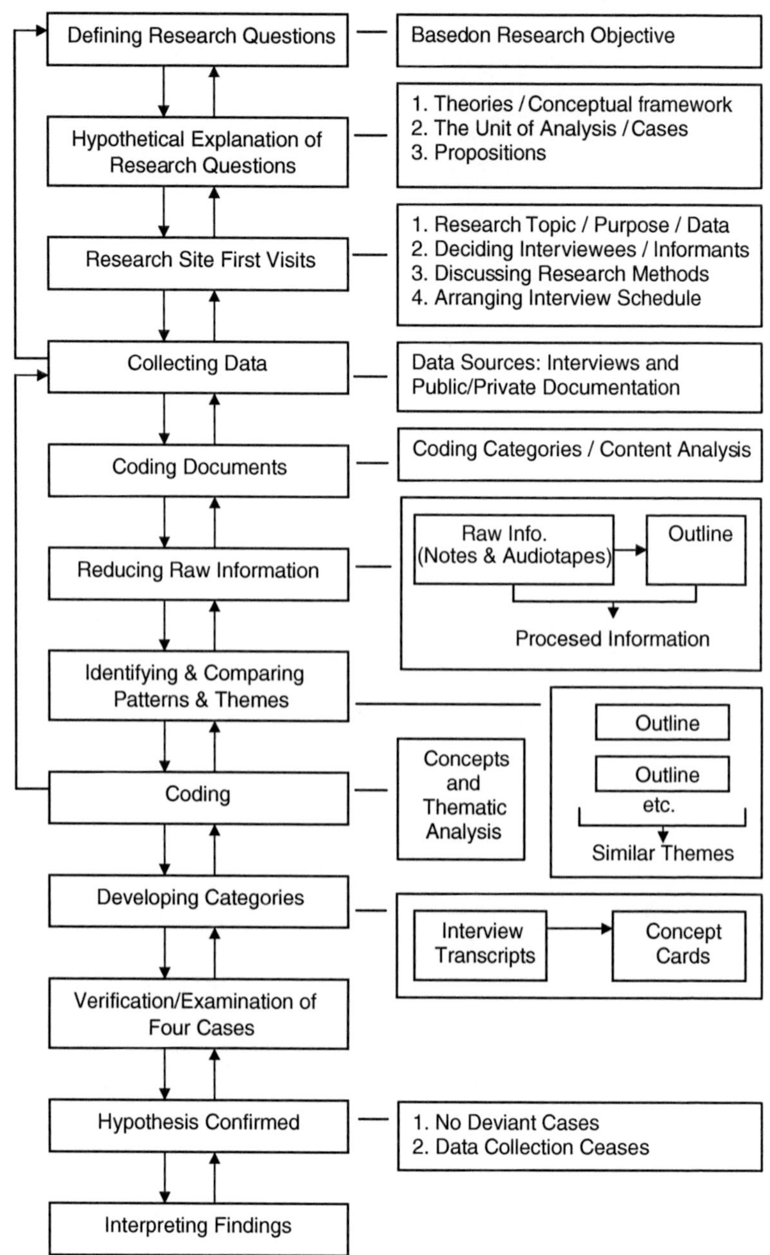

Appendix D   Reducing the texts of interviews – success subsample

Data Source	Interviewee	Incident, Quotation, Opinion, Event
Case A: Interview No.1	CEO	Research Question 1: Belief → Human nature is essentially good → 'Me too' is not my style (constant emphasis on R&D/NPD) → High reputation of innovation (full-involvement) → Making decisions, taking responsibilities → Decentralisation, partnership, agreement, common goal + independent personal style (profit sharing) → 'If the lips are gone, the teeth will be cold' (joint ventures) → 'What is a workman without his tools?' (qualified Resources – involved and support, not set up) → Perception as a team/team-member → Assign PM, PM 'suggests/picks' members (decision rights) Research Question 2: Strategy → Performance measurement system (PMS) is a strategy, for specific purposes (but not for controlling) → New tax regulation – retirement plans → Some difficult to measure, dispute about who to measure, so give up, consider whole company → Not right time to incorporate it (external factors) Research Question 3: Purposes/Impacts → Firing unqualified people – company's down-sizing, shaping, restructuring, reengineering → A sign: what we need is qualified, self-responsible people → A new teamwork environment Research Question 4: Fairly + Objectively + Reasonably
Case A: Interview No.2	HR	Research Question 1: → All-related team-members attend meeting for measures Research Question 2: → 'It is easier to move a mountain than to change a person's character' → New pension plans July 1, 2005 (a heavy cost for company) → "In Co. A, our system is ok, if there is a problem, the problem is 'imple menting by the wrong people' Research Question 3: → 'Participants themselves cannot see clearly, onlookers can see the whole game' – who is qualified, who is free-rider Research Question 4: → PM measures his team-members, only for that project; functional dept. managers measure their people → PM arranges and discusses with functional dept. managers, time allocation, so functional manager knows who work

Appendix D   – *Continued*

		longer – whole consideration
Case A: Interview No.3	PM	Research Question 1: → 'Through experience, wisdom is nurtured' → A project: requirement → specification → planning → implementing → reviewing → 'A poor workman blames his tools' Research Question 2: → One step closer to success → Depends on the purpose of team – new market, reputation, technology (patents) → Failure Management Evaluating Analysis (FMEA) Research Question 3: → A responsible + qualified PM is primary Research Question 4: → Only measure this project, not per-year evaluation
Case A: Interview No.4	R&D -Mechanical -Software -Firmware -Hardware	Research Question 1: → Communication through meeting/email/phone… whenever Research Question 2: → Discussing my performance with my Sir, get agreement Research Question 3: → Company's policy. System is ok, the problem is 'measurer' Research Question 4: → Dept. manager measures
Case A: Interview No.5	QA -Quality Assurance -Quality Reliability	Research Question 1: → Dept. manager assigns Research Question 2: → Based on each process of quality insurance system Research Question 3: → Communication/Control/Improvement Research Question 4: → play as a supporting part, so Dept. manager measures
Case A: Interview No.6	Sales	Research Question 1: → Brand management: Regional office – Sales – channel Research Question 2: → Profit margin %, understanding customer needs Research Question 3: → Supervision, comparisons (internal vs external) Research Question 4: → Dept. manager measures (PM can complain or compensate)
Case A: Interview No.7	Market Researcher (MR)	Research Question 1: → Market research is the first step for breakthrough products Research Question 2: → Post-evaluation, market development & evaluation Research Question 3: → Feedback, inspection Research Question 4: → Dept. manager measures
Case A: Interview No.8	Procurement	Research Question 1: → Supporting job, on-time component supply Research Question 2: → Cost (quantity) & Quality (testing, customer acceptance) Research Question 3: → Feedback, Improvement Research Question 4: → Supporting job, Dept. manager measures

Appendix D   – *Continued*

Data Source	Interviewee	Incident, Quotation, Opinion, Event
Case B: Interview No.1	Associate Vice President (AVP)	Research Question 1: → Trend + tax advantages + government funding for Innovative R&D → 'You cannot make bricks without straw' (basic factor) → 'Tension makes difference' (emphasis on innovation) → 'Unlimited salary' strategy (motivating professionals) → Trustworthiness & respect: 'Don't use whom you doubt, don't doubt who you choose to use' → 'With determination and purpose, anything can be achieved' (common goal) → Propose a project or assign a PM for a specific project → Teamwork environment + involvement in NPD Research Question 2: → Amenable to match environment or purposes → Respect HR Research Question 3: → Specific purposes – improvement, direction, goal, signal → Positive effect, system + implementation + feedback Research Question 4: → Div. managers, one of their job is measuring people, any problem, they need to take responsibility, so they measure their people
Case B: Interview No.2	HR	Research Question 1: → Div. as an measurable unit Research Question 2: → Individual: every one has his/her specific (different) KPI, discuss with his/her direct supervisor about individual objectives + performance target + weighting (%) → Team: speed, cost, sales volume, patents (new technology), value Research Question 3: → 'If you have money you can make the ghosts and devils turn your grind stone', policy, management style → Motivation, caution, feedback (implementation), signal → Unqualified (did not reach the objective) employee will fill in an 'improvement form', still cannot improve, then quit (signed an agreemert for leaving) Research Question 4: → Project: PM; six-month & per-year evaluation: Div.
Case B: Interview No.3	PM	Research Question 1: → 'What you don't want to be done to yourself, don't do it to others' → 'A bad workman quarrels with his tools' – inadequate or difficult working conditions → 'Show me the future' → PM has an idea – propose a project plan Research Question 2: → Agreement, open, evaluation form returned for feedback & improvement Research Question 3: → Keep qualified, sweep unqualified, a sign, s style Research Question 4: → Team-member came to you, you must help.

Appendix D – *Continued*

Case B: Interview No.4	R&D	Research Question 1: → Job assignment by Div., 'take responsibility for myself' → Co-work, work as a team, respect, communication Research Question 2: → Discussing with Div. & PM, allocate time, flexible Research Question 3: → Next project assignment, challenging job Research Question 4: → Div. manager measures, more than ten cases on hand
Case B: Interview No.5	QA	Research Question 1: → Quality info. collection, solution, prevention Research Question 2: → 1) sample, 2) prototype testing, 3) mass production → 'No news is good news; if we speak, then must be bad news' → A part of job: going well, no bonus; if there is a problem, PM will complain to Div. Research Question 3: → Continuously improvement Research Question 4: → Div.: Supporting job, it's a part of job
Case B: Interview No.6	Sales	Research Question 1: → Channel, opportunity, potential Research Question 2: → KPI Research Question 3: → Salary Research Question 4: → Div. manager
Case B: Interview No.7	MR	Research Question 1: → Market research, market quality information Research Question 2: → Post-evaluation assessment, updating on-time new info. Research Question 3: → Feedback/responsibility Research Question 4: → Div. manager
Case B: Interview No.8	Manufacturing	Research Question 1: → Supporting, assigning Research Question 2: → Checking Schedule Research Question 3: → Communication with QA, R&D Research Question 4: → Div. manager measures
Case B: Interview No.9	Procurement	Research Question 1: → Supporting Research Question 2: → On-time supply + order cost Research Question 3: → Standard, feedback Research Question 4: → Div.

Appendix E Reducing the texts of interviews – failure subsample

Data Source	Interviewee	Incident, Quotation, Opinion, Event
Case C: Interview No.1	CEO	Research Question 1: Management Philosophy → Global view, marketing, expansion (so decentralisation) → Wish be a sole leading innovator in the entire industry → Technology + environment protection concepts → 'Good luck seldom comes in pairs but bad things never walk (occur) alone', not only main business went wrong, but also bad investment decisions → Losing qualified people Research Question 2: → PMS is ok, but bad implementation, no feedback → HR set measures or forms, CEO & GM review it Research Question 3: → Measuring – paying for performance – returning results for future improvement → Did not work, so employees complain unfair, distrust Research Question 4: → Dept. manager
Case C: Interview No.2	HR	Research Question 1: → Authority ≠ responsibility Research Question 2: → Measurer did not do his job well, personal emotions → Report to GM, seems improved, actually the same Research Question 3: → Dysfunctional behaviours to team and company → Not worth to work hard Research Question 4: → Dept. manager measures and then send it to HR
Case C: Interview No.3	PM	Research Question 1: → 'Baseball wrong. Man with four balls not able to work' → Money + time → Authority delegation, but how to arrange team-members is PM's 'ability + reputation' Research Question 2: → Depends on each team's goal, purpose → Setting individual KPI with direct supervisor → cost vs. benefit of measurement Research Question 3: → Unfair, ambiguous bonus, everyone has it, angry → Disbelieve any more, difficult to improve, no motivation Research Question 4: → Dept. manager
Case C: Interview No.4	R&D	Research Question 1: → Dept. assigns, tight time schedule, report to superior Managers (communication? bad feeling), sometimes team-member involved personal feelings, conflicts Research Question 2: → Team-evaluation: self-evaluation (individual KPI) + team-member Dept. evaluation → Implementing badly, just paperwork, no feedback Research Question 3:

Appendix E   *– Continued*

		→ Official procedures, I don't know how they (senior management) use it, not clear, so no use Research Question 4: → Dept. manager, or what else he (Dept. manager) should do? It is a part of Dept. manager's job.
Case C: Interview No.5	QA	Research Question 1: → Make sure the sample, prototype, product is high-quality, test & report, depends on personal experience Research Question 2: → QA is supporting, everything we do is our job description, review accepted, then OK; argument, then PM, R&D, or manufacturing complain → Cross-dept. evaluation so called 360° evaluation Research Question 3: → Co-work, communication Good idea, reasonable, but implement badly, so no effect Research Question 4: → QA Dept. manager
Case C: Interview No.6	Manufacturing	Research Question 1: → A part of job, meeting Research Question 2: → Cross-Dept. evaluation, Dept. evaluation, schedule set Research Question 3: → For feedback, confirmation, improvement purposes Research Question 4: → Dept. manager
Case C: Interview No.7	Sales	Research Question 1: → Propose an idea – review – discuss – assess – implement Research Question 2: → KPI, objective achievement, professional ability, self-improvement ability Research Question 3: → Good measurement design, but not really like that Research Question 4: → Dept. manager
Case C: Interview No.8	Procurement	Research Question 1: → It is my job, meeting, discussing, & setting time schedule, potential components, collecting pricing info. Research Question 2: → Cost, timing & quality of components Research Question 3: → Feedback: internal vs. external → Nothing happens if bad performance Research Question 4: → Dept. manager

Appendix E   – *Continued*

Data Source	Interviewee	Incident, Quotation, Opinion, Event
Case D: Interview No.1	VP	Research Question 1: Background → be the leader in innovation, R&D, efficient production, quality insurance & marketing → create humanised high-tech & customer's need products → innovation, quality, honesty, efficiency, enthusiasm, passion → upgrade technology: the development of advanced technologies & technology transfer → 'One step in the wrong direction will cause you a thousand years of regret' → Cannot keep qualified professionals, they don't think it is fair and then don't feel it is worth to work hard Research Question 2: → Meeting to decide KPI & team progress → Must consider whole company, not just the team Research Question 3: → 'War not determine who is right; war determine who is left', even you are really good, but cannot co-work with others, then you must leave Research Question 4: → Each Dept. manager
Case D: Interview No.2	HR	Research Question 1: → Cannot cooperate & communicate between each members → Performance measurement problem, no effect, nobody wants to take responsibility Research Question 2: → KPI Research Question 3: → 'To cultivate trees, you need ten years; to cultivate people, you need 100 years' → The purpose of PMS is to motivate qualified employees, but it is impossible to 'motivate' wrong people → No effect, because didn't return the form back, and everybody get bonus Research Question 4: → Dept. manager
Case D: Interview No.3	PM	Research Question 1: → Assign a PM from PM Dept., negotiate & choose R&Ds with R&D Dept. manager → Company emphasise on NPD, qualified resources is not the problem; reward plans, bonus is fine too, because we compare with other companies, there is a 'standard' → the thing is there is no clear and effective PMS for us to follow, don't feel it is fair, or worth, so cannot motivate related members Research Question 2: → Actually the design of PMS is OK, every measure is reasonable & acceptable, but not right person to implement it, no feedback, no motivation Research Question 3: → At first for feedback, qualification of bonus, improvement

Appendix E   – *Continued*

		for next project Research Question 4: → Discuss with Dept. manager
Case D: Interview No.4	R&D	Research Question 1: → Dept. manager & PM, depends on time allocation, meeting for team schedule Research Question 2: → Individual KPI evaluation Research Question 3: → Measures is meaningful, but don't trust measurer Research Question 4: → Dept. manager
Case D: Interview No.5	Sales & Marketing	Research Question 1: → Market research for applicable, potential opportunity, customer needs Research Question 2: → KPI, changed every six-months, focused on individual performance, correct judgement or suggestion Research Question 3: → Basic salary is low, bonus depends on your performance, good idea, but (after two months) found that everyone got bonus, just paperwork Research Question 4: → Dept. manager
Case D: Interview No.6	QT	Research Question 1: → Review, meeting, quality assurance system Research Question 2: → Management style Research Question 3: → Feedback, deciding salary Research Question 4: → Dept. manager
Case D: Interview No.7	Manufacturing	Research Question 1: → Meeting for schedule, practical application Research Question 2: → Checking each process, on time, cost, quality Research Question 3: → Feedback, Improvement Research Question 4: → Dept. manager
Case D: Interview No.8	Procurement	Research Question 1: → Supporting job Research Question 2: → Cost, quality, timing Research Question 3: → Feedback, cost control, no punishment, everybody the same Research Question 4: → Dept. manager

Author Index

Subject Index

Note: Page numbers in italics denote figures